although it does allow for depreciation which other methods sometimes exclude.

accounting ratios. See FINANCIAL RATIOS.

Account of Her Majesty's Exchequeur. See CONSOLIDATED FUND.

account rendered. A statement or bill (invoice) informing customers of the amount owing in respect of goods or services supplied to them.

accounts code (accounting code). Code letters or numbers used in classifying income or expenditure according to BUDGET headings or other categories in a system of accounting.

accounts payable. A statement of all money currently owed by a firm for goods and services not yet paid for. Mainly used in the USA. See CREDITOR.

accounts receivable. A statement of all money currently owed to a firm which has a short settlement term. Mainly used in the USA. See DEBTOR.

accretion. The process whereby income (either from interest payments or direct additions) builds up investment funds.

accrual. An accounting principle covered by both EEC and UK law (e.g. the British Companies Act 1985) which requires that all income and expenditure over a financial year shall be included in the accounts, irrespective of when it was received or paid.

accruals method. See ACCRUAL.

accrued asset (accrued revenue). In accounting, the amount accumulated over a period but which is received only at fixed times – such as the receipt of quarterly interrest.

accrued expense. See ACCRUED LIABILITY.

accrued liability (accrued expense). In accounting, the amount owing which has accumulated over the financial year (up to the date of payment) but which is payable at fixed times only – for example, as quarterly interest payments.

accrued revenue. See ACCRUED ASSET.

accumulated depreciation. See DEPRECIATION.

achievement motivation. A form of MOTIVATION theory developed by David MCCLELLAND which suggests that individuals are driven by varying degrees of a need for achievement (nAch). Individuals with a high nAch constantly require proof of their having made their mark – for example, financial rewards. This principle is described in McClelland's book, *The Achieving Society* (New York: Van Nostrand Rheinhold, 1961).

achievement motivation test. One of several PSYCHOLOGICAL TESTS developed for achievement. The most widely-used is the Thematic Appreciation Test (TAT).

acid test ratio (quick ratio). The FINANCIAL RATIO of liquid assets against CURRENT LIABILITIES. So-called because the result provides an 'acid test' of whether a business is or is not viable, since it indicates how far a firm is able to pay its debts.

ACME Directorate. A special directorate, set up within the SCIENCE AND ENGINEERING RESEARCH COUNCIL in the UK to promote the application of computers in manufacturing and engineering.

acquisition. The purchase of a firm or of its assets.

across-the board settlement. A form of pay settlement in which all employees receive the same proportional increase (i.e. wages go up across the board). Such an arrangement maintains DIFFERENTIALS.

ACT. See ADVANCE CORPORATION TAX.

action-centred leadership. A phrase, originally coined by John Adair, a UK management writer, to describe his view of leadership training. This argues that leadership can be developed by training people to carry out the particular set of actions expected of a leader. This approach is described in several of Adair's books and articles – for example, *Training for Leadership* (London: Macdonald, 1968).

action learning. A MANAGEMENT DEVELOPMENT concept originated by Reg Revans in the UK, which is based on the idea that managers learn by doing and reviewing what they have done, and on providing opportunities for them to carry out this activity in a variety of different circumstances. For example, an action learning programme might involve managers exchanging jobs for a short period so as to provide them with new insights and experience. Particular features of action learning projects include the fact that participants work on a real, rather than an artificial, problem, and the use of a group or 'set' of managers who bring their different experiences and perspectives to bear on an individual's project. A good reference book on the subject is R. Revans, *Action Learning – New Techniques for Management* (London: Blond & Briggs, 1980).

action research. A form of research into organizations which differs from controlled experiment in that it explicitly recognizes that the act of doing research will have an influence on the organizations being studied. Action research projects aim to contribute both to the development of the organization under study and the theoretical body of knowledge. This approach is described by Peter Clark in *Action Research and Organizational Change* (London: Harper & Row, 1970).

activities analysis. One of three key forms of organizational analysis suggested by Peter DRUCKER which examines organizational functioning in terms of the activities of the business. The other two are DECISION ANALYSIS and RELATIONAL ANALYSIS.

activity. A term used in PROJECT NETWORK TECHNIQUES to describe the work required to complete a specified EVENT.

activity chart. A chart which sets out the various components of a process of a project, plotted against time.

activity on arrow (arrow diagram). A form of NETWORK plan in which activities are indicated as arrows.

activity on node (node diagram). A form of NETWORK plan in which activities are indicated as nodes.

activity ratio (efficiency ratio). A FINANCIAL RATIO, usually based on the ratio of sales REVENUE to ASSETS (cash, fixed assets etc). So-called because it gives an indication of how well a firm uses its assets.

activity sampling (work sampling). A research technique which records observations of events at specific times. It is often used in WORK STUDY to observe actions performed by a worker or machine. The intervals used may be fixed or randomly varied to eliminate bias.

ACTT. *See* ASSOCIATION OF CINEMATOGRAPH, TELEVISION AND ALLIED TECHNICIANS.

actual costs. An accounting term used to distinguish between the actual costs of producing an item and those indicated by BUDGETTED COSTS or STANDARD COSTS.

actuarial return. The return on investment measured by DISCOUNTED CASH FLOW techniques. *See* INTERNAL RATE OF RETURN.

actuary. An INSURANCE worker whose task it is to calculate premiums.

ADA. A high-level computer language, originally developed for the US Department of Defense, mainly used in scientific applications.

adaptive control (self-optimizing control). A type of control in which the set points/control targets alter in response to changing conditions so as to achieve optimum performance under varying conditions.

added hours. In cases where employees work overtime, the amount paid is calculated by adding hours to the normal working week for which the employee is paid. For example, two hours worked at double time would add four hours' payment at the standard rate.

added value (value added). The increase in value of a good or service as a result of operations involved in producing them. It is represented by the difference between the selling price and the initial raw material or labour cost.

address. In computing, the area where a particular item of information is located in a computer's memory.

adjusting entry. A type of entry used in accrual accounting in which transactions are not entered directly; instead the accounts are adjusted to bring the financial position up to date. Thus, in preparing a FINANCIAL STATEMENT or BALANCE SHEET adjusting entries will be made to cover items like DEPRECIATION or interest payments.

administrative management theory. An approach to management theory, particularly associated with Henri FAYOL, Mary Parker FOLLET and Lyndal URWICK and popular in the 1930s. It followed the SCIENTIFIC MANAGEMENT tradition of Frederick Winslow TAYLOR and was in turn followed by the HUMAN RELATIONS SCHOOL OF MANAGEMENT TRAINING. The main emphasis in this theory is on formal organizational structures and hierarchies, and the particular defined responsibilities and accountabilities associated with them. Good overviews of the work of these theorists can be found in D. Pugh (ed.), *Organization Theory: Selected Readings* (Harmondsworth: Penguin, 1976) and J. Child, *Organizations: A Guide to Theory and Practice* (2nd edn, London: Harper & Row, 1982).

adoption theory. The body of knowledge concerned with the responses individuals and organizations make to innovations. In the diffusion of innovations − whether new products or processes − adoption over time tends to follow a normal distribution across the population. Everett Rogers identifies five groups of adopters: the innovators, early adopters, early majority, late majority and laggards. (*See* E. Rogers, *The Diffusion of Innovations* (2nd edn, London: Macmillan and New York: Free Press, 1982)). If the adoption data is plotted on a cumulative basis over time it gives rise to the characteristic S-shaped curve for adoption of innovations.

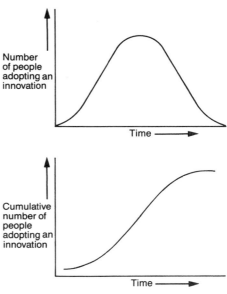

adoption curves

ad valorem (Lat.: 'according to the value'). A phrase used to indicate the value of something.

ad valorem tax. A tax based on the value of something − for example, a VALUE ADDED TAX.

Advance Corporation Tax. The tax paid by a UK firm when it chooses to distribute the profits (e.g. as dividends) instead of retaining them in the company. This is usually paid before the main payment of CORPORATION TAX (sometimes known as mainstream corporation tax) and the ACT payment (which must not exceed 30 per cent of taxable profits) deducted from that sum. The current rate is $\frac{3}{7}$ of the amount distributed as profits, and is always calculated in line with the basic rate of income tax.

advance factory. An approach to stimulating investment in certain regions which qualify for some form of ASSISTED AREA status. Advance factories are purpose-built factory units built with government or local authority money and made available under conditions attractive to investors (e.g. rate-free, reduced rent etc).

advertising. The activities associated with publicizing and promoting a product, service or company.

advertising agency. A business specializing in creating, preparing and placing advertisements for its clients. Such an agency specializes in advertising on a freelance basis, as distinct from a department within an organization.

advertising coverage. The extent of market or segments which is covered in an advertising campaign.

advertising executive. An individual responsible for advertising work within a department or agency. This often involves taking responsibility for particular customer accounts and planning overall advertising strategy and campaigns.

advertising goals. *See* ADVERTISING OBJECTIVES.

advertising objectives (advertising goals). The targets towards which an advertising campaign is directed — for example, increased customer awareness, increased market share, increased sales etc.

Advertising Standards Authority. An independent body, set up in 1962, responsible for monitoring the content of advertisements published in the UK across all media except television, which is covered by the Independent Broadcasting Authority (IBA). Advertisements are judged against the British Code of Advertising Practice or the IBA Code, and both codes contain the basic principle that advertisements in the UK should be 'legal, decent, honest and truthful'.

advice note. A document, detailing quantity, price, delivery date etc, which is sent to a buyer to indicate that the goods or services requested have been despatched.

Advisory Conciliation and Arbitration Service (ACAS). A UK body set up in 1975 as a statutory body to provide an ARBITRATION service in industrial disputes.

Advisory Council on Research and Development (ACARD). A UK government body set up to provide policy advice and guidance in matters of industrial, science and technology policy.

affidavit. A legally-sworn statement which is affirmed as true by the individual making it in the presence of an authorized agent (such as a Commissioner for Oaths in the UK).

affiliated company. A company which is under the same ownership as another.

AFL. *See* AMERICAN FEDERATION OF LABOR.

AFL—CIO. *See* AMERICAN FEDERATION OF LABOR — CONGRESS OF INDUSTRIAL ORGANIZATIONS.

afternoon shift. A shift in which the bulk of the work is done in the afternoon: the middle shift of a three-shift day, or the last of a two-shift day. The term can occasionally mean a part-time shift.

after-sales service. Various kinds of support provided to the customer by the seller after purchase of an item. Typical kinds of after-sales service include maintenance support, software updating (in computer systems) and technical advice.

AG. *See* AKTIENSGESELLSCHAFT.

agency. An arrangement in which a firm or individual acts on behalf of another to perform certain specified services. For example, an overseas agent represents the interests of a firm in countries where it has no facilities of its own for marketing, customer support etc.

agenda. A list of topics which are to be dealt with during a formal meeting.

agent. *See* AGENCY.

aggregate demand. The total demand for goods and services in an economy made up of demand for consumer goods and services, capital goods, producer services, public sector demand and export demand.

AGM. *See* ANNUAL GENERAL MEETING.

AGV. *See* AUTOMATIC GUIDED VEHICLE.

AI. *See* ARTIFICIAL INTELLIGENCE.

AIBD. *See* ASSOCIATION OF INTERNATIONAL BOND DEALERS.

AIDA ('Attention, Interest, Desire, Action'). An acronym used in some sales training approaches to describe the ideal sequence of responses which a buyer should exhibit when deciding to buy something – and which a salesman should try and elicit.

aided recall. A technique used in psychological testing in which individuals in interviews are prompted to talk about something by reminding them of associated things. It is particularly used in MARKET RESEARCH.

aksjelskap (A/S). The Norwegian equivalent of a PUBLIC LIMITED COMPANY in the UK.

aktiebolag (AB). The Swedish equivalent of a PUBLIC LIMITED COMPANY in the UK.

Aktiensgesellschaft (AG). A form of company in West Germany equivalent to a PUBLIC LIMITED COMPANY in the UK. German law requires such firms to have a minimum of DM 100,000 CONTRIBUTED CAPITAL and a two-tier board system involving an AUFSICHTSRAT (supervisory board) elected by shareholders and employees, and a VORSTAND, which is responsible for the day-to-day direction and management, much as a board of directors does in the UK. AG is also used in Switzerland and Austria to denote a public limited company and there are similar legal requirements regarding minimum contributed capital and, in Austria, the need for a two-tier board structure.

aktieselskab (A/S). The Danish equivalent of a PUBLIC LIMITED COMPANY in the UK.

ALGOL. A high-level computer language whose name derives from the term 'Algorithmic Language'. It was originally developed in the late 1950s, and different versions exist – such as ALGOL 58, 60, 68 – which correspond to the year in which the specifications were published. It has been largely superseded by newer, more powerful languages such as PASCAL.

algorithm. A set of rules for solving a problem. Algorithms are used extensively in SYSTEMS ANALYSIS and computer programming.

all-in rate. A wage rate in which all the extras – such as bonuses – are included in the standard rate per hour.

allocation of overheads. In ABSORPTION COSTING, the process of assigning the OVERHEADS in producing something to different COST CENTRES.

allonge. A piece of paper added to a BILL OF EXCHANGE to make room for further signatures by endorsers.

all-or-none embargo. In INDUSTRIAL RELATIONS, a demand that any privileges (bonuses, opportunities for overtime etc) should be available to all, otherwise none of the workforce will co-operate.

allotment. In a new SHARE or SECURITIES issue, the process whereby the issuer accepts offers from buyers. In a public offer the process may involve a ballot to decide how many shares should be allotted and to which applicants.

allotment letter. A letter sent to allottees accepting their offer to buy SECURITIES and containing details of how many and the terms of acceptance. Most letters of allotment allow allottees to sell the securities on to someone else who then becomes the allottee; such letters are termed 'provisional' or 'renouncable'.

allottee. One to whom SECURITIES are allotted.

allowed time. A WORK STUDY term for the time allowed for performance of a standard task. *See* STANDARD TIME.

All-Share Index. *See* FINANCIAL TIMES–ACTUARIES ALL-SHARE INDEX.

alphanumeric. A term used in computing to describe characters which are letters and numbers and other characters such as spaces or punctuation. An example of an alphanumeric keyboard would be that usually found on a traditional typewriter.

alpha securities. The most actively-traded shares on the Stock Exchange, with ten or more MARKET MAKERS in each. Market makers are obliged to deal at the quoted price.

alternate standard (alternative standard). A WORK STUDY term. If there are different ways of carrying out a task, then, when setting STANDARD TIMES, an alternate standard is also set for each different way.

alternating shift. A two-shift system in which workers work a period on days and then a similar period on nights.

alternative standard. *See* ALTERNATE STANDARD.

Alvey Directorate (Alvey Programme). A special directorate set up jointly by the UK DEPARTMENT OF TRADE AND INDUSTRY and the SCIENCE AND ENGINEERING RESEARCH COUNCIL in response to the findings of the Alvey Committee on so-called FIFTH-GENERATION COMPUTER systems. It currently funds a number of major research projects in this area.

Alvey Programme. *See* ALVEY DIRECTORATE.

AMA. *See* AMERICAN MANAGEMENT ASSOCIATION.

Amalgamated Engineering Union (AEU). *See* AMALGAMATED UNION OF ENGINEERING WORKERS.

Amalgamated Union of Engineering Workers (AUEW). The former name for the main UK trade union representing engineering workers. In 1985 it changed its name to the Amalgamated Engineering Union (AEU).

amalgamation. The process of coming together voluntarily — for example, of two companies. *See* MERGER.

amendment. (1) Any form of change.

(2) In the context of formal meetings, conferences etc, an amendment involves some change in the wording of a motion — as distinct from an addition to the end of a motion, which is called an addendum.

American Federation of Labor (AFL). One of the main US trade union groupings.

American Federation of Labor — Congress of Industrial Organizations (AFL−CIO). The US equivalent of the TRADES UNION CONGRESS in the UK. It was formed by a merger in 1955 of the two major US trade union groupings.

American Management Association (AMA). An organization of managers, similar to the BRITISH INSTITUTE OF MANAGEMENT (BIM) in the UK in its structure and aims.

American National Standards Institute (ANSI). A US body which sets and monitors standards for industry — the equivalent of the BRITISH STANDARDS INSTITUTE in the UK.

American Standards Association (ASA). The US body responsible for setting and monitoring standards within the computer industry.

amortization. (1) The setting aside on a BALANCE SHEET of the amount by which an INTANGIBLE ASSET expires.
(2) In the USA, the equivalent of DEPRECIATION.
(3) In a production context, the recouping of fixed costs (e.g. tooling) by spreading them across a large quantity of output.

amortize. To pay off a loan gradually.

Amstel Club. The name given to a small group of European banks and finance houses which operate a reciprocal financing of imports and exports between member countries.

AMT. The acronym for advanced manufacturing technology. It is also used as an abbreviation for a range of financial and consultancy support available from the UK Department of Trade and Industry under its AMT Scheme to promote the adoption of such technology.

analog computer. An early form of computer in which information was represented in analog form (e.g. by voltages or resistances in an electrical circuit) rather than as binary digits, as is the case in a digital computer. It is still used in cases where speed is important but it is limited by its inability to store data.

analytical estimating. In production management and WORK STUDY, an alternative to full-scale WORK MEASUREMENT for jobs when information is needed about the costs or times for jobs in production, based on estimating requirements for each component of the job.

analytic job evaluation. An approach to JOB EVALUATION which involves comparing common elements which comprise each job.

ANCOM. See ANDEAN COMMON MARKET.

Andean Common Market (ANCOM). A COMMON MARKET involving Bolivia, Chile, Colombia, Ecuador, Paraguay and Venezuela.

annual capital charge. A financial management technique which involves comparing regular cash flows on a yearly basis with the cost of capital as a way of assessing how well the organization is performing.

annual general meeting (AGM). There is a legal requirement on all REGISTERED COMPANIES in the UK to hold a meeting once a year of all members at which the directors make a report. This includes an income statement, balance sheet, auditor's report and directors' report and is usually published in one volume as the ANNUAL REPORT for the company. The interval between AGMs must not exceed 15 months.

annual percentage rate (APR). The figure for the annual rate of interest which, in the UK, must be disclosed by law to prevent consumers being misled by credit agencies quoting flat rates which appear low. It is covered by the CONSUMER CREDIT ACT.

annual premium costing. In PENSION calculations the premium payable can be calculated in two ways – annual premium costing or SINGLE PREMIUM COSTING. In the former,

costs are worked out on the basis of a standard annual payment made every year until retirement. In single premium costing the premium costs are worked out on the basis of the amount of pension earned in a year on a year-by-year basis, which means that the premium varies as retirement is approached.

annual report. A legally-required report by a REGISTERED COMPANY in the UK which contains a BALANCE SHEET, a PROFIT AND LOSS ACCOUNT, an auditor's report and a directors' report as a minimum. This document is made available to shareholders and anyone expressing interest in the company. In the USA the SECURITIES AND EXCHANGE COMMISSION requires audited financial statements, a five-year summary of earnings with an accompanying management analysis, a description of the business and of the main markets in which the company's securities are traded, a management report identifying directors and executives and details of the market prices and dividends on securities over the past two years.

annual return. A legally-required return detailing activities of all REGISTERED COMPANIES which must be sent to the REGISTRAR OF COMPANIES, where it remains available for public inspection.

annual usage value. A term used in INVENTORY CONTROL to describe the total cost of the quantity of different categories of stock used during a year.

annuity. A form of PENSION which is bought on retirement by paying a lump sum. In many cases annuities are bought on the proceeds of a maturing endowment assurance policy which may also form part of a pension scheme.

ANSI. See AMERICAN NATIONAL STANDARDS INSTITUTE.

anthropometry. In WORK STUDY, the study of human body measurements.

anticipation. If a customer pays a debt early, he may receive a discount from the supplier, or, alternatively, he may deduct something from the price paid himself; this latter is known as anticipation. The practice is common in the USA but less well-known in the UK.

anticipation stocks. (1) Stocks of raw materials which are bought in anticipation of rises in prices.

(2) Finished goods etc which are stockpiled ahead of favourable market movements.

anti-featherbedding. Actions taken to prevent FEATHERBEDDING.

anti-trust. An action, legislative or otherwise, taken to prevent or restrict MONOPOLISTIC practices. It is widely used in the USA – for example, in the long battle between ATT and IBM over computing and telecommunications activities.

AOQ. *See* AVERAGE OUTGOING QUALITY.

AOQL. *See* AVERAGE OUTGOING QUALITY LIMIT.

APEX. *See* ASSOCIATION OF PROFESSIONAL, EXECUTIVE, CLERICAL AND COMPUTER STAFF.

APL. A high-level computer language whose name derives from 'A Programming Language'.

application program (applications software). A type of computer program which performs a particular function for the user, such as WORD PROCESSING, SPREADSHEET, or utilities.

applications software. *See* APPLICATION PROGRAM.

appraisal interview. *See* PERFORMANCE APPRAISAL.

appraisal method. (1) *See* PERFORMANCE APPRAISAL.

(2) A financial technique used in calculating DEPRECIATION. At the start and finish of each account period asset values are appraised and the depreciation is calculated on the basis of differences between the two.

apprentice. A person who takes a form of employment (an apprenticeship) in which he receives training for a craft or trade. Apprentices are usually paid at lower rates than skilled workers until they finish their apprenticeship, and may be INDENTURED to a particular employer for that period. The tradition of apprenticeships goes back to the craft guilds of mediaeval times.

appropriation. The allocation of money in a BUDGET for a particular activity.

approximation of laws. *See* EUROPEAN COMMUNITY.

APR. *See* ANNUAL PERCENTAGE RATE.

aptitude test. A test used to assess a person's aptitude for particular tasks or jobs.

AQL. *See* ACCEPTABLE QUALITY LEVEL.

arbitrage. The practice of using different market prices to advantage by entering into multiple contracts simultaneously, buying at a lower price and selling at a higher. It can be practised with securities, commodities, currencies etc. Simple or one-part arbitrage involves only one pair of prices; compound or two-, three- or more-part arbitrage refers to complex multiple deals.

arbitrageur. One who practises ARBITRAGE. Since arbitrage requires being able to move in and out of investments quickly, there is a temptation for arbitrageurs to engage in INSIDER TRADING. In 1986 the Boesky scandal in the USA, which had repercussions throughout the stock exchanges of the world, emerged through the confessions of Ivan Boesky, an arbitrageur, about a variety of insider deals.

arbitration. A process whereby disputes can be resolved by the intervention of a third, neutral party. Arbitration procedures are often specified − for example, as clauses in contracts − to allow for the situation where disputes might arise.

Arbitration Acts 1950, 1975, 1980. Various pieces of UK legislation covering the arbitration of industrial relations disputes. Broadly, they offer the opportunity to refer difficult disputes to independent arbitration; the 1975 Act set up the ADVISORY,

CONCILIATION AND ARBITRATION SERVICE (ACAS) as a statutory body for this purpose.

Argyris, Christopher. US psychologist and management researcher whose work has particularly focused on the relationship between the individual and the organization. He has made a number of contributions to the development of the theory and practice of ORGANIZATION DEVELOPMENT, some of which are described in *Intervention Theory and Method* (Reading, Mass.: Addison Wesley, 1970). For a review of his work, see D. Pugh, et al, *Writers on Organizations* (3rd edn, Harmondsworth: Penguin, 1986) and C. Handy, *Understanding Organizations* (Harmondsworth: Penguin, 1976).

arithmetic mean. *See* MEAN.

arrears. Overdue or unpaid debts.

arrow. A feature of a NETWORK connecting two nodes and representing an ACTIVITY or a relationship between EVENTS, and indicating the direction of movement through the network.

arrow diagram. *See* ACTIVITY ON ARROW.

articles of association. A formal set of rules setting out the relationship within a UK REGISTERED COMPANY between its members and directors. Items covered include the rights of various classes of shareholder, arrangements for general meetings and voting eligibility. In the USA equivalent rules are called articles of incorporation. Articles of association are held at COMPANIES HOUSE by the REGISTRAR OF COMPANIES and are available for public inspection.

articles of incorporation. *See* CERTIFICATE OF INCORPORATION.

artificial intelligence (AI). The field of study in computing and information technology which attempts to model the information processing characteristics of the human brain. AI is particularly concerned with the development of expert systems in which the experience, accumulated knowledge and judgmental rules which human experts deploy can be simulated by computer systems.

A/S. (1) *See* AKSJELSKAP.
(2) *See* AKTIESELSKAB.

ASA. (1) *See* ADVERTISING STANDARDS AUTHORITY.
(2) *See* AMERICAN STANDARDS ASSOCIATION.

ASEAN. *See* ASSOCIATION OF SOUTH EAST ASIAN NATIONS.

'A' shares. A class of non-voting ordinary SHARE, rarely used nowadays.

ASLEF. *See* ASSOCIATED SOCIETY OF LOCOMOTIVE ENGINEERS AND FIREMEN.

ASLIB. *See* ASSOCIATION OF SPECIAL LIBRARIES AND INFORMATION BUREAUX.

assembler. A low-level computer language in which instructions are written in the form of mnemonics for the actual machine code instructions.

assembly. (1) The manufacturing of products based on putting different components together.
(2) The assembled arrangement of components.

assembly chart. *See* GOZINTO CHART.

assembly-line production. A form of production, particularly developed by Henry Ford in his Model-T car plants, for carrying out assembly work. In an assembly line operations are carried out in sequence, building up the product as it flows along the production line, each worker adding components or performing operations on them.

assertiveness training. A form of MANAGEMENT DEVELOPMENT which is designed to improve an individual's command over a situation so as to achieve his or her goals. Assertiveness does not necessarily require aggressiveness or authority but involves developing INTERACTIVE SKILLS which ensure that the individual's point of view is communicated clearly in a variety of different situations.

asset. In accounting, something owned by a person or company and which represents (or will represent at some future date) an economic benefit to them. Assets are classed as fixed − such as capital equipment − and current − such as cash, stocks, or debtors. Liquidity is an indicator of how quickly assets can be turned into cash and thus current assets − which can be easily converted − are sometimes known as liquid assets. A distinction is also drawn in the above assets between those considered as tangible and intangible, the latter having an apparent value as far as the books of the company are concerned but in practice not realizable − for example, the GOODWILL of a firm.

asset stripping. The process of taking over a firm in order to dispose of its ASSETS or to use them elsewhere. After this, the original organization is usually closed down, having been stripped of its assets.

assign. (1) To transfer rights (e.g. of ownership) to another, or to transfer obligations − such as in a contract − to another, usually called the assignee. The person who assigns is called the assignor.
(2) To allocate something or some task to someone − for example, the performance of specific duties within an organization.

assignable variable. In process control, an observed departure from expected performance which may be attributed (assigned) to a known cause.

assignment analysis. In JOB EVALUATION, a type of analysis which is based on skills or experience required etc.

assisted areas. Regions of the UK which have been given special status by the DEPARTMENT OF TRADE AND INDUSTRY in recognition of their particular need for industrial development. Several classes of assisted area exist, such as intermediate areas and development areas, and in each conditions are set up to facilitate development − for example, via reduced regulation, building and investment grants etc.

associated company. In the UK, a company which is associated with (but not a subsidiary of) another − for example, in some form of JOINT VENTURE. Under the Companies Act 1985 an associated company is defined as

one in which the investing company can exert a significant influence over the associated company in terms of policy and decision-making.

Associated Society of Locomotive Engineers and Firemen (ASLEF). The UK trade union representing the above group and one of two major rail unions, the other being the National Union of Railwaymen (NUR).

associated states. *See* EUROPEAN COMMUNITY.

Association of Broadcasting Staffs (ABS). One of two major trade unions in broadcasting, the other being the ASSOCIATION OF CINEMATOGRAPH, TELEVISION AND ALLIED TECHNICIANS.

Association of Cinematograph, Television and Allied Technicians (ACTT). One of two major trade unions in the broadcasting industry, the other being the ASSOCIATION OF BROADCASTING STAFFS.

Association of International Bond Dealers (AIBD). An organization, formed in 1969, based in Zurich, which acts as a self-regulatory body for dealers in EUROBONDS.

Association of Professional, Executive, Clerical and Computer Staff(APEX). The main UK trade union of white-collar workers in office and clerical activities.

Association of Scientific, Technical and Managerial Staffs (ASTMS). One of two main white-collar unions in the UK, the other being the ASSOCIATION OF PROFESSIONAL, EXECUTIVE, CLERICAL AND COMPUTER STAFF.

Association of South East Asian Nations (ASEAN). An organization set up to represent the political and economic interests of a number of countries in the region (Brunei Darussalam, Indonesia, Malaysia, Philippines, Singapore, Thailand) which attempts to co-ordinate trade policy within the region and with the rest of the world.

Association of Special Libraries and Information Bureaux (ASLIB). A UK organization concerned with improving the use of information in industry, commerce and the public sector.

Association of Teachers of Management (ATM). A UK specialist group representing those with an interest in management education in colleges, business schools, industry etc. The main purpose of the ATM is to promote – through research, conferences, seminars and publications – the study and practice of management education.

assurance. An alternative term for INSURANCE.

ASTMS. See ASSOCIATION OF SCIENTIFIC, TECHNICAL AND MANAGERIAL STAFFS.

ATA carnet. A customs document, which is accepted in many countries signatory to the ATA Convention, which allows items to be imported free of duty if the importation is of a temporary nature – for example, a salesman carrying samples which he will take back with him at the end of his visit.

at call. Money lent on the understanding that it is a demand deposit – that is, that it can be withdrawn on demand at any time.

ATE. See AUTOMATIC TEST EQUIPMENT.

ATM. (1) See ASSOCIATION OF TEACHERS OF MANAGEMENT.
    (2) See AUTOMATED TELLING MACHINERY.

at sight. A characteristic of BILLS OF EXCHANGE, SECURITIES etc which are payable immediately rather than requiring acceptance or clearing procedures.

Attachment of Earnings Act 1971. A UK law which under certain circumstances permits CREDITORS to obtain repayment of their debts at the source of a debtor's earnings.

attendance bonus. A bonus paid for regular attendance and/or good timekeeping.

attendance time. The total time spent working by an employee, on the basis of which his wages are calculated.

attended time. The measure of the utilization of a machine, calculated by subtracting the unattended time (when no operator or maintenance person is using the machine) from the total time period involved.

attest. A legal term meaning to affirm the authenticity of a signature on a contract or other document by countersigning it.

attitude. The set of factors – including personality and experience – which predisposes behaviour in human beings.

attitude survey. A survey carried out to determine individual attitudes towards the subject in question – for example, asking employees about their satisfaction with working conditions. Attitude surveys are used extensively in market research to identify consumer attitudes to new or existing products. They can either be carried out via questionnaire or interview approaches, or a combination of both.

attorney. A person appointed to act on behalf of another, either by being given power of attorney or, as in the USA, being appointed as a legal representative.

attribute listing. A technique used in problem-solving to explore attributes of an idea by listing them systematically. A description of the technique can be found in T. Rickards, *Problem Solving Through Creative Analysis* (Aldershot: Gower Press, 1974).

auction. The process of selling in which the price of items is not fixed but instead the potential buyers bid and the items are sold to the highest bidder.

audit. (1) A process of detailed examination of a company's accounts to assess their accuracy. For legal purposes, an audit must be carried out by an independent auditor from outside the firm, but it is also possible to carry out periodic internal audits using accountants within the company.
    (2) Any detailed and critical examination of other aspects of a company's business – for example, manpower or technology.

audit by rotation. A process of systematically auditing aspects of a company's financial or general performance on a cyclical basis. The period between audits is called an audit cycle.

Audit Commission. A UK body set up under the Local Government Act 1982 to take responsibility for all local authority auditing work in the public sector.

audit cycle. *See* AUDIT BY ROTATION.

audit methods. *See* PANEL INTERVIEW METHODS.

auditor's report. A legally-required report from independent and qualified auditors which must be attached to any INCOME STATEMENT or BALANCE SHEET prepared by a UK REGISTERED COMPANY. It must give the opinion of the auditors as to whether the accounts present 'a true and fair view' of the financial affairs of the company.

audit trail. A process of following a transaction through all the stages of a company's financial accounting system.

AUEW. *See* AMALGAMATED UNION OF ENGINEERING WORKERS.

Aufsichtsrat (Ger.: 'overseeing council', but usually translated as 'supervisory board'). All West German, Swiss and Austrian AKTIENGESELLSCHAFT companies must appoint such a board whose members are chosen by employees and shareholders. The board (which must have at least three members) supervises the *Vorstand* (board of management) although its role is advisory, not executive. It does, however, have the power to appoint directors and determine their salaries, to require a report from them on any aspect of the business and to convene a general meeting of shareholders. It forms the top tier of the so-called 'two-tier' system of management.

autarchy. *See* AUTARKY.

autarky (autarchy). An economic term used to describe a state of self-sufficiency of a company or country. It is particularly used in the context of international trade.

authoritarian management (autocratic management). A style of management which emphasizes non-consultation and acceptance without challenge of directives issued by a manager. Often associated with such a style is the belief that people require an element of strong discipline and control.

authorized capital (nominal capital). The total nominal or stated value of all the shares which a company is authorized to issue.

authorized depository. A firm or individual authorized to take custody of various kinds of BEARER SECURITIES. Exchange control laws require that such securities be kept by authorized depositories on behalf of the real owners.

authorized stock. The maximum amount of all classes of stock which may be issued by a corporation. This authorization is contained in the CERTIFICATE OF INCOPORATION.

autocracy. A type of power structure in which one individual — an autocrat — has power over all the others.

autocratic management. *See* AUTHORITARIAN MANAGEMENT.

automatic telling machinery (ATM) (through-the-wall banking). Equipment designed for automated banking services allowing customers self-service facilities outside banking hours.

automated test equipment (ATE) (automatic test equipment). Equipment, usually computer-based, which carries out testing of components and products automatically. It is extensively used in the electronics industries.

automatic guided vehicle (AGV; autonomous guided vehicle). A driverless or robot cart which travels around a factory floor carrying components, materials and finished products. It has the advantage that the route which it follows is determined by computer and is not fixed like a conventional conveyor.

automatic test equipment. *See* AUTOMATED TEST EQUIPMENT.

autonomous bargaining. A bargaining position in industrial relations in which trade unions and employers' federations as organized representatives have little influence over the negotiation process.

autonomous guided vehicle. *See* AUTOMATIC GUIDED VEHICLE.

autonomous work groups. A pattern of work organization which gives a group of workers considerable scope and responsibility for planning and carrying out production. It is an important element in SOCIO-TECHNICAL SYSTEMS.

autonomy. The property of self-determination in individuals or in an organization. It can refer specifically to the degree to which an individual or group is free to make decisions without having to refer to others.

available to promise. The uncommitted portion of a company's inventory or planned production, usually calculated from the MASTER PRODUCTION SCHEDULE.

aval. An endorsement on a BILL OF EXCHANGE which is not made out to the drawer.

average. A statistical term normally used to describe the arithmetic MEAN of a set of results. Other ways in which statistical average is expressed include the MODE and the MEDIAN.

average adjuster. A type of insurance loss adjuster whose task is to assess the extent of a liability to meet a claim for a general average contribution or when there is a particular average loss.

average cost. The total cost of producing an item divided by the number of units produced. *See also* UNIT COST.

average cost pricing. A pricing policy based on an average cost plus some level of MARK-UP.

average outgoing quality (AOQ). In quality management, the average number of errors in the output from a production process after ACCEPTANCE SAMPLING. It is usually expressed as a percentage.

average outgoing quality limit (AOQL). The maximum number of errors acceptable in production after ACCEPTANCE SAMPLING. It is usually expressed as a percentage.

average salary pension scheme. A form of PENSION scheme in which the final pension is based on the average income throughout a person's working life rather than on his final salary. Premiums are based on a percentage of that salary paid annually.

avoidable costs. A class of costs which are the consequence of a particular decision made by management – such as entry into a new market or the development of a new product. They differ from unavoidable costs in that different decisions might avoid such costs whereas some costs – like salaries and buildings and equipment – are unavoidable.

B

back orders. Orders outstanding for delivery or production.

back selling. In MARKETING, a form of SALES PROMOTION where the product or service is promoted at a point elsewhere in the selling chain. For example, a component manufacturer may promote his goods by promoting products which incorporate them.

back shift. The AFTERNOON SHIFT in a three-shift system.

backward integration. The process of adding more activities to a company's PORTFOLIO of products or processes by moving further back along the supply chain. For example, an assembler might move into production of components, or a processor might acquire interests in raw material supply.

backward pricing. A situation on the Stock Exchange in which MARKET MAKERS' quotations are out of line such that a profit could be made by buying and selling simultaneously (i.e. the best BID is higher than the best OFFER).

BACS. *See* BANKS AUTOMATED CLEARING SYSTEM.

bad debts. Debts which are not likely to be paid and are consequently written off as a loss on the company PROFIT AND LOSS ACCOUNT.

balance of payments. A statement of the debits and credits of a trading nation over a period of time. There can be various classes of debits and credits — for example, visible and invisible exports, or current and capital payments — but their total must balance. If there is more on the credit than the debit side, this is known as a balance of payments surplus; if the reverse is true, it is a balance of payments deficit.

balance of trade. A statement of the difference in value between the value of imports to and exports from a country.

balance quantity. In INVENTORY CONTROL, the number of components or sub-assemblies which are needed by a specified stage of production in order to guarantee the planned output of finished products.

balance sheet (position statement). A statement expressing the financial position of a firm at a particular point in time, as distinct from a PROFIT AND LOSS ACCOUNT which is published annually. It usually contains details of ASSETS and LIABILITIES expressed in a balanced form which is legally defined under the Companies Acts in the UK.

balance sheet ratios. *See* FINANCIAL RATIOS.

balancing allowance. The amount of money which can be deducted from taxable profits when an asset is sold at a time when the tax WRITTEN DOWN value of an asset is less than the sales value received.

balancing time. The means of obtaining some measure of flexibility in working hours in production by changing the hours worked during a period without altering the overall number.

balloon note. A type of loan in which repayment is made by a series of small instalments culminating in one large final payment.

ballot. (1) A vote taken on an issue in which individuals record their preference on a piece of paper which is placed in a ballot box and counted later — as distinct from other forms of voting, such as a show of hands.
(2) When a new issue of SECURITIES is oversubscribed, the selection of who is to receive how many shares is often done on the basis of a ballot in which all eligible names are put into a pool and then withdrawn one by one until all of the issue is allocated.

Baltic Exchange. One of the London-based exchanges, dealing with chartering and freight movements in shipping and aircraft.

Banca d'Italia. The CENTRAL BANK of Italy.

Banco de Portugal. The CENTRAL BANK of Portugal.

Banco d'España. The CENTRAL BANK of Spain.

banding. An approach to payment structures which involves grouping different rates together into a series of bands into which jobs are then classified.

bandwidth. (1) In telecommunications, the limits in frequency terms which define a particular communications band.
(2) In FLEXIBLE WORKING HOURS, the total working day, composed of core time and flexible hours.

bank bill. A type of BILL OF EXCHANGE drawn on a bank.

bank draft (bankers' draft). A PROMISSORY NOTE issued by a bank promising to pay the stated sum on demand, usually at a named office.

bankers' draft. *See* BANK DRAFT.

Bank for Industrial Settlements (BIS). An organization set up in 1930 to permit international settlements of debts and also to provide a forum for discussion of important financial affairs by the central banks of major countries. Current membership is around 30 countries and the headquarters are in Switzerland.

Banking, Insurance and Finance Union (BIFU). The main UK trade union representing employees in the financial industry.

Bank of England. The CENTRAL BANK for the UK which performs a number of key financial roles in the economy. Formally, it is a branch of the Treasury and is managed by a Court of Directors, including 16 directors plus a Governor and a Deputy Governor, all of whom are appointed by the Crown. Functions of the Bank of England, as defined under the Banking Act 1979, include: (*i*) the issuing of bank notes; (*ii*) the sale of Treasury Bills; (*iii*) acting as a banker to both government and UK clearing and

commercial banks; (*iv*) regulating the dealings of UK government stocks; (*v*) regulating the behaviour of UK banks (including advising and directing on lending policy, interest rates etc); and (*vi*) regulating the market for foreign exchange and, when these are in force, the operation of exchange controls.

Bank of Greece. The CENTRAL BANK of Greece.

bank of issue. A bank which issues the bank notes which form a national currency.

bank rate. A figure which indicates the minimum rate at which the Bank of England will DISCOUNT BILLS OF EXCHANGE. It was used up until 1972 to indicate to the other UK banks the rates of interest they should use, but was then replaced by the MINIMUM LENDING RATE.

bankrupt. A legal status in which an individual is declared INSOLVENT. The word can be used as both a verb – to bankrupt – or a noun, describing an individual in a state of bankruptcy. Conditions attached to being bankrupt include the placing of the individual's property in the hands of a TRUSTEE who will use it to pay off creditors.

bankruptcy notice. The legal notice which precedes an act of bankruptcy in which a judgment debtor is given seven days to pay his debt (or guarantee that it will be paid). Failure to do so results in his being declared bankrupt.

Banks Automated Clearing Service (BACS). A UK network payments system for making credit transfers and payments automatically between banks.

banque d'affaires (universal bank). A type of bank which handles the business of both a MERCHANT BANK and a CLEARING BANK, often taking an EQUITY STAKE and an active role in managing the businesses to which it lends.

Banque de France. The CENTRAL BANK of France.

bar chart. A way of representing information in graphical form, using rectangles or bars to illustrate different magnitudes – for example relative proportions or percentages.

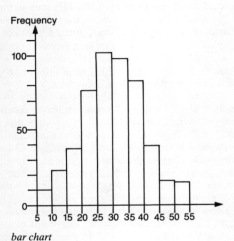

Frequency

bar chart

bar code. An identifying label on an item which enables it to be read by a scanning system – for example, a light pen linked to a computer. The stripes of black and white represent binary numbers which provide a convenient way of storing information about the item – for example, in a retail product this might include price, sell-by date, supplier, stock code etc. Bar codes are used in stock control, production control and particularly retailing. *See* LASER SCANNING.

bargain. (1) A Stock Exchange transaction.

(2) A form of agreement or any advantageous purchase.

(3) To negotiate – for example, in bargaining over terms of a CONTRACT or in COLLECTIVE BARGAINING between employers and trade unions.

Barnard, Chester. A US management writer in the 1930s who made a number of contributions to the CLASSICAL MANAGEMENT SCHOOL. He was particularly interested in the functions of the executive, making the point that 'executive work is not that of the organization but the specialized work of maintaining the organization in operation . . . the executive functions serve to maintain a system of co-operative effort'. His work is described in *The Functions of the Executive* (Cambridge, Mass.: Harvard University Press, 1938) and summarized in D. Pugh, et al, *Writers on Organizations* (3rd edn, Harmondsworth: Penguin, 1986).

barriers to entry. In FREE TRADE systems it may still not be possible for a new firm to enter a market because of barriers such as the high costs of research and development, the need for sufficient volume to obtain scale economies or the high capital investment requirements.

barter. A form of trade in which goods are exchanged for each other rather than for cash.

Barth system. A term used in WORK STUDY originally developed in the USA by Carl Barth. It is a system of PAYMENT-BY-RESULTS in which payment due is calculated on the basis of STANDARD TIMES per unit of work according to a particular formula.

base rate. The basic rate of interest offered by the major banks in a country.

BASIC (Beginners' All-purpose Symbolic Instruction Code). A high-level computer language developed to provide a relatively simple general-purpose programming language and widely used on personal computers.

bar code

basic minutes. *See* WORK STUDY.

basic motion time (BMT). A form of WORK MEASUREMENT similar to the PREDETER-MINED MOTION-TIME SYSTEM.

basic rate. The basic hourly rate of pay for a job.

basic time. *See* WORK STUDY.

basic work data (BWD). A form of WORK MEASUREMENT system similar to the PRE-DETERMINED MOTION-TIME SYSTEM.

basket of currencies. A notional grouping of different currencies against which a nation's own currency is sometimes valued to give a broader view of its value than simply comparing it against another single currency. For example, comparing £ sterling to a group of European currencies instead of against the US dollar.

batch mode. (1) A mode of producing goods in groups with similar characteristics − batches − rather than continuously. Batch processing is used when the production process is interrupted − for example, by the need to move to different machines for different operations, or by the need to wait for such machines to be reset to make different batches. *See* FLOW PRODUCTION.
(2) In computing, batch mode or batch processing refers to operations which are not carried out sequentially in real time but are stored up and then executed as a batch −for example, when the computer is not busy processing other work.

baud (baud rate). The measure of the speed of transmission of information, usually from a computer. One baud is equivalent to one BIT of information per second. Most computer communications begin at 300 baud and go up to several thousand baud using high-speed data transfer techniques.

baud rate. *See* BAUD.

Bayesian analysis. Statistical techniques which use and establish probability curves to help in decision-making by exploring potential outcomes of different options.

Bayes theorem. A statistical theorem which is used in DECISION TREES as an aid to calculating the EXPECTED MONETARY VALUE of a particular course of action. It argues that the value of outcome (A) multiplied by its probability (P) plus the value of outcome (B) multiplied by its probability (P) and so on for all outcomes will be equal to the total expected monetary value, since the probability of all things happening will add up to 1. Expressed algebraically, this is

$$P_A(A) + P_B(B) + P(...) = 1\,(E)$$

where E is the expected monetary value and A, B etc the expected values of the different outcomes of a decision.

BDA. *See* BUNDESVEREIN DER DEUTSCHEN ARBEITGEBERVERBÄNDE.

bear. An individual who adopts a short position in stockmarket trading in SECURITIES. He promises to sell at a future date securities which he does not yet hold but the price of which he anticipates to fall, so that he can buy and sell at a profit.

bearer. An individual possessing some form of financial instrument which is payable to the bearer.

bearer bond (coupon clipping). A type of BOND which differs from a registered bond in that ownership is not specified by the issuer, thus making it transferable simply by passing on the certificate.

bearer debenture. A type of bond similar to a BEARER BOND, but involving a debenture rather than a bond.

bearer security. A type of security similar to a BEARER BOND which is easily transferable by passing on the certificate.

bearer share (share warrant). A type of SHARE whose proof of ownership is a bearer security.

bear market. A market for securities, commodities etc in which prices are falling. The opposite of BULL MARKET.

bear position. A Stock Exchange term for when a dealer's sales exceed his purchases.

bed and breakfast deal. A UK Stock Exchange dealing which is based on selling shares and then buying them back again. In the process it is possible to minimize the costs in STAMP DUTY, CAPITAL GAINS TAX and COMMISSIONS payable. In its original form this practice is now prohibited by the UK INLAND REVENUE which requires that buying and selling securities be considered as two separate DEALS.

Bedaux system. A type of incentive BONUS scheme originated in the USA by Charles Bedaux in the early 1900s. It is usually calculated on the basis of time saved as a percentage of the STANDARD TIME for a job. This money is added to a central fund and divided up among all the indirect workers in a plant.

Beginners' All-purpose Symbolic Instruction Code. *See* BASIC.

behavioural sciences. The name given to a group of academic disciplines, such as sociology, psychology and economics, which deal with aspects of human behaviour, such as the functioning of groups or organizations.

behavioural theory of the firm. A theory originally developed by Richard Cyert and James March and expounded in their book *A Behavioural Theory of the Firm* (Englewood Cliffs: Prentice-Hall, 1963), which argues that organizations are coalitions of different interest groups and have multiple goals representing their different views. This influences the pattern and outcome of decision-making in a way which introduces considerable uncertainty and challenges the assumptions about rational behaviour which are often found in classical management theory or in economic models of the firm.

below the line. *See* ABOVE THE LINE.

benchmark. A basis for comparison between things – for example, the performance of two computer systems. Originally it was used in surveying and was a mark made on a surface to identify a measured altitude which acted as a reference for all other measurements. Now the term is widely used for any comparison – as in benchmark tests – to evaluate the performance of different items of equipment or of individual workers.

benchmark job. In JOB EVALUATION, a job with which others are compared.

bereavement pay. A payment made to an employee while on bereavement leave due to a death within his family.

Betriebsrat. A WORKS COUNCIL in West German firms; a legal requirement in organizations employing more than 500 employees.

b/f. Brought forward.

bid. (1) An offer to buy something at a certain price – for example, at an auction.
(2) An offer to sell something at a price – as in tendering for a contract.

bid price. The price at which a MARKET MAKER will buy stock on the Stock Exchange.

BIFU. *See* BANKING, INSURANCE AND FINANCE UNION.

Big Bang. The colloquial term given to the day (27 October 1986) when the London Stock Exchange made a number of changes aimed at opening up the market to greater competition and which was characterized by the introduction of several automated dealing and information systems. One of the key changes made was the elimination of the traditional distinction between a JOBBER and a STOCKBROKER.

bill. (1) An INVOICE.
(2) A BILL OF EXCHANGE.
(3) A set of legislative proposals offered for discussion prior to becoming a statute.

bill broker. An individual or firm which deals in BILLS OF EXCHANGE, buying them at a discount and then holding them for payment or rediscounting them.

bill of exchange. A document which the drawer signs and addresses to the drawee which requires the drawee to pay – either on demand or at some future specified time – a specific sum of money to a specific person called the payee. Bills payable on demand are sometimes called sight bills; these differ from time bills which are not paid until they reach a maturity date − a specified time period after the bill is drawn. Time bills are often traded before they become due; in this process the payee endorses the bill and sells (discounts) it to another person who becomes the payee. A CHEQUE is the most common form of bill of exchange in domestic use which is drawn on a bank and payable on demand.

bill of lading. A document covering all details of freight carried by various means − ship, air, train etc − which is signed by the master of the vessel or other responsible person and is held by the consignee − the individual who has paid for the goods and is awaiting delivery. Information on such a bill includes the name of the carrier, departure and arrival ports, a full description of the goods in transit, the rate for carriage and the name of the consignee.

bill of material. A list of the quantities and types of material input to a product − components, sub-assemblies etc. It is often held as a computer file − the BOM file − in systems where it provides the basis for MATERIALS REQUIREMENTS PLANNING.

bill of sale. Documentary evidence of new ownership when the ownership of goods is transferred to another individual or organization, although the actual goods remain in the possession of the original owner.

BIM. *See* BRITISH INSTITUTE OF MANAGEMENT.

binary system. A number system based on powers of two rather than the familiar decimal system based on powers of ten. Since in binary all numbers are represented by a combination of one or zero, this system is suitable for computers based on electronic switches.

bin card. In INVENTORY CONTROL, a record card kept at the place of storage on which details of stock movements in and out of that part of the stores are recorded.

binomial distribution. A form of FREQUENCY DISTRIBUTION in statistics which is of particular use in analysis of cases which involve either/or decisions.

biotechnology. The generic name given to the expanding field of biologically-based processes, such as fermentation and genetic engineering, which in many cases offer radically-improved low-energy routes to traditional processes.

BIS. *See* BANK FOR INTERNATIONAL SETTLEMENTS.

bit. In computing, one item of information. The term is derived from binary digit, the smallest unit of information in computers working on the BINARY SYSTEM.

black. A practice in industrial relations disputes in which members of a union refuse to handle or have dealings with a firm or its products.

black box. Any system in which the inputs and outputs are known but the internal workings are not. For example, automatic controllers could be described as black box for most people: the inputs − control instructions − and outputs − control of the process − are known, but how the system actually operates is unknown.

black economy. The informal sector of the economy where work is done but no record of it is officially available and on which no tax is paid. *See* MOONLIGHTING.

black-hole engineering. In designing complex assemblies (such as vehicles) the assembler may leave the detailed design of a particular sub-system − such as a steering system − to a specialist supplier, on the basis that the supplier has more expertise in that area. On the drawing (or, more commonly, the computer model in a COMPUTER-AIDED DESIGN system) the assembler will leave a 'black hole' into which the supplier inserts his detailed systems design.

blackleg (scab). A colloquial term for a worker who does not support industrial action being taken by the remainder of a workforce.

blacklist. The process of setting up a list of people or firms against whom some form of discrimination is to be practised. For example, an employee blacklist would contain names of those to whom employment would be refused while another form of blacklist might identify those to whom credit will not be given.

Blake, Robert. One of the originators of the MANAGERIAL GRID.

blanket agreement. An agreement in industrial relations which covers all firms in an industry or country.

blanket order. A PURCHASE ORDER containing an open-ended contract for the supply of specified goods. Such an order contains agreements on price, approximate delivery requirements and other terms of trading. The actual delivery volumes are subsequently specified by the customer on a MATERIAL CONTROL SCHEDULE and prices may be subsequently amended by revisions to the purchase order. *See* VENDOR SCHEDULING.

blind test. A form of MARKET RESEARCH in which consumers are asked to test a product which has all identifying markings removed — often in comparison with other similar competing products which are also disguised.

```
           ┌──────────────────┐
           │ Raw materials in │
           └──────────────────┘
                    │
                    ▼
           ┌──────────────────┐
           │ Initial treatment│
           └──────────────────┘
                    │
                    ▼
           ┌──────────────────┐
           │ Assembly stage (1)│
           └──────────────────┘
                    │
                    ▼
           ┌──────────────────┐
           │ Assembly stage (2)│
           └──────────────────┘
                    │
                    ▼
           ┌──────────────────┐
           │ Inspection and   │
           │ testing          │
           └──────────────────┘
                    │
┌──────────────┐    ▼
│ Rejects/rework│◄──┤
└──────────────┘    │
           ┌──────────────────┐
           │ Packaging and    │
           │ despatch         │
           └──────────────────┘
```

block diagram

block diagram. A diagram which sets out the relationship between elements of a system but does not specify in detail what goes on inside each block. It is often used in computer programming and SYSTEMS ANALYSIS.

block release (day release). A form of training release in which employers allow employees a sustained period away from work (but on full pay) to undertake some form of training.

block vote. A form of voting at large meetings or conferences where delegates representing the interests and views of large groups not at the meeting indicate as they vote the size of the block of votes which they represent. *See also* CARD VOTE.

blue chip. (1) A company which represents a safe and reasonably profitable long-term investment — a reputation earned by a history of good performance and management. A blue chip security is a share in such a firm.
   (2) Anything which has the characteristics of being a good and reliable risk.

blue-collar workers. Manual workers, as distinct from those workers involved in clerical or supervisory tasks, who are termed white-collar workers. The name originally derives from the overalls worn by shop-floor workers in some US factories.

blueprint. (1) A detailed engineering drawing or plan. The name orginates in the process used to copy such drawings which reproduces them on a blue background.
   (2) A plan or layout of something.

blue sky research. Long-term high-risk research which involves a high level of speculation (both financial and intellectual) but which might yield significant gains by opening up totally new fields of opportunity.

blue sky laws. US laws which govern the practice of dealing in securities. The name derives from a legal decision which once classed securities dealing as 'speculative schemes that have no more basis than so many feet of blue sky'.

BMT. *See* BASIC MOTION TIME.

Board of Trade. Now part of the DEPART-MENT OF TRADE AND INDUSTRY, this UK body was responsible for matters concerning the regulation, support and development of trade in the UK.

Bolton Report. An influential report produced in 1971 by a committee chaired by John Bolton which was set up by the Board of Trade (now the DEPARTMENT OF TRADE AND INDUSTRY). Entitled *Small Firms* (London: HMSO (Cmnd 4810), 1971), it examined the role of the small firm (less than 200 employees) in the UK economy, the problems it faced and the contribution it could make to the national economy, levels of employment etc.

bond. (1) A deed by which an individual (obligator) acknowledges an obligation to do something for another (the obligee).

(2) A type of security which is redeemable by the holder. In the UK this refers only to government securities, but in other countries like the USA the term also refers to securities issued by the private sector. Bonds have a nominal value and interest is paid on them by the issuer until the bond is redeemed, at which point the nominal value is returned to the bondholder. Sometimes a premium (called the redemption or call premium) is paid when the bond is redeemed. The maturity term of bonds is generally ten years for long-term bonds, five to ten years for medium-term bonds, and less than five years for short-term bonds. The rates of interest may be fixed or floating.

bonded goods. A class of goods (e.g. cigarettes or alcohol) on which some form of customs or EXCISE DUTY is payable.

bonded store (bonded warehouse). A place of storage for BONDED GOODS before the duty on them is paid. The name derives from the BOND given by the proprietors of such stores that the duty will be paid before the goods are released.

bonded warehouse. *See* BONDED STORE.

bondholder. One holding a BOND.

bond rating. In the USA, the ability of a firm to redeem and pay interest on securities which it issues in the form of bonds.

bonus. (1) An extra payment made to an employee which may be conditional on achieving or exceeding some performance target (e.g. better quality, more output), or which may be given at the discretion of management as a form of incentive. Bonuses may also be awarded at seasonal intervals — such as a Christmas bonus — in which the amount paid reflects the performance of the company as a whole.

(2) Something extra.

bonus increment. In payment systems, an addition to STANDARD TIME which is used as an incentive.

bonus schemes (incentive bonus schemes). Schemes which reward extra effort — expressed in factors like improved output, quality etc — with extra payment. Various formulas exist for implementing bonus schemes, some of which are proprietary systems.

bonus shares (CAPITALIZATION ISSUE; SCRIP). Extra shares given to shareholders who fulfil certain conditions — such as a loyalty bonus for keeping their investment for a long period of time.

books. The financial statements and accounts of a firm.

book-to-bill ratio. A term used in some sectors, notably the semiconductor industry, to indicate the health of the sector and its short-term future prospects. It refers to the ratio between the order book (i.e. future business) and the bills (invoices) issued for work done or currently being carried out (i.e. current operating levels). A high book-to-bill ratio means that future prospects are very healthy, while a low one implies a slump coming. Book-to-bill ratios are particularly used in industries with a rapid boom/slump cycle.

book value. An indication given in the accounts of the value of the firm and its assets. This often differs from the current market value or replacement cost of those assets.

boom. In economics, a period of rapid growth in output, bringing with it growth in employment and an increase in living standards.

boom or bust cycle. A BUSINESS CYCLE which involves alternating periods of rapid growth followed by severe slumps.

borrowing allocation. The level which a board of directors sets as the upper limit on borrowing to finance capital investment in a firm.

borrowing requirement. The amount an organization needs to borrow in order to finance all its commitments during a financial year. In the national sense the government has a public sector borrowing requirement (PBSR) which indicates the amount of borrowing necessary to finance public spending.

borrowing time. In PAYMENT-BY-RESULTS systems it is possible for workers to 'borrow' time from that allocated for one task and use it to complete another task.

Boston box. A matrix diagram developed by the Boston Consulting Group in the USA in the 1960s to help explain their theories about business strategy. The principle is that companies can break their product range down into four categories — stars, cows, dogs and question marks — and develop a strategy accordingly. The breakdown is carried out by plotting the position of products on two axes — one for market share and one for market growth; this gives a matrix or 'Boston box'.

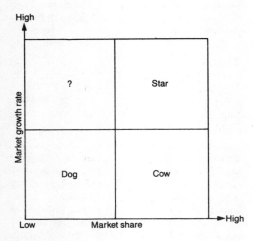

Boston box

Dogs are poorly-performing, old products which should be disposed of from the range; cows are mature products which continue to earn regular revenue; stars are new, high-performing products which require considerable strategic effort to exploit while they are still stars in the market; and question marks are newer products about which the market pattern is not yet clear.

In recent years this approach has come under attack from alternative views of strategy, notably that offered by Michael PORTER and his team at the Harvard Business School.

bottom-up approach. An approach to planning or decision-making which is based upon consultation with those at the bottom of an organizational hierarchy — as opposed to top-down approaches in which instructions and decisions come down from the top.

bought in. *See* BOUGHT OUT.

bought ledger. A part of the ledger of transactions of a firm which deals with purchases made by the firm.

bought out (bought in). (1) Components or sub-assemblies purchased from a source outside the firm rather than produced in-house.
(2) Sub-contracted skills or other services.

Boulwarism. In industrial relations, a position in which an employer makes an analysis of what it considers reasonable — in terms of wages, conditions etc — and then refuses to negotiate beyond this position in COLLECTIVE BARGAINING. The term takes its name from a former vice-president of the General Electric Company in the USA.

bourse. From the French; the name used by many European countries for their STOCK EXCHANGES.

boycott. A refusal to participate in something on grounds of principle. For example, refusing to use a particular service or buy a product because the firm involved in its supply is in breach of an agreement, or practises some form of discrimination.

Box—Jenkins methods. Statistical techniques which are used in forecasting. They are particularly used in computer-based curve extrapolation forecasts.

brainstorming. An approach to problem-solving originally developed by Alex Osborn, a US advertising executive. The basis of the technique is to suspend criticism and evaluation of ideas put forward by a group and to aim for as many ideas (fluency) and as many different types of idea (flexibility) as possible – even if many seem strange or silly. One of the strengths of the approach is that one silly idea may spark off other more useful ideas elsewhere in the group. At a later stage the ideas can be evaluated and, if necessary, further developed by brainstorming or other techniques. Brainstorming provides the basis for a series of idea generation/problem-solving techniques and is widely used in marketing, product development, organization development and group training. A good description of brainstorming and other related techniques appears in T. Rickards, *Problem-solving Through Creative Analysis* (Aldershot: Gower Press, 1974).

branching network. In project networks, a condition in which the network branches to a series of optional routes. The choice of which route to take depends on information obtained when that point is reached in the project and cannot be planned in advance; it is left up to the discretion of the project manager as to which course will be most suitable.

brand. In marketing, a product or service sold under a particular name in order to differentiate it in the marketplace.

brand leader. In marketing, the product with the most prominent image as far as consumers are concerned and which is assumed to lead the market in its development.

brand loyalty. The degree to which customers in a market remain committed to buying a particular brand of goods or services even if the cost difference is disadvantageous.

brand manager. A marketing manager with responsibility for a particular BRAND.

break-even analysis. A method for finding the break-even point (BEP) (i.e. where the firm receives as much from sales as it spends in making something) by calculating revenue and costs of different volumes of production of an item. *See* BREAK-EVEN CHART.

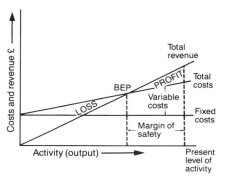

break-even analysis

break-even chart. A chart for calculating the break-even point (BEP) in which the lines for expected sales revenue and for production costs (fixed and variable) are plotted. The point of intersection is the break-even point – that is, the point where costs of production are exactly met by incoming revenue and the FIXED COSTS are covered. The margin of safety is the region beyond the break-even point which indicates how far the firm is from making a loss.

break-up value. The value of ASSETS on the LIQUIDATION of a firm, assuming they are converted into cash.

Bretton Woods. In 1944 a United Nations conference was held at Bretton Woods in the USA which discussed economic policies and co-operation in the world. It led to the setting up of the INTERNATIONAL MONETARY FUND and the WORLD BANK.

Bridlington Principles. A set of principles laid down by the UK TRADES UNION CONGRESS (TUC) in 1939 (and subsequently amended and expanded) to prevent inter-union arguments arising from DEMARCATION DISPUTES, negotiation rights etc, by requiring that they be referred to a Disputes Committee within the TUC.

Brisch classification. A coding system for the engineering industry which aims to assign particular codes to all items of resources — materials, manpower, equipment etc.

British Bankers' Association. An organization which represents the interests of all recognized banks in the UK.

British Business. A weekly publication of the DEPARTMENT OF TRADE AND INDUSTRY which includes details of government activity relevant to business and provides basic statistical data for the performance of various industrial sectors.

British Code of Advertising Practice. A code of practice set out by the ADVERTISING STANDARDS AUTHORITY.

British Computer Society. A professional association for the computer and information technology industry.

British funds. *See* CONSOLS.

British Institute of Management (BIM). An organization representing the interests of professional managers in the UK. Its activities include co-operating in the publication of the journal *Management Today*.

British Standard (BS). A certification given to indicate compliance with established standards or procedures by the BRITISH STANDARDS INSTITUTE.

British Standards Institute (BSI). An organization responsible for setting and monitoring standards in products and practice in UK firms.

British Technology Group (BTG). An organization set up in 1981 as a result of the merger of the National Research and Development Corporation (NRDC) and the National Enterprise Board (NEB) to provide support to innovative activities in the UK. The BTG is part of the DEPARTMENT OF TRADE AND INDUSTRY (DTI) and funds research and development in new products and processes either as a loan or as an equity partner; it currently holds over 2000 patents and 600 licences.

broad-band. In communications, a channel — for example, a cable in a telecommunications system — which can carry a wide variety of different frequency signal traffic. Thus a broad-band cable system based on fibre optics would be able to carry voice, image, television, data and other traffic — as distinct from a narrow-band system which would be limited to a small range.

broad-line strategy (full-line strategy). In strategic management, a strategy based on having a high variety within a product line.

broker. A go-between; someone who arranges something (usually a transaction) between two parties. This service is often paid for by a commission on the value of the transaction rather than by a flat fee. Examples of areas where brokers operate include insurance, commodity, stock (securities), information and money. Following the BIG BANG in the London Stock Exchange, any member can act as either a dealer or a broker or in both of these capacities.

brokerage. (1) The activity of broking.
(2) The commission paid.

BS. *See* BRITISH STANDARD.

BS5750. The BRITISH STANDARD setting out the requirements for certification for QUALITY ASSURANCE and control within a firm. If a firm is 'approved to BS5750' this is a guarantee of the quality of its products and its control over quality aspects in its manufacturing process.

BSI. *See* BRITISH STANDARDS INSTITUTE.

BTG. *See* BRITISH TECHNOLOGY GROUP.

bucket shop. An organization which operates outside the official organized market to offer something at a low price, for example, airline tickets, securities or futures contracts on commodities. Because it is outside the organized market framework it is not subject to regulation, and dealings with bucket shops are consequently riskier but prices offered may be significantly lower.

budget. (1) A financial plan which sets out expected income and expenditure over a future period. This can be for a firm or department but also for a nation; the Budget for the UK is announced every March by the Chancellor of the Exchequeur who explains plans for public expenditure and income from taxes etc.

(2) An authorization for certain types of expenditure (e.g. for stationery or travel). In this connection it is sometimes called an AP-PROPRIATION.

budget allocation. *See* APPROPRIATION.

budgetary control. A form or organizational control based on comparing actual financial performance against budgets for particular activities considered as budget centres.

budgetted costs. Costs included in a BUDGET. *See* STANDARD COST.

budgetting. The process of preparing a BUDGET.

buffer stock (safety stock). Stock held to cover production or sales demand when unforeseen circumstances arise — such as machines breaking down, suppliers unable to deliver etc.

bug. In computing, an error in a piece of software which causes a program to malfunction. In complex systems such bugs can remain hidden long after the system has been developed, since the particular part of the program containing the bug may be rarely used. For this reason, efforts are made to debug software — that is, to remove bugs — while it is being developed.

building society. A UK organization which uses money from one class of members (investors) to lend to others (borrowers) for the purchase of property for them to live in and on which they make repayments on a mortgage basis. Investors receive interest on their money and the savings are secured on the borrower's property. Building societies are defined as non-profit-making and are covered by legislation to this effect. However, the Building Societies Act 1986 considerably expanded the range of financial services which building societies can offer, and also provided a new regulatory framework covering their operation.

bull. A Stock Exchange term for an individual who buys SECURITIES in the anticipation that prices will rise — as distinct from a BEAR who undertakes to sell them at a future date and anticipates that the price will fall in the short term, enabling him to buy at a lower price and sell later at a higher price.

bulldog bond. A bond denominated in sterling and used by non-UK residents in the UK market.

bulletin board. A term originally used to describe a notice board but rapidly taking on the more specific meaning of an electronic notice board in an ELECTRONIC MAIL system on which computer users within a network can leave or collect messages.

bullion. A form of gold or silver (usually ingots) which are not coins with a face value but instead whose value is directly related to the quantity of metal itself.

bull market. A market for SECURITIES etc in which prices are rising. *See* BEAR MARKET.

Bullock Report. A report published in 1976 by a committee under the chairmanship of Lord Bullock which investigated the question of industrial PARTICIPATION within UK organizations. Its recommendations were broadly similar to systems operating in countries like West Germany (such as worker representation on the boards of companies). However, despite considerable discussion, little has been done to implement its findings.

bull position. A Stock Exchange term for when a dealer's purchases exceed his sales (i.e. in anticipation of a rise in prices).

Bundesverein der Deutschen Arbeitgeberverbände (BDA). A union of West German employers' federations which conducts negotiations with the federation of trade unions, the DEUTSCHE GEWERKSCHAFTSBUND, at a national level.

burden. The US equivalent of INDIRECT COSTS.

bureaucracy. A term coined by the German sociologist Max Weber to describe a form of organization which has a clearly-defined hierarchical structure, high levels of specialization, highly-defined roles, responsibilities and tasks, extensive reliance on rules and procedures, and which operates on the basis of top-down authoritarian control. Such organizational forms are attractive for the control and administration of large organizations, such as the civil service or large companies.

bureaucratic management. A style of management based on the principles of bureaucracy, emphasizing rules, procedures and hierarchical authority. A good description of the basic principles underlying bureaucratic management is given in J. Child, *Organizations: A Guide to Theory and Practice* (2nd edn, London: Harper & Row, 1982).

Bureau of Standards. A US government agency, equivalent to the BRITISH STANDARDS INSTITUTE, responsible for establishing and maintaining standards in industrial products.

burn in. A form of test, used particularly in the electronics industry, which allows a component or system to run for a sustained period in order to ensure its reliability and adherence to required performance specifications.

Burns, Tom and Stalker, George. Authors of an important work in organization theory titled *The Management of Innovation* (London: Tavistock, 1961). Their theory was based on work carried out in the Scottish electronics industry and explored the appropriateness of different kinds of organization structures for the tasks being undertaken. They concluded that bureaucratic and rigid structures which emphasized procedures − 'doing things by the book' − were best suited for routine tasks, such as production. These they termed MECHANISTIC ORGANIZATIONS. By contrast, activities like research required a high degree of flexibility in their structures, since so much work was of a non-routine nature. These they termed ORGANIC structures.

business agent. In the USA, a union official who acts as the local (branch) treasurer and who represents the union in negotiations with employers.

business cycle. A regularly recurring pattern of economic activity moving from boom to recession and back again over a period of time. Several types of business cycles have been identified with differing periods, ranging from long waves (*See* KONDRATIEV LONG WAVES) of 45−50 years' duration to short-run cycles of 3−5 years. Extensive discussion of the causes of such cyclical behaviour can be found in economics literature.

business game. A form of training in which elements of a business situation are given to participants who then must use this information as the basis for making decisions as to how to manage that situation. Many business games are now computer-based or computer-moderated − the decisions are fed into a computer and it calculates the outcomes and presents the next round of information with which the participants must work. Business games have been developed to simulate a wide variety of business activities, including marketing, industrial relations, research and development, and financial management.

business indicators. Statistics providing information about business performance and particularly those which chart the activity of key factors likely to influence business performance.

business interruption insurance. A form of INSURANCE which covers against losses due to specified causes of business interruption − such as the inability to produce due to rebuilding work after a fire or explosion. *See* CONSEQUENTIAL LOSS.

Business Monitor. A periodical report produced by the UK Government Statistical Office and published by HMSO giving statistical data on particular industrial sectors. Around 200 sectors are currently covered.

business park. *See* SCIENCE PARK.

business planning. *See* CORPORATE PLANNING.

Business Week. A US weekly publication covering a wide variety of issues related to business and industry.

Butcher Committee. A committee set up in 1985 by the UK government under the chairmanship of John Butcher, a minister in the DEPARTMENT OF TRADE AND INDUSTRY (DTI), to examine the problems of skill shortages and training provision throughout UK manufacturing industry at all levels, and to make recommendations for improving the supply of trained manpower in the future.

buyer. A manager with responsibility for PURCHASING within a firm.

buyer behaviour (consumer behaviour). A branch of marketing involving the study of why consumers purchase particular items and what influences their choices.

buyers' market. A condition when goods or services are in such plentiful supply that it favours the buyer rather than the seller who cannot get an advantageous price for them.

buzz group. A form of BRAINSTORMING group used in management problem-solving.

BWD. *See* BASIC WORK DATA.

byte. In computing, a quantity of information. One byte is equivalent to eight BITS.

C

C. A high-level computer language.

CA. *See* CHARTERED ACCOUNTANT.

CACM. *See* CENTRAL AMERICAN COMMON MARKET.

CAD. *See* COMPUTER-AIDED DESIGN.

CAE. *See* COMPUTER-AIDED ENGINEERING.

callable bond. A BOND which is redeemable on demand.

callable loan (call loan). A loan from a COMMERCIAL BANK payable on demand by the lender and repayable at any time by the borrower.

call analysis. A technique used in marketing to measure the performance of different salesmen by examining the frequency and effectiveness (e.g. conversion of enquiries to orders) of calls made to customers.

call-back pay (call-in pay). A special wage sometimes paid to a worker who has been laid off and then called back to the firm.

called-up capital. The amount of money actually paid − called up − by shareholders for a SHARE issue. This may only be a proportion of the total cost of the share, with the remainder being due at some future date or when the company in question is LIQUIDATED.

calling cycle. In marketing, the average time between calls made by salesmen.

call-in pay. *See* CALL-BACK PAY.

call loan. *See* CALLABLE LOAN.

call-off. A form of materials purchase in which a supplier is given a schedule of goods likely to be required over a future period − say one year. The actual number of goods are called off against that schedule in batches, as and when needed by the producer.

call option. The possibility, in securities dealing, to buy the right to make a later purchase (an option) at a specified price by a specified date.

call premium. A premium which an issuer may have to pay to a bondholder on surrender if a redeemable BOND is called in.

call rate. In marketing, the number of calls made to customers over a period of time.

call-up. In securities dealing, the act of asking for the remaining proportion of money unpaid on shares. *See* CALLED-UP CAPITAL.

CAM. *See* COMPUTER-AIDED MANUFACTURING.

CAP. Common Agricultural Policy. *See* EUROPEAN COMMUNITY.

capacity cost. The cost of production when a plant is working at its full capacity.

capacity planning. A part of the planning process in manufacturing which seeks to balance the forecast demand against the available capacity for performing various operations.

capital. The money involved in a business enterprise which is invested in goods, equipment, buildings, stock etc. Investment capital is the money available to invest in these items and comes from many sources − equity, loan capital, grants, overdrafts and retained earnings.

capital account. (1) In national economics, any payments in the balance of payments which are not covered in the current account − for example, loans of capital between nations.
(2) In accounting, an account recording for a class of share capital.

capital allowance. An allowance made against a company's tax payments to compensate for the DEPRECIATION of capital equipment (e.g. machinery). The level and rate of capital allowances varies with government economic policy; in the UK this favours new investment, since allowances are high in the first year of purchase. In other countries − for example West Germany − allowances are made against certain types of equipment or plant such as those used for research and development purposes in smaller firms.

capital appropriation. The allocation in a budget of capital for future investments. *See* APPROPRIATION.

capital asset pricing model (CAPM). In PORTFOLIO analysis the CAPM provides a mathematical model of the various different kinds of risk involved in the market and thus a means of identifying suitable avenues for diversification.

capital budget. A budget which provides details of capital requirements for future investment.

capital commitment. The amount of capital expenditure which is earmarked against investment commitments but not yet paid out by a firm.

capital consumption allowance. A measure of DEPRECIATION used in the context of a country's national accounts.

capital duty. A tax paid when a company is set up in the UK. It is also payable when firms expand by increasing their CONTRIBUTED CAPITAL.

capital employed. (1) An indication of the amount of capital invested in a business. Capital employed can be calculated as gross or net, the former referring to all the fixed and current assets, and the latter these items less the current liabilities.

(2) On balance sheets, the total of a shareholder's equity plus long-term debts.

capital equipment. An umbrella name for the several different kinds of equipment used to produce products or services, such as machinery, office equipment, test equipment etc.

capital expenditure. Capital that is spent on assets, as distinct from revenue expenditure, which is spent on revenue items such as travel or stationery.

capital flight. The transfer of currency from one country to another to obtain benefits (or to avoid problems) due to economic, political or military developments.

Capital Gains Tax (CGT). A UK tax introduced in 1965 and levied on capital gains as opposed to income. Capital Gains Tax becomes applicable when an asset is sold and the cash realized. It applies to most items of capital gains although exceptions include motor vehicles and some government securities.

capital goods. Goods, such as machine tools, which form part of capital investments − as distinct from consumer goods.

capital intensity. A measure of the amount of capital employed compared to the amount of labour employed − usually a direct ratio. A capital-intensive firm is one in which there is a high level of capital investment − for example, in automated plant − and a low level of labour intensity.

capital investment appraisal. The process of comparing the return likely to accrue from capital investment projects. Different techniques for doing this are available which enable estimates of the future financial returns to be calculated in a variety of ways − for example, ACTUARIAL rate of RETURN, INTERNAL RATE OF RETURN and NET PRESENT VALUE. The latter two have the advantage that they take into account the changing value of money over time and are often called DISCOUNTED CASH FLOW techniques.

capitalization. (1) *See* CAPITAL STRUCTURE.

(2) Market capitalization is the total value of all issued shares in a company.

capitalization issue. When a bonus issue is made by converting retained profits and earnings into share capital.

capital market. (1) The various sources of capital funds available for investment – from banks, finance houses, VENTURE CAPITALISTS etc.
(2) The market for SECURITIES.

capital output ratio. In economics, the link between capital investments made and changes in the flow in the goods and services produced by a firm. In general, increases in capital investment – in machinery etc – lead to a rapid increase in the flow of goods or services – a low capital output ratio. By contrast, a high capital output ratio is found in cases where investments do not bring a rapid increase in this flow – for example, investment made in developing the infrastructure of an organization.

capital productivity. The ratio of value added to capital employed – a measure of how efficiently capital is used when making investments.

capital stock. The US term for share capital – that is, capital raised by selling stock.

capital structure. The make-up of a company's funding – via borrowing, share issues etc. *See also* GEARING.

capital surplus. When a company's capital is increased – for example, when assets are revalued.

capital turn. The financial ratio linking sales to CAPITAL EMPLOYED.

capital transfer tax (CTT). A UK tax levied on the process of transferring wealth, introduced in 1975. The amount payable depends on the wealth of the person or organization making the transfer but can be paid by either party.

CAPM. *See* CAPITAL ASSET PRICING MODEL.

card steward. A trade union official responsible for collecting dues from members.

card vote. A form of BLOCK VOTE in which the number of votes for which a DELEGATE has a MANDATE are indicated on a card.

Careers and Occupational Information Centre (COIC). Part of the MANPOWER SERVICES COMMISSION in the UK which provides guidance, information, reference materials and other support for careers guidance.

Caribbean Community (CARICOM). A loose economic and political grouping of Caribbean states, established in 1973, with some characteristics of a COMMON MARKET. Its headquarters are in Guyana.

Caribbean Free Trade Area (CARIFTA). A CUSTOMS UNION and FREE TRADE AREA operated within the Caribbean region to promote economic development.

CARICOM. *See* CARIBBEAN COMMUNITY.

CARIFTA. *See* CARIBBEAN FREE TRADE AREA.

carry-back. A reduction to tax paid during the present period to balance an overpayment of tax in an earlier period.

carry forward (carry over). The process of moving an entry in a BALANCE SHEET or accounts book to another column or page.

carrying charge. A type of interest charged on instalment payments on the remaining balance owed.

carrying costs. The various costs incurred through carrying a particular item in stock – capital tied up, warehousing costs, insurance etc. *See* STOCKHOLDING COST.

carry over. *See* CARRY FORWARD.

cartel. A form of restrictive trade practice similar to a MONOPOLY in which a market is controlled – via price fixing, sharing out of segments etc – by a few firms so as to eliminate competition between them and to prevent entry by other firms into the market.

cartogram. A map which is marked in such a way which assists management information and decision-making – for example, indicating sales performance by geographical territories.

cascade network. A form of PROJECT NETWORK diagram related to CRITICAL PATH ANALYSIS.

CASE. *See* COMPUTER-AIDED SOFTWARE ENGINEERING.

case method. An approach to management training which is based on detailed analysis of case studies. Case studies can be of real or fictitious companies and are presented in sufficient detail to enable students to examine particular issues in context. The cases can by used in a variety of ways − for example, ROLE PLAYING as part of a BUSINESS GAME. Case studies are particularly associated with the teaching approach of the Harvard Business School in the USA.

case study. *See* CASE METHOD.

cash. Money which is readily available for spending − either in hand or in current accounts at a bank or financial institution.

cash before delivery (CBD). An arrangement which requires payment for goods before they are delivered − as opposed to CASH ON DELIVERY.

cash book. A basic record of all transactions − credits and debits − from which a more complex BALANCE SHEET analysis can be built up.

cash budget (cash forecast; cash flow forecast). A form of BUDGET which identifies expected future cash receipts and payments.

cash cow. A concept originally developed by the Boston Consulting Group as part of their matrix analysis of products and markets. Cash cows are products which are profitable in steady, slow-growing markets in which the company has a high market share − and thus regular revenue. Cash cows can be 'milked' for funds to support other more risky ventures − for example, new products or to help develop other markets for the company. *See* BOSTON BOX.

cash flow. Cash which flows in and out of a business. Negative cash flow is when a company pays out more than it receives in cash and positive cash flow is the reverse of this. Having a negative cash flow does not necessarily mean the company is in trouble, since it may have considerable amounts tied up in assets such as stocks; however, it cannot

continue for long in this position without realizing some of these assets in order to pay its debts.

cash flow accounting. A form of accounting based on recording the cash flows in and out of a business − as distinct from accrual accounting, which also considers long-term items like inventories, debtors and creditors.

cash forecast (cash flow forecast). *See* CASH BUDGET.

cash on delivery (COD). An arrangement which requires payment for goods when they are delivered. *See also* CASH BEFORE DELIVERY.

cash on shipment (COS). An arrangement which requires payment for goods when they are despatched (shipped) to the purchaser.

cash ratio (liquidity ratio). (1) The financial ratio of current assets to current liabilities, giving an indication of how much cash the company has available at any time.
(2) The amount of cash reserves which a bank has on hand or with the central bank to satisfy the demands of its customers and its liabilities. The figure for cash ratio is not legally specified in most countries (in the UK it is about eight per cent), but in practice it is controlled by signals from the relevant central banks.

casting vote. In a formal meeting, a second vote which the chairman can cast in situations where voting is tied in order to reach a decision.

casual labour. Workers not employed on a permanent basis but taken on and laid off as and when required. Many industries − for example, construction or docking − work largely on a casual-labour basis, employing a small core group of permanent staff and coping with demand fluctuations via casual labour.

caveat emptor (Lat.: 'let the buyer beware'). An established principle in COMMON LAW which puts the onus on the purchaser of something to ensure that it is good quality, value for money etc.

caveat subscriptor (Lat.: 'let the signer beware'). A phrase used in the context of signing contracts.

CBA. *See* COST BENEFIT ANALYSIS.

CBD. *See* CASH BEFORE DELIVERY.

CBI. *See* CONFEDERATION OF BRITISH INDUSTRY.

CCA. *See* CURRENT COST ACCOUNTING.

CCITT. *See* COMITÉ CONSULTATIF INTERNATIONAL TÉLÉGRAPHIQUE ET TÉLÉPHONIQUE.

CCLB. *See* COMMITTEE OF LONDON CLEARING BANKS.

CD. (1) *See* CERTIFICATE OF DEPOSIT.
(2) *See* COMPACT DISC.

CEEFAX. A videotext system operated by the BBC in the UK.

CEI. *See* COUNCIL OF ENGINEERING INSTITUTIONS.

cell organization. A form of organization based on grouping activities and workers together into a cell concerned with one particular product or sub-assembly. *See* AUTONOMOUS WORK GROUPS; GROUP TECHNOLOGY.

cellular radio. A form of mobile communications in which radio telephones are linked to a computer system which constantly changes frequency so that the signal remains strong despite moving around of the equipment.

CEng. *See* CHARTERED ENGINEER.

census of production. Data on industrial performance and activity collected annually by the UK government.

Central American Common Market (CACM). A COMMON MARKET with no TARIFF BARRIERS and a CUSTOMS UNION among a number of Central American countries including Costa Rica, Guatemala, Honduras, Nicaragua and El Salvador.

central bank. A national bank which acts as banker to other banks within the financial system in a country and which exerts control over the operation of the financial system and markets. Examples are the Bank of England in the UK and the Federal Reserve Bank in the USA.

Centrale Générale des Syndicats Libéraux de Belgique (CGSLB). The major grouping of Belgian trade unions.

Central Office of Information (COI). A UK government information service providing publicity and information on all government department activities.

central processing unit (CPU). The main information processing unit − the 'brain' − of a computer. In computer architecture there are a number of other functional units concerned with activities such as input/output and memory storage; the CPU is the unit which carries out the actual computing operations.

Centre for Inter-firm Comparison. A non-profit-making organization in the UK which offers expert inter-firm comparison against a number of yardsticks on a confidential basis.

centronics interface. A standard PARALLEL INTERFACE extensively used in connecting peripherals − mainly printers − to computer systems.

CEO. *See* CHIEF EXECUTIVE OFFICER.

certificate of assurance. A document given to an employee leaving a company pension scheme which has been contracted out of the STATE GRADUATED PENSION scheme giving details of his pension entitlement. This is forwarded to the Department of Health and Social Security and the benefits due are added into the employee's pension due under the state scheme.

certificate of deposit (CD). A form of negotiable interest-bearing certificate issued by a bank, usually, but not exclusively, for 90 days' maturity.

certificate of incorporation. A document issued in the UK to a company which registers as legally incorporated with the REGISTRAR OF COMPANIES. Similar procedures operate in the USA.

certificate of non-participation. A certificate issued by the Registrar of Non-participatory Employment to UK companies who operate an employee pension scheme and who wish to contract out of the STATE GRADUATED PENSION scheme.

certificate of origin. A document required by customs officials which indicates the country of origin of imported goods. It is used to calculate tariff rates and duties payable on those goods.

certified accountant. A recognized accountancy qualification in the UK denoting a member of the Association of Certified Accountants.

certified public accountant (CPA). A recognized accountancy qualification in the USA denoting a member of the American Institute of Certified Public Accountants.

CET. *See* COMMON EXTERNAL TARIFF.

CFDT. *See* CONFÉDÉRATION FRANÇAISE DÉMOCRATIQUE DU TRAVAIL.

CFI. Cost, freight and insurance. *See* COST, INSURANCE AND FREIGHT.

CFTC. (1) *See* COMMONWEALTH FUND FOR TECHNICAL CO-OPERATION.
(2) *See* CONFÉDÉRATION FRANÇAISE DES TRAVAILLEURS CHRÉTIENS.

CGIL. *See* CONFEDERAZIONE GENERALE ITALIANA DEL LAVORO.

CGSLB. *See* CENTRALE GÉNÉRALE DES SYNDICATS LIBERAUX DE BELGIQUE.

CGT. (1) *See* CAPITAL GAINS TAX.
(2) *See* CONFÉDÉRATION GÉNÉRALE DU TRAVAIL.

CGT−FO. *See* CONFÉDÉRATION GÉNÉRALE DU TRAVAIL − FORCE OUVRIÈRE.

chain store. A retailing operation with a number of shops. *See* MULTIPLE.

chain of command (line of command). In an organization hierarchy, the line down which instructions and information pass from senior management.

chamber of commerce (chamber of industry and commerce). An association set up for the promotion of trade in an area. Chambers of commerce are voluntary organizations and membership includes local tradespeople and business representatives. There is also a Junior Chamber of Commerce for younger business people, and the idea − which originated in France − has become accepted and chambers have been established in most European countries. In the UK the activities of chambers of commerce are co-ordinated by the Association of British Chambers of Commerce.

chamber of industry and commerce. *See* CHAMBER OF COMMERCE.

champion. *See* PROJECT CHAMPION.

change agent. An individual who acts as a catalyst in changing some aspect of an organization, for example, in carrying through an ORGANIZATION DEVELOPMENT programme.

change of practice principle. In INDUSTRIAL RELATIONS, an agreement that changes in working methods will bring corresponding changes in payment systems.

channel of distribution. *See* DISTRIBUTION CHANNELS.

CHAPS. *See* CLEARING HOUSES AUTOMATED PAYMENTS SYSTEM.

characteristics of easy movement. In MOTION STUDY, the basic principles on which easy human movement are based. They were originally developed by Frank and Lilian Gilbreth and Ralph Barnes in the 1920s.

character reader. A device for CHARACTER RECOGNITION.

character recognition. Methods of reading data into computer-based systems as alternatives to typing them in. Two main systems dominate − optical character recognition

(OCR) and magnetic ink character recognition (MICR).

charge account. A form of CREDIT account for the purchase of goods or services.

charge hand. *See* FOREMAN.

charismatic authority. *See* CHARISMATIC MANAGEMENT.

charismatic management (charismatic authority; charismatic style). A MANAGEMENT STYLE based on the authority accepted by members of an organization due to personal qualities – charisma – of the manager.

charismatic style. *See* CHARISMATIC MANAGEMENT.

charm price. *See* PSYCHOLOGICAL PRICING.

charter. (1) To hire the capacity of a means of transport – boat, plane, bus etc – for carrying cargo and/or passengers.
(2) The documents setting out terms and conditions of operation – for example, in a CHARTERED COMPANY.

chartered accountant (CA). A UK accountant who is a member of the Institute of Chartered Accountants.

chartered company. A historical type of company in the UK given permission to trade through a Royal Charter granted by the Crown.

chartered engineer (CEng). A professional engineer in the UK who is qualified according to the examinations of 1 of the 14 engineering institutions and who has in addition a specified period of practical experience. Since the establishment of the ENGINEERING COUNCIL, proposals have been put forward to replace chartered engineers with some alternative form of certification which will help raise the status of engineers in the public eye.

Chartered Institute of Patent Agents. The professional institute to which UK patent agents belong.

check. The US spelling of CHEQUE.

checking account. The US equivalent of a UK CURRENT ACCOUNT.

checking service. In the USA, services offered to holders of a CHECKING ACCOUNT.

check-off agreement. An agreement between employers and trade unions that the former will deduct union dues directly from employees' wages on behalf of the latter.

cheque. An order to a bank to pay a specified amount to a named individual or organization from an account held by the person signing.

cheque account. *See* CURRENT ACCOUNT.

Chicago School of Economists. A group of economists following a liberal tradition in economics, particularly associated with the University of Chicago. Among famous people belonging to this group are the Nobel prize-winner Herbert Simon, and Milton Friedman, one of the best-known protagonists of MONETARISM.

chief executive officer (CEO). The most senior executive in a company – the managing director in the UK, *Geschäftsführer* in West Germany, president in the USA etc.

CHIPS. *See* CLEARING HOUSES INTERBANK PAYMENTS SYSTEM.

Chi-squared test. A test for significance in statistics used when comparing data from different sources.

CIF. *See* COST, INSURANCE AND FREIGHT.

CIM. *See* COMPUTER-INTEGRATED MANUFACTURING.

CIO. *See* CONGRESS OF INDUSTRIAL ORGANIZATIONS.

circular flow of income. The way in which money (or, more exactly, the purchasing power conferred by money) moves around the economy as goods and services are bought and sold.

circulating assets. *See* CURRENT ASSETS.

circulating capital *See* WORKING CAPITAL.

CISAL (CISL; CISNAL). *See* CONFEDE-
RAZIONE ITALIANA AUTONOMI SINDICATI
LAVATORI.

City Code on Take-overs and Mergers. The
self-regulatory code imposed by the Stock
Exchange in the UK to oversee and advise
on the conduct of take-over bids and mergers. It operates through the Panel on Take-
overs and Mergers. Up to 1986 this was the
only form of regulation in the City, but since
the BIG BANG deregulation of the Stock Exchange and the introduction of the FINAN-
CIAL SERVICES ACT a new watchdog organization – the SECURITIES AND INVEST-
MENTS BOARD – has been established.

City of London (The City). The name used
to describe the concentration of financial institutions in the area around the square mile
of the old city of London. These include the
Stock Exchange, the BANK OF ENGLAND,
the major commodity and metal exchanges
and the headquarters of the major banks.

Civil and Public Servants Association
(CPSA). One of two main UK trade unions
for the civil service, the other being the Civil
Service Union.

Civil Service Union (CSU). One of two main
UK trade unions for the civil service, the
other being the Civil and Public Servants
Association.

CKD. *See* COMPLETELY KNOCKED DOWN.

Classical Management School. The name
given to a group of early researchers and
writers in the field of organizational behaviour and management. This group includes
Chester BARNARD, Mary Parker FOLLETT,
Frederick Winslow TAYLOR and Lyndall
URWICK.

**Classification of Occupations and Directory
of Occupational Titles** (CODOT). A system
operated by the MANPOWER SERVICES
COMMISSION within the DEPARTMENT OF
EMPLOYMENT to classify job types, and to
offer an information data base for reference
use by those concerned with career planning
and training.

Clean Air Acts. Various UK pieces of legislation aimed at pollution control.

clearing bank. A type of bank which belongs
to a network (in England the London Bankers' Clearing House) through which
cheques are settled between member banks.
Rather than carrying out a large number of
individual transactions, these are added together to produce a single total and are settled on the basis of single large cheques
drawn on the Bank of England. In Scotland
a similar system operates through the Committee of Scottish Clearing Banks.

**Clearing Houses Automated Payments Sys-
tem** (CHAPS). A computer-based system in
the UK linking the major clearing banks
which allows them to transfer and clear
cheques on the same day via electronic communication rather than by physical transfer.

Clearing Houses Interbank Payment System
(CHIPS). An automated interbank clearing
system for clearing international cheques,
based in New York.

clerical aptitude test. A selection test designed to measure abilities in clerical activities, such as classification of information.

clerical work evaluation. A technique used
in WORK STUDY to measure work carried out
in offices.

clerical work improvement programme. A
technique for work measurement in offices
based on PREDETERMINED MOTION–TIME
SYSTEMS.

clerical work measurement. The analysis of
clerical work.

clock card. A card which is punched on a
time clock by an employee when arriving at
or leaving work.

clocking-in (clocking-on). A method of recording time spent working by employees
whereby a clock card is punched on starting
and finishing work (also sometimes at the
start and finish of breaks for meals etc). The
system is usually, but not exclusively, used
by blue-collar workers, though it is becoming decreasingly popular.

clocking-on. *See* CLOCKING-IN.

close company. A form of company which is controlled by a small number (a maximum of 5) of shareholders and in which the maximum amount of shares held by others is 35 per cent. Company law requires such companies to distribute most of their profits and investment income.

close corporation. The US equivalent of a CLOSE COMPANY.

closed-loop control. A form of control in which the input is constantly modified on the basis of information feedback from the output stage. Such control systems are self-correcting and the principle is widely applied to both physical and organizational controls – for example, quality control.

closed shop (union shop). An arrangement whereby all employees in an organization must belong to a specified trade union. Two kinds of closed shop exist – pre-entry, in which employees must be members of the union before they are allowed to join the firm, and post-entry, in which becoming a member is a condition of joining the firm.

closure. The process of bringing a meeting, or part of the business of a meeting dealing with a particular agenda item, to a close. This is often specified as a formal procedure in the rules of an organization for conducting meetings. An example of such a closure would be taking a vote on a motion which has been discussed.

cluster analysis. A statistical technique used to sort large quantities of information into clusters having some similar elements which have been identified in FACTOR ANALYSIS. It often makes use of complex computer-based techniques to search for clusters in multiple dimensions.

cluster sampling. A MARKET RESEARCH technique which involves sampling within a population using clearly-defined clusters or groups – for example, all residents in a particular area or the parents of children attending a local school.

CMEA. *See* COUNCIL FOR MUTUAL ECONOMIC ASSISTANCE.

CNAA. *See* COUNCIL FOR NATIONAL ACADEMIC AWARDS.

CNC. *See* COMPUTER NUMERICAL CONTROL.

CNPF. *See* CONSEIL NATIONAL DU PATRONAT FRANÇAIS.

coalition bargaining. A form of bargaining similar to COLLECTIVE BARGAINING but involving two or more unions acting in coalition in negotiation with an employer.

COBOL (Common Business-Oriented Language). A high-level computer language developed for business applications.

COCOM. *See* INTERNATIONAL CO-ORDINATING COMMITTEE.

COD. *See* CASH ON DELIVERY.

Code du Commerce. The French legal code covering aspects of business.

co-determination (*Mitbestimmung*). A principle behind West German legislation on industrial democracy which allows for the participation of employees and others in the decision-making of their organizations. Under the co-determination law employees can sit on the upper board (the *Aufsichtsrat* – supervisory board) of the two-tier system and have other rights to participate in the management of their firms.

CODOT. *See* CLASSIFICATION OF OCCUPATIONS AND DIRECTORY OF OCCUPATIONAL TITLES.

cognitive dissonance. A concept in psychology which describes the condition in which a person's attitudes conflict with their behaviour. The theory, originally developed by Leon Festinger, suggests that the individual will change his behaviour or attitudes to try and remove the dissonance between them.

COHSE. *See* CONFEDERATION OF HEALTH SERVICE EMPLOYEES.

COI. *See* CENTRAL OFFICE OF INFORMATION.

COIC. *See* CAREERS AND OCCUPATIONAL INFORMATION CENTRE.

cold call. A visit or telephone call by a salesman to a previously unapproached (cold) potential customer.

cold turkey. A colloquial term for the process of moving over to a new computer system without keeping the old system running parallel – a high-risk venture unless carefully planned.

collateral. A form of GUARANTEE given for a loan. Examples include property, securities, or a cash guarantee by a third party.

collective bargaining. A process in INDUSTRIAL RELATIONS whereby agreement is reached on factors like wages, working conditions etc by negotiations between employers and trade unions acting collectively on behalf of their members, leading to some form of collective agreement. Such bargaining takes place at a number of levels, from the individual plant, through regional and up to national level. *See also* COMPANY AGREEMENT; FACTORY AGREEMENT; WORKPLACE BARGAINING.

collective contract. A form of autonomous worker control of production or part of production in which the group takes collective responsibility for standards, work organization etc. *See* AUTONOMOUS WORK GROUPS.

colour vision test. A test to check for the existence of and the extent of colour blindness.

column diagram. *See* HISTOGRAM.

COM (Computer Output to Microfilm). A form of data storage whereby computer output is converted to MICROFILM images.

COMAL (Common Algorithmic Language). A high-level computer language.

combine committee. A central SHOP STEWARDS' committee representing a number of plants within a large organization.

COMECON. *See* COUNCIL FOR MUTUAL AND ECONOMIC ASSISTANCE.

Comité Consultatif International Télégraphique et Téléphonique (CCITT). An international organization based in Geneva concerned with establishing and maintaining standards in telecommunications. Its membership includes the PTTs (post and telecommunications authorities) of major countries. The CCITT is a member of the International Telecommunications Union, part of the United Nations system.

comité d'entreprise. A form of WORKS COUNCIL required by French law in firms employing more than 50 people.

commercial arbitration. A mechanism for resolving disputes between customers and suppliers. In the UK these disputes can be negotiated at a number of non-statutory tribunals (many of which are based upon CHAMBERS OF COMMERCE) set up for the purpose.

commercial bank (joint stock bank). A form of bank which offers basic services for deposits and short-term loans to individuals and organizations. They do not generally offer the more specialized services of investment banks or merchant banks. In the UK they are called CLEARING BANKS, in the USA MEMBER BANKS, and in most other European countries, CREDIT BANKS.

commercial paper. A type of PROMISSORY NOTE which is negotiable. It is usually a short-term instrument (up to 270 days in the USA) and is unsecured. The main disadvantage of such a paper is that it does not allow for extension of the period of the loan.

Commercial Relations and Exports Division. *See* DEPARTMENT OF TRADE AND INDUSTRY.

commission. A form of payment made to someone who obtains business for a firm – often a percentage of the value of that business.

commission agent. An agent paid on a COMMISSION basis. This differs from a DEL CREDERE AGENT who takes a business risk with the supplier.

commissione interna. A WORKS COUNCIL required under Italian law in all firms employing more than 40 people.

committed costs. Costs to which a company is committed once a project has started — as opposed to MANAGED COSTS where some element of managerial control over their extent remains.

Committee for Industrial Technologies. *See* DEPARTMENT OF TRADE AND INDUSTRY.

committee of inspection. A committee appointed by CREDITORS involved in BANKRUPTCY proceedings to represent their interests in the case.

Committee of London Clearing Banks (CLCB). An organization representing the major clearing banks in England.

Committee of Permanent Representatives. *See* EUROPEAN COMMUNITY.

commodity. (1) Something produced for sale.
(2) Items bought and sold in bulk, like sugar, grain or metals. Commodities are traded in two forms, actual and futures, the former referring to items available for delivery immediately and the latter to contracts for delivery on some specified future date. Dealing takes place at a variety of specialist commodity exchanges such as the Corn Exchange or the London Metal Exchange.

commodity broker. A BROKER who deals in COMMODITIES.

Common Agricultural Policy (CAP). *See* EUROPEAN COMMUNITY.

Common Algorithmic Language. *See* COMAL.

common budget. *See* EUROPEAN COMMUNITY.

Common Business-Oriented Language. *See* COBOL.

common carrier. A company whose business is to provide transport or communications facilities. The term was originally used for US transport companies working between states, but has increasingly come to be applied to the field of telecommunications with the growth of deregulation and hence competition.

Common Commercial Policy. *See* EUROPEAN COMMUNITY.

common customs tariff. *See* EUROPEAN COMMUNITY.

common external tariff (CET). An agreed policy pursued by members of a COMMON MARKET to help protect against imports from non-member states by an agreed tariff levied on incoming items. *See* EUROPEAN COMMUNITY.

Common Fisheries Policy. *See* EUROPEAN COMMUNITY.

Common Industrial Policy. *See* EUROPEAN COMMUNITY.

common law. A UK body of law which is based not on statutes but on precedent from earlier cases and judgments.

common market. An agreement between two or more countries to establish a CUSTOMS UNION and the removal of TARIFF BARRIERS between them and to establish a COMMON EXTERNAL TARIFF against imports from other countries. Specifically the term refers to the European Economic Community which was established in 1957 under the Treaty of Rome. *See* EUROPEAN COMMUNITY.

Common Monetary Policy. *See* EUROPEAN COMMUNITY.

Common Regional Policy. *See* EUROPEAN COMMUNITY.

Common Social Policy. *See* EUROPEAN COMMUNITY.

common stock. A US term for ordinary SHARES in a company.

Common Tax Policy. *See* EUROPEAN COMMUNITY.

Common Technology Policy. *See* EUROPEAN COMMUNITY.

Common Transport Policy. *See* EUROPEAN COMMUNITY.

Commonwealth Fund for Technical Co-operation. A UK fund administered by the COMMONWEALTH SECRETARIAT which provides technical advice and support to member states of the British Commonwealth.

Commonwealth Secretariat. A branch of the UK Foreign Office concerned with the interests and affairs of the member states of the British Commonwealth. These include providing advice and support, both financial and information, for business and industry.

Community. See EUROPEAN COMMUNITY.

Community Agricultural Fund. See EUROPEAN COMMUNITY.

Community law. See EUROPEAN COMMUNITY.

compact disc (CD). A storage medium for computer data etc which utilizes the principle of optical storage whereby a pattern representing bits of information is etched into the surface of a special disc by means of a computer-controlled laser. The pattern can then be read by another machine which also incorporates a laser. This is the same principle as in a videodisc used in INTERACTIVE VIDEO.

companía collectiva. A form of PARTNERSHIP under Spanish law.

Companies Acts. The various pieces of legislation in the UK which cover LIMITED LIABILITY COMPANIES. Issues dealt with under these laws include the arrangements for formation and operation of limited companies.

Companies House. The place in London where records of all UK companies registered with the REGISTRAR OF COMPANIES are held and are available for public inspection.

company agreement. An agreement reached between management and unions after COLLECTIVE BARGAINING at the level of an individual company (including companies with more than one plant). *See also* FACTORY AGREEMENT.

company bargaining. A COLLECTIVE BARGAINING process leading to a COMPANY AGREEMENT.

company limited by guarantee. *See* GUARANTEE COMPANY.

company model. A model − usually computer-based − of a firm which can be used in simulation work to assist forecasting and planning.

company secretary. The person in a REGISTERED COMPANY with responsibility for ensuring compliance with the various legal requirements of the COMPANIES ACTS.

company-wide quality control. A concept in which the quality of a product or service becomes the responsibility of every member of that company. It was developed originally, along with other ideas associated with Japanese quality management − such as QUALITY CIRCLES − by W. Edward Deming and Jospeh Juran. *See* TOTAL QUALITY CONTROL.

comparative estimating. In WORK STUDY, analytical estimating based on comparisons with similar jobs done previously.

compensating rest. *See* RELAXATION ALLOWANCE.

compiler (translating routine). A computer program which translates instructions written in HIGH-LEVEL LANGUAGE into low-level MACHINE CODE.

complementary products. Goods which are often sold with each other, the demand for one affecting the other (e.g. cameras and film, fish and chips etc).

completely knocked down (CKD). Products that are shipped as kits of parts for assembly at their destination (e.g. automobiles).

component bar chart (compound bar chart). A bar chart which divides each bar up into component parts to show the composition of some statistics − for example, the performance of four companies per year for the

42   composite motion

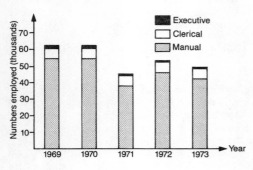

component bar chart

past five years, or as in the diagram, the numbers of different types of employee in a firm.

composite motion. The grouping together of two or more motions concerning a particular subject in a meeting or conference.

composite rate. An interest rate paid to depositors with financial institutions, such as BUILDING SOCIETIES, which deduct income tax at source.

composition. A response made by a person who is made BANKRUPT in which he offers to pay all creditors a fixed amount which is approved by the court.

comptroller (controller). The senior financial manager in a company.

Comptroller and Auditor General. The UK government official responsible for auditing the accounts of government departments and, where required, of other public bodies, with the particular motive of ensuring efficient use of resources.

compound arbitrage. *See* ARBITRAGE.

compound bar chart. *See* COMPONENT BAR CHART.

compound interest. A form of INTEREST which is calculated on the basis of a proportion of the original sum loaned plus the value of the interest so far accrued if it had been invested (i.e. compounded). This can be calculated from the equation

$$S = P(1 + i/100)^n$$

where P is the present value of the sum invested, i the compound interest rate, n the number of years (or other time periods) and S the future sum after that time.

compulsory licence. A licence issued by a court overriding an objection by a patentee who refuses to allow his patent to be used.

computer-aided design (CAD). A design system which involves drawing using a visual display screen linked to a computer rather than a pencil and paper. Images can be stored and manipulated electronically and can also be converted into electronic information via some form of digitizing device. CAD systems offer considerable advantages over conventional design systems in terms of speed, flexibility and the ability to make minor changes quickly.

computer-aided engineering (CAE). A computer-aided process of moving from design (via computer-aided design) through to computer aided-manufacture. This involves converting design data into control programs, for example, for CNC tools.

computer-aided manufacturing (CAM). Various forms of computer control of manufacturing processes, sometimes linked under a supervisory computer control system, sometimes operating as autonomous stand-alone controllers.

computer-aided production management (CAPM). Various forms of production management activity − such as inventory control, purchasing, production control − which can be carried out by suitable computer software. Such systems are often available in the form of integrated suites of software, since many of them use the same information base.

computer-aided software engineering (CASE). An umbrella term for techniques for writing, testing, debugging and coding computer software which are supported by various computer-based software engineering tools.

computer-integrated manufacturing (CIM). Advanced factory automation in which all

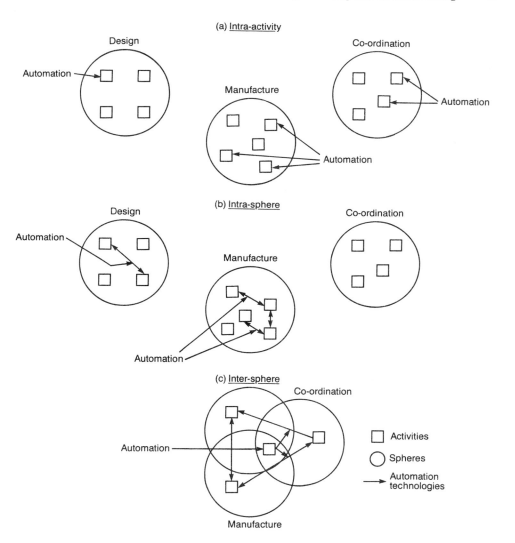

trends towards factory integration

aspects of manufacturing – from design and production planning, through the various production operations to testing, and final packaging and inspection – are controlled and co-ordinated by computers. A particular feature of CIM systems is that there is some form of shared use of information – either via a NETWORK or a DISTRIBUTED PROCESSING system. The diagram above shows how over time there has been integration of activities, first within the main areas of manufacturing, and, more recently, with the aid of computers between these areas. Full CIM is still some way off but integration between areas such as computer-aided design and manufacture or flexible manufacturing systems, linking production with co-ordination, is now well-established. A good review of

CIM is given in J. Jarvis, *Computer-integrated Manufacturing and Status* (London: Institution of Electrical Engineers, 1986).

computer numerical control (CNC). A form of computer control of equipment such as machine tools.

Computer Output to Microfilm. *See* COM.

concentration analysis. A type of analysis in which the major elements are separated out (e.g. major customers, most regularly used stock items etc). *See* ABC ANALYSIS; PARETO ANALYSIS.

concession request form. *See* ENGINEERING CHANGE NOTE.

conditions of employment. Issues such as wages, benefits, hours of work etc, usually covered in an employee's CONTRACT OF EMPLOYMENT.

Confédération Française Démocratique du Travail (CFDT). One of the major groupings of French trade unions, equivalent to the TRADES UNION CONGRESS in the UK.

Confédération Française des Travailleurs Chrétiens (CFTC). One of the major groupings of French trade unions.

Confédération Générale du Travail (CGT). One of the major groupings of French trade unions.

Confédération Générale du Travail – Force Ouvrière (CGT–FO). One of the major groupings of French trade unions.

Confederation of British Industry (CBI). In the UK, the main representative body for industrial employers. It offers a wide range of advisory and practical services to members and lobbies on their behalf at national level. The CBI was formed in 1965 by amalgamating the major employers' federations for different industries, and it now represents about 11,000 companies as well as all the major nationalized industries, most trade associations and other smaller employers' organizations.

Confederation of Health Service Employees (COHSE). A major UK trade union representing health service workers.

Confederation of Shipbuilding and Engineering Unions (CSEU). A grouping of 24 trade unions in the shipbuilding and engineering industries in the UK.

Confederazione Generale Italiana del Lavoro (CGIL). The major grouping of Italian trade unions, equivalent to the TRADES UNION CONGRESS in the UK.

Confederazione Italiana Autonomi Sindicati Lavatori (CISAL; CISL; CISNAL). One of the major groupings of Italian trade unions.

confirming house. An organization which operates in the area of international trade and acts as a go-between between overseas buyers and domestic exporters in a country. Its main role is to confirm orders placed by the buyer and to undertake to pay for those goods when shipped, thus removing the risk from the exporter.

conformance testing. Testing to ensure conformance to agreed national or international standards.

conglomerate. An organization with a wide variety of business interests, often grouping several companies under one name.

conglomerate merger. A merger of companies to form a conglomerate.

Congress of Industrial Organizations (CIO). A US trade union federation. *See* AMERICAN FEDERATION OF LABOR.

conscientious objector. (1) An individual who refuses to participate in something for reasons of conscience.
(2) In industrial relations, an individual who objects to joining a union or to contributing to its funds.

conseil d'entreprise. A form of WORKS COUNCIL required under Belgian law in all firms employing more than 150 people.

Conseil National du Patronat Français (CNPF). The main EMPLOYERS' FEDERATION in France.

consequence analysis. A technique used in project evaluation to explore the outcomes of different options.

consequential loss. In addition to problems caused by physical damage for which insurance can be taken out — such as fire, water etc — other losses may be incurred — such as interruption of work due to lack of premises. Such consequential losses can be insured against, usually to compensate for loss of earnings or profits. *See also* BUSINESS INTERRUPTION INSURANCE.

consignment account. In a business involving a seller and an agent, the ownership of the goods involved must be clearly documented. If they remain the actual property of the seller, even though the agent has them in his possession, they are termed 'on consignment' (consignment stocks) and a special class of accounts — consignment accounts — are kept on them.

consignment distributor. A distributor operating on the basis of paying the original seller for goods only when the distributor has resold them.

consignment note. The documentation accompanying an order when delivered, which lists details like quantity and nature of all goods in that consignment.

consignment stocks. Goods which are being handled by an agent. *See* CONSIGNMENT ACCOUNT.

consolidated accounts (consolidated financial statements). Accounts submitted by a holding company which consolidate the individual accounts of all subsidiaries within a group.

consolidated financial statements. *See* CONSOLIDATED ACCOUNTS.

Consolidated Fund (Account of Her Majesty's Exchequer). The account at the Bank of England into which government revenues are paid.

consol. A form of government stock which is not redeemable but which represents a safe investment. *See* GILT-EDGED STOCK.

consortium. A group of individuals and/or companies which join together to undertake a specific project.

conspicuous consumption. Highly-visible expenditure — such as new cars or big houses — which is undertaken not out of need but in order to impress.

Construction Industry Training Board. A UK organization responsible for training and staff development in the construction industry.

constructive conflict. *See* CREATIVE CONFLICT.

constructive dismissal. A type of UNFAIR DISMISSAL referring to the case of employees who technically leave employment of their own free will but who are in fact pushed into doing so by action or conditions in their workplace.

consultative management. A management style which emphasizes consultation in order to secure views and attempts to achieve some measure of participation by others before taking decisions.

consumer acceptance test. A form of MARKET RESEARCH in which new products are tried out in the field to determine their acceptability (and other reactions) to consumers.

consumer action. *See* CONSUMERISM.

consumer behaviour. *See* BUYER BEHAVIOUR.

consumer credit. A range of credit facilities extended for the purchase of consumer goods and services — such as hire purchase, credit cards etc.

Consumer Credit Act. UK legislation covering terms and conditions of consumer credit arrangements, aimed at protecting the consumer.

Consumer Credit Protection Act. A US law covering terms and conditions of consumer credit arrangements, aimed at protecting the consumer.

consumer disposable. *See* CONSUMER DURABLE.

consumer durable. Consumer goods designed for long-term use, such as washing machines, refrigerators or hi-fi systems – as opposed to consumer disposable, designed for one-time or short-term use, such as foodstuffs.

consumer expendable. *See* CONSUMER DURABLE.

consumerism (consumer action). The growing and often highly-organized response of consumers to the supply of goods and services. Consumerism takes the form of pressure for legislation on issues like quality, extent of provision, prices etc and sanctions can be applied to force suppliers to change their practices or products – for example, via boycotts, lobbying, adverse publicity etc.

consumer panel. A market research tool which involves setting up a group of consumers' representatives of the target population and then seeking their views, reviewing their purchases, and discussing their responses to new product ideas.

Consumer Product Safety Commission. The US agency responsible for setting and maintaining standards of consumer product safety.

consumer promotion. A form of sales promotion targetted directly at the consumer – for example, cut-price sales – as distinct from trade promotions which are aimed at retailers and distributors.

Consumer Protection Advisory Committee. An organization set up in the UK under the terms of the 1973 FAIR TRADING ACT to monitor issues concerning consumer protection and to report to the DIRECTOR-GENERAL OF FAIR TRADING. In particular, it is responsible for overseeing the implementation of various pieces of consumer protection legislation including the above act, the TRADES DESCRIPTION ACTS 1968, 1972 and the CONSUMER SAFETY ACT 1978.

Consumer Protection Bill 1986. A UK law which provides legislation on product liability to protect the individual consumer. It was enacted in response to a EUROPEAN COMMUNITY Directive of 1985 which required member states to implement protective legislation against defective goods.

Consumer Safety Act 1978. UK legislation aimed at providing extra protection for consumers in respect of defective products.

Consumers' Association. A UK organization set up in 1956 as an early consumer action group which, with the growth of consumerism, has become an important focus. It remains an independent body and among other advisory and research activities it carries out comparative tests on a variety of products and services. The results are publicly available and may appear in the magazines in the *Which?* series, published by the Association.

Consumers' Union. A long-established US organization responsible for protecting the interests of consumers.

containerization. An approach to the storage, handling and transport of goods using standard-sized containers which can be manipulated by special-purpose machinery and transported on specially-designed vessels, rail trucks or lorries. Its advantages include the systematization of freight movement to permit easy flow between different transport media.

Contango Day. A Stock Exchange term for the end of a stock market period on which all accounts must be settled.

contango facilities. If someone dealing on the Stock Exchange does not wish to pay his account at the end of a period, he may take advantage of contango facilities which enable him to pay interest on the value of the shares he has bought and settle his account at the end of the next period.

Continental shift system. A shift system involving frequent changes of shift among workers.

contingency allowance. In WORK STUDY, an allowance for other occasional tasks not studied when establishing a STANDARD TIME for a job.

contingency planning. Forward planning to cater for unexpected eventualities in the life of a project.

contingency theory. A theory in organizational behaviour which suggests that the structure of an organization is determined by a number of factors, such as size, nature of technology employed, market environment etc − in other words, it depends on the operating contingencies of the firm. Selection of a suitable structure is the subject of management exercising strategic choice. A good description of contingency theory appears in J. Child, *Organizations − A Guide to Theory and Practice* (2nd edn, London: Harper & Row, 1982).

contingent liability. A liability which depends on something happening as a result of some future event.

continuous credit. See REVOLVING LOAN.

continuous movements. In MOTION STUDY, those smooth movements which require no sudden changes in direction.

continuous production. See FLOW PRODUCTION.

continuous shift work. A shift system which permits operation of a plant on a continuous basis, 24 hours a day, 7 days a week.

continuous stationery. Computer stationery which is supplied on a continous roll or folded, suitable for repetitive work such as printing invoices.

continuous timing. See CUMULATIVE TIMING.

contract. (1) A legal agreement between two or more parties.
(2) In financial markets, a unit of trading for a financial future.

contracting in. See CONTRACTING OUT.

contracting out. (1) In the context of UK trade unions, various pieces of legislation have made it possible for trade unions to raise a levy on their members to support a political party (which has invariably been the Labour party). At times this has been on a contracting-in basis, where an individual chooses to pay the levy − and at times on a contracting-out basis, which requires the individual to choose to opt out and declare this intention. Legislation in the 1980s forced unions to ballot their members on this practice and the principle of contracting out was reinforced with a considerable majority.
(2) The term is also used in the context of employee PENSION schemes.

contract of employment. A legal agreement given to an emplyee which sets out the terms and conditions of his employment − such as the period of notice required by employee and employer etc. UK legislation supporting this is in the Contracts of Employment Acts 1963 and 1972, and the Employment Protection (Consolidation) Act 1978.

contracts preference schemes. Preferential purchasing policies by public agencies introduced in the UK as part of a support package in areas with ASSISTED AREA status, such as DEVELOPMENT AREAS. Subject to satisfactory conditions on price, quality, delivery etc, these contracts favour firms in these areas.

contributed capital. See PAID-IN CAPITAL.

contribution. The contribution a particular product or service makes to fixed costs and the profits of a firm. This figure is obtained by subtracting the costs associated with producing the product from the sales revenue generated by it.

contribution analysis. In accounting, a form of analysis used to establish the CONTRIBUTION made by each of a firm's products or services to its overall financial performance.

contribution pricing. An adjustment made to price levels, after CONTRIBUTION ANALYSIS, to improve the contribution of different products or services to the overall financial performance of a firm.

contributory negligence. See EMPLOYEE'S CONTRIBUTORY NEGLIGENCE.

contributory pension scheme. A form of PENSION scheme which involves employees paying a fixed proportion of their income into a scheme to which their employer also contributes. *See* PENSION FUND; SUPERANNUATION.

control. A basic function of management whereby management compares actual performance against planned performance and takes appropriate action when necessary.

controllable costs. Types of cost which are under the direct control of a manager or department.

controlled circulation publication. A form of publication which is sent free to a list of readers whose membership is controlled. The publication is paid for by advertising and selection of names for the list is on the basis of those likely to be able to make or influence purchase of the advertised goods or services. Such publications are monitored by the independent Audit Bureau of Circulation.

controlled daywork. *See* MEASURED DAYWORK.

controlled report. *See* PERFORMANCE APPRAISAL.

controlled work. Work which has been organized and measured by agreed WORK STUDY. *See* OPERATOR PERFORMANCE.

controller. *See* COMPTROLLER.

controlling interest. Ownership of a sufficient number of voting shares in a company to be able to exert control over its activities and direction by virtue of being able to outvote any other shareholders.

convenor. The senior SHOP STEWARD in an enterprise, elected as leader by other shop stewards and acting as their representative in dealings with employers and local and national trade unions.

conversational programming. A form of computer programming in which users interact with a computer directly to produce a program, rather than prepare instructions beforehand.

conversion training. An approach to retraining for performance of new but related

tasks in a firm. For example, an electrical maintenance fitter may be given training in electronics to enable him to deal with new generations of computer-based equipment.

convertibility. The indication of how far a currency can be converted into other currencies or gold.

convertible bond. A BOND which can be converted at the holder's option into shares in the issuing company, usually within a specified time period.

convertible debenture. *See* CONVERTIBLE SECURITY.

convertible loan stock. Stock which is taken out as a fixed-interest security but which includes an option to convert at a subsequent date into ordinary shares.

convertible security. A SECURITY which can be converted into other securities under certain agreed conditions on which the holder has an option.

cooling-off period. In industrial relations disputes, a period of time (sometimes voluntary, sometimes legally required) before industrial action is taken. It provides a breathing space in which both sides in dispute may reconsider their positions.

co-operative. Any form of organization in which producers or purchasers get together to set up a business within a regulated system. Among the typical rules under which a co-operative works are: (*i*) members must benefit from the conduct of the business; (*ii*) there must be equal control of the business — one man, one vote; (*iii*) interest repayments are limited in any one year; (*iv*) surplus distribution may be wholly retained or distributed among members; and (*v*) membership is open to anyone satisfying clearly set-out criteria. In the UK these legal requirements are set out under the terms of the Industrial Common Ownership Act 1976.

Co-operative Development Agency. An organization set up in the UK in 1978 by the government to promote the concept of CO-OPERATIVES and to advise on their setting up and operation.

co-ownership. A shared ownership of something in which the shareholders have a stake in the venture.

co-partnership. A form of CO-OWNERSHIP.

copy brief. The main document setting out an advertising campaign – objectives, strategy, measures of success etc.

copyright. The exclusive rights governing written material in terms of what it may be used for subsequently.

CORAL (Computer On-Line Real-Time Applications Language). A high-level computer language.

core group. A central group of workers in an organization operating some form of FLEXIBLE MANNING who have long-term security of employment and constitute the permanent core, as opposed to peripheral workers who are taken on and laid off as and when required.

core time. Particular periods in FLEXIBLE WORKING HOURS during which all employees must be in attendance. Outside this core time employees are free to choose their working hours.

Corfield Report. A report, published in 1979, of a committee under the chairmanship of Sir Kenneth Corfield into the practice of industrial design and its management in the UK.

corporate identity. *See* CORPORATE IMAGE.

corporate identity programme. A programme aimed at raising awareness of or focusing attention on a company or aspect of its business.

corporate image (corporate identity). The image a company presents to the outside world.

corporate management. The overall management of an organization, as opposed to departmental or sectional management.

corporate planning (business planning). A planning process which takes into account the whole organization as a set of resources and considers future development in the context of markets, competitive environment, legislative environment, new technologies etc. A major element is developing corporate strategy in which the company's strengths and weaknesses are analysed in the context of environmental threats and opportunities and decisions regarding future action are taken in the light of overall corporate objectives which set out the goals and philosophy of the company.

corporate secretary. The US equivalent of a COMPANY SECRETARY.

corporate strategy. *See* CORPORATE PLANNING.

corporation. (1) A group of people acting as a corpus – a body.
(2) A collection of individuals acting as a single entity which has a legal status and autonomy in business dealings.

corporation tax (mainstream corporation tax). The basic tax levied on the profits of all companies in the UK, subject to various kinds of allowances which change over time. The rate varies with the current financial legislation but is usually around 50 per cent of profits, reducing to a lower level (around 30 per cent) if profits do not exceed a specified amount.

correlation. In statistics, the degree of linkage between two or more variables. Expressed as a correlation coefficient, a figure approaching 1.0 means that there is a strong linkage, while a negative coefficient which approaches -1.0 shows there is a negative relationship between items.

correspondent banking. A relationship between large and small banks where the former hold money and perform specialist services for the latter.

COS. *See* CASH ON SHIPMENT.

CoSIRA. *See* COUNCIL FOR SMALL INDUSTRIES IN RURAL AREAS.

cost, insurance and freight (CIF). An arrangement whereby the seller of goods includes the costs of shipping and insurance to a specified destination in the price. *See* FREE ON BOARD; FREE ON RAIL.

cost absorption. *See* ABSORPTION COSTING.

cost accountant. An accountant specializing in recording and analysing cost data in order to advise on future cost control with business.

cost benefit analysis (CBA). Techniques used in assessing possible projects which an organization might undertake. Various methods exist but the general aim is to quantify as many of the expected costs and benefits associated with the project as possible.

cost centre. (1) *See* COST CENTRE APPROACH.
(2) In an organization, a department or group which does not normally produce any income (revenue) but which represents a cost borne by the organization in order to secure provision of particular services — for example, research and development.

cost centre approach. A form of organizational financial control based on identifying defined areas of operations to which costs can be attributed. This provides a useful way of identifying where and how costs are being incurred.

cost effectiveness. A measure of the extent to which money has been well-spent on something which is derived by comparing the benefits produced with other ways of achieving them.

costing. The process whereby costs are assigned.

costing system. An organizational control system which keeps track of the actual costs and controls them against budgetted costs.

cost of goods sold. *See* COST OF SALES.

cost of sales (cost of goods sold). The total costs associated with producing and selling goods.

cost-plus pricing. An approach to pricing an item based on adding a fixed amount or percentage to the actual cost of producing that item. In practice this covers a range of approaches to pricing based on variants of the above formula.

cost price squeeze. A situation in which prices cannot easily be raised but where costs of producing an item cannot be kept down. An example might be the smaller firms in the motor components industry which do not buy enough raw materials, energy etc to be able to keep costs of factor inputs low — but which depend too much on their final market to be able to risk raising prices, since this would result in someone else taking the business at a lower price.

cost push inflation. INFLATION caused by rising costs — for example, of raw materials or energy, such as the 1974−5 oil crisis. *See* DEMAND INFLATION.

cost reduction plan. A form of PAYMENT-BY-RESULTS scheme where cost savings are agreed by employers and employees. Any extra savings achieved are translated into a bonus for employees.

cost variance. The difference between ACTUAL COSTS and STANDARD COSTS.

cost/volume/profit analysis (CVP analysis). The examination of the effect of producing in differing volumes on the costs of production and the profit achieved from higher sales. It is used to determine optimum levels of operation.

Council for Mutual Economic Assistance (CMEA; COMECON). A trading network for economic co-operation among the major socialist states in Europe and the USSR. Members include Bulgaria, Czechoslovakia, the German Democratic Republic, Hungary, Mongolia, Poland, Romania and the USSR.

Council for National Academic Awards (CNAA). In the UK, the body which is responsible for overseeing the curricula and courses and the award of degrees and other educational qualifications from further and higher education institutions in the public sector.

Council for Small Industries in Rural Areas (CoSIRA). A UK organization set up to help small firms (defined as firms with a turnover of less than £10,000 and employing less than 20 skilled people) in manufacturing and services industries located in rural areas. The range of services offered includes advice on technical and commercial matters, workshops and premises, finance, training and some grants.

Council for the Securities Industry (CSI). An organization set up in 1978 by the Bank of England which has a co-ordinating role for all matters relating to the London securities market, including, up until 1986, the operation of its own self-regulatory system. It is financed by contributions from affiliated bodies and a levy on the equity collected by stockbrokers.

Council of Engineering Institutions (CEI). An umbrella organization comprising the major engineering institutions in the UK, such as the electrical, mechanical, civil, chemical and so on, which speaks as the representative voice of the engineering profession. *See* ENGINEERING COUNCIL.

Council of Europe. An organization, established in 1949, with headquarters in Strasbourg, as the first pan-European political organization. Its aims are to bring about closer European unity, protect democracy and human rights and improve living conditions. There are currently 21 member states, including the 12 members of the European Community (Austria, Belgium, Cyprus, Denmark, France, Germany, Greece, Iceland, Ireland, Italy, Liechtenstein, Luxembourg, Malta, the Netherlands, Norway, Portugal, Spain, Sweden, Switzerland, Turkey, and the UK). The Council has no executive powers but makes recommendations and drafts European treaties (Conventions) in a variety of fields, including health, social welfare, education, local government and justice. Over 100 Conventions have been drawn up, including the European Convention on Human Rights, which makes it possible for individuals to take their case to the Court of Human Rights in Strasbourg. The work of the Council is directed by a Committee of Ministers drawn from the foreign ministers or deputies from the member states, and this body is influenced in turn by the Parliamentary Assembly which includes members of parliament from the member states.

Council of Ministers. *See* EUROPEAN COMMUNITY.

counselling. The act of listening and giving advice on problems. It is especially used in personnel and careers guidance.

counter purchasing. An arrangement in international trade whereby trade in one direction is balanced by a flow in the other. Thus, if a supplier sends one type of goods to one country, another firm may buy other goods to the same value from that country. Although similar to BARTER, the difference is that goods are bought and sold rather than simply exchanged. The practice is common in trade with countries in the Eastern bloc.

countervailing duty. A special form of import duty which is designed to counter the effects of export subsidies. This duty is in addition to any normal duties imposed on that type of goods.

country of origin. In international trade, the source of an item in a transaction, or of goods being imported.

coupling up. The overlapping of two shifts during changeover in shiftwork to ensure continuity.

coupon (coupon rate). The annual rate of interest on a SECURITY.

coupon advertising. The form of ADVERTISING in which the reader of a paper or journal completes and sends off a coupon for further information.

coupon clipping. *See* BEARER BOND.

coupon rate. *See* COUPON.

covariance. A statistical term, derived from common variance, which describes the extent to which two variables vary at the same rate.

covenant. A CONTRACT or a clause in a contract.

covenants in restraint of trade. Clauses in an employee's CONTRACT OF EMPLOYMENT which secure against his disclosing knowledge obtained during his employment which might be of value to a competitor. Employers must have good reason for inserting such clauses.

· **cover.** *See* EARNINGS/DIVIDEND RATIO.

coverage analysis. A technique used in INVENTORY CONTROL which identifies an ideal stock level representing the minimum cost of working capital tied up in stocks to provide an acceptable level of customer service.

Coverdale training. A form of management development, originally developed in the UK by Ralph Coverdale, based on group dynamics, which emphasizes the performance of real tasks in a group.

covered. (1) Business transactions where the risk of loss is minimized.
(2) In foreign exchange markets, dealings in which spot and forward contracts are balanced in such a way that no loss will be incurred whichever way exchange rates move during the forward contract period.

CPA. (1) *See* CERTIFIED PUBLIC ACCOUNTANT.
(2) *See* CRITICAL PATH ANALYSIS.

CPM (critical path method). *See* CRITICAL PATH ANALYSIS.

CP/M (Control Program for Microcomputers). A widely-used, relatively standard operating system for microcomputers which is being superseded by the more powerful MS/DOS.

CPSA. *See* CIVIL AND PUBLIC SERVANTS ASSOCIATION.

CPU. *See* CENTRAL PROCESSING UNIT.

craftsman. A skilled worker who has acquired skills during an apprenticeship and/or some form of technical or craft training.

craft union. A trade union, the majority of whose members are drawn from skilled craftsmen as distinct from other groups such as white-collar workers, blue-collar wokers etc.

creative conflict (constructive conflict). The idea that under certain circumstances conflicts can be resolved to the benefit of all concerned by the opening out and confrontation of the issues involved, rather than by agreeing a compromise or smoothing over the conflict so that it emerges again later. The concept originated with Mary Parker FOLLETT but has been widely used and developed by workers in the field of ORGANIZATION DEVELOPMENT. A good discussion of conflict resolution in organization development can be found in W. French and O. Bell, *Organization Development* (2nd edn, Reading, Mass.: Addison Wesley, 1982).

credit. (1) An entry in an ACCOUNT to indicate a payment by a DEBTOR.
(2) The entry in the right-hand side of a ledger.
(3) The positive balance in a CURRENT ACCOUNT.
(4) A period of time allowed before money borrowed or the purchase price of goods or services must be repaid.
(5) A certificate awarded on completion of part of a course of study. *See* CREDIT ACCUMULATION.

credit accumulation. The process of studying for a degree or diploma or other qualification in which credits are awarded for completion of units or modules of the course. The qualification is awarded when sufficient credits have been accumulated.

credit agency (credit bureau). An agency specializing in checking credit-worthiness of individuals and organizations and providing this information to potential sources of credit.

credit approval. The process of checking the extent to which an individual or organization will be able to repay credit.

credit bank. The European equivalent of a clearing bank in the UK. *See* COMMERCIAL BANK.

credit bureau. *See* CREDIT AGENCY.

credit control. (1) At a national level, an element of fiscal policy which exerts various forms of control over the availability of credit offered by banks and other institutions.

(2) The process of controlling who is eligible for credit and how much and under what conditions this is provided – for example, setting spending limits on credit cards.

credit factoring. A form of factoring in which sales which have been invoiced are bought from a supplier for less than their face value, the difference being the factor's profit.

credit insurance. An INSURANCE cover guaranteeing payment of debts incurred through purchase of goods or services on credit.

credit line. See LINE OF CREDIT.

credit note. A form of compensation given to a customer in lieu of cash if he returns goods or complains about goods or services. A credit note is equivalent to the same amount of cash but entitles the holder to goods or services from the supplier issuing it to the value of the note.

creditor. (1) One who is owed money, as opposed to a DEBTOR who owes it.

(2) A heading in financial accounts indicating to whom money is owed. Also known, especially in the USA, as ACCOUNTS PAYABLE.

credit outstanding. See LINE OF CREDIT.

credit rating. An indication of the creditworthiness of an individual or company, based on an assessment of their ability to repay the amount of credit advanced.

credit sale. A sale based on extending credit to the buyer rather than requiring the whole price of something to be paid in cash.

credit squeeze. A part of a government's credit control policy which involves limiting the availability of credit in order to reduce the risk of inflation due to too-rapid spending.

credit union. An organization set up to act as a co-operative bank, able to take deposits and make loans to members. Credit unions are common in the USA where they perform a similar role to BUILDING SOCIETIES in the UK.

crisis management. See MANAGEMENT BY CRISIS.

critical incident analysis. See CRITICAL INCIDENT METHOD.

critical incident method (critical incident analysis). A technique in which key aspects of past performance are analysed to derive guidelines for better performance in the future. For example, the characteristics of the best and worst new product launches might be analysed in order to identify strategies for improving this process in the future.

critical path analysis (CPA). An approach to planning which involves a PROJECT NETWORK indicating the various stages which must be gone through and the sequence in which these must take place. The technique is used to highlight those activities which are critical to the project's progress and to identify a critical path through the project.

critical path method (CPM). See CRITICAL PATH ANALYSIS.

cross booking. The practice of booking time against different jobs where some times booked are less than the actual time taken, and some more. It is used to even out overall work rates.

cross charging. See TRANSFER PRICING.

cross impact analysis. See CROSS IMPACT MATRIX.

cross impact matrix (cross impact analysis). A forecasting method which looks at the impact a number of different developments have upon each other by listing them on both axes of a matrix. In each cell of the matrix the cross impact of these on each other can then be examined.

cross subsidizing. The process of using profits from one company or plant or profit centre to subsidize a loss made elsewhere in the organization.

cross trading. A form of FLEXIBLE MANNING in which craftsmen are trained for more than one craft area − often by CONVERSION TRAINING − and then move between these areas. For example, increasingly automated plant in factories is requiring a breadth of skills in maintenance rather than the traditional single skills and this need is being met by cross trading.

Crown Agents (for Overseas Governments and Administrations). A UK body which acts as a purchasing and managing agent for various countries within the Commonwealth.

CSEU. *See* CONFEDERATION OF SHIPBUILDING AND ENGINEERING UNIONS.

CSU. *See* CIVIL SERVICE UNION.

culture. The collection of attitudes, values, beliefs, norms etc which underpin an organization and shape the behaviour of its members. Put simply, it is 'the way we do things 'round here'. A good description of organization culture can be found in C. Handy, *Understanding Organizations* (Harmondsworth: Penguin, 1976).

cumulative preference share. A form of PREFERENCE SHARE on which dividends may be accumulated if profits are poor in one year and then paid at the end of the next year when they improve.

cumulative timing (continuous timing). A WORK STUDY technique for job timing in WORK MEASUREMENT which uses a continuous monitoring of a job over time, as opposed to a FLYBACK TIMING approach.

current account. (1) A bank account held by individuals or organizations from which transactions can be immediately effected. In many cases current accounts bear no interest. It is known as a checking account in the USA.
(2) At a national level, the balance of payments where currency transactions − imports and exports − are recorded.

current assets (floating assets; liquid assets). ASSETS of an essentially short-term nature − cash, stocks, money owed etc − as opposed to FIXED ASSETS which are longer-term in nature, such as buildings.

current cost accounting (CCA) (current cost convention). A convention in accounting which values ASSETS amd measures COSTS and REVENUE on a current basis rather than on a historical one. This accounting is done using the current value to the business of assets.

current cost convention. *See* CURRENT COST ACCOUNTING.

current liabilities. LIABILITIES of a short-term nature which will be paid within the financial year − such as debts, overdraft charges, interest etc.

current ratio (working capital ratio). A FINANCIAL RATIO relating current assets to current liabilities.

current use value. *See* EXISTING USE VALUE.

current yield. The return offered by SECURITIES, expressed as a percentage, obtained by dividing the amount received as dividend by the price of the shares.

curriculum vitae (CV). A document which sets out a record of an individual's experience, qualifications and achievements. When given to a prospective employer, it offers a brief background to the individual on which an assessment of his suitability for a post can be partially based.

Customs and Excise. The agency responsible for collecting customs duties levied in the UK.

customs union. One of the basic foundations for establishing a COMMON MARKET, whereby participating countries agree to eliminate customs and other tariff barriers between them. They may also choose to establish a

COMMON EXTERNAL TARIFF barrier against non-members. *See* FREE TRADE.

customs drawback. *See* DRAWBACK.

CV. *See* CURRICULUM VITAE.

CVP. *See* COST/VOLUME/PROFIT ANALYSIS.

cybernetics. The study of the principles and practice of control. The word takes its name from the Greek work for steersman.

cycle billing. The sending out of invoices on a cyclic basis so that work, and hopefully revenue, is evenly spread.

Cyert, Robert and March, James. *See* BEHAVIOURAL THEORY OF THE FIRM.

D

daily contracted hours. The number of hours per day specified in an employees' CONTRACT OF EMPLOYMENT.

daisy-wheel printer. A computer printer which operates by a hammer striking a wheel which contains all the print characters and which spins round, under computer control, to select the character to be printed. Although slower than matrix or laser printers, daisy-wheel printers produce typewriter-quality output because of their similar action.

damages. Payments made in compensation for some form of injury — physical or otherwise (e.g. damage to a reputation, loss of GOODWILL etc).

dangle. In NETWORK PLANNING, an arrow in an activity which has no preceding or succeeding event in an arrow on activity network. *See* ACTIVITY ON ARROW.

data base. A collection of information stored on a computer — for example, a list of customer names and addresses or the payroll details of employees within a firm. Data bases range from simple, card-index types for small computer usage through to complex relational data bases in which many different combinations of data can be stored and manipulated; these tend to require extensive memory and processing power and are to be found on larger, more advanced computer systems.

data base management. The process of building, maintaining and using a DATA BASE.

data base management system (DBMS). Computer software for DATA BASE MANAGEMENT.

data compression. A family of software techniques for reducing the volume of data to be transmitted in a communications system without affecting its integrity.

data flow chart (procedure flow chart). A chart which maps the way in which information flows through a system and identifies who and what is involved in the flow.

data logger. A device (usually electronic) for collecting (logging) data about the performance of a process or production system.

data logging. The collection of data about various performance characteristics in a production system or item of equipment — for example, production rate, machine utilization, time lost for breakdown etc. It is used as an input to production management.

data processing (DP). The manipulation of data by a computer.

Data Protection Act 1984. UK legislation covering the storage of personal data on computers in DATA BASES. It was introduced to protect the rights of individuals about whom data might be held in the form of computer records, and to give them details of what data is held on them and why. The act requires all organizations (except the Police Force and other specified institutions) which hold such data to register with the DATA PROTECTION REGISTRAR who is the individual empowered to oversee the implementation of the act.

Data Protection Registrar. The individual given the responsibility for implementing the requirements of the DATA PROTECTION ACT 1984.

dawn shift. The early-morning shift in a three-shift system.

day book (journal). In accounting, the record of all transactions carried out by an individual or firm — debits and credits — on a daily basis.

day release. *See* BLOCK RELEASE.

day shift. The morning or middle shift in a three-shift system.

days off in lieu. *See* LIEU DAYS.

days of grace. A generally accepted additional allowance of time before a debt must be repaid.

daywork. A payment scheme based on a rate per hour and the amount of time worked, to which other additional payments – such as bonuses – may be added.

dB(A) (decibel, adjusted). A measure to approximate the effect of noise on the human ear. Under an EEC code of practice, 90 dB(A) is the maximum level in industry.

DBMS. *See* DATA BASE MANAGEMENT SYSTEM.

DBS. *See* DIRECT BROADCASTING SATELLITE.

DCF. *See* DISCOUNTED CASH FLOW.

dead hand. *See* MORTMAIN.

dead time. In PAYMENT-BY-RESULTS payment systems, the time spent by workers waiting for work for which there may be a negotiated payment rate.

deal. (1) Any kind of transaction.
(2) A trade in SECURITIES.

debenture. (1) A type of SECURITY on which interest is paid as a percentage of its nominal value. This interest payment is also guaranteed by the company issuing the security in its assets. The company may also redeem the debentures by payment of a fixed sum (usually on a fixed date, which is termed a maturity), although some debentures are available as perpetual and have no fixed date by which time they must be redeemed.
(2) In international markets, BONDS which are secured only against the unpledged assets of a company.

debenture bond (debenture stock). The US equivalent of UNSECURED LOAN STOCK.

debenture capital. Money received by a firm in exchange for DEBENTURES.

debenture holder. One holding DEBENTURES.

debenture trust deed. A deed entitling a trustee to act on behalf of debenture holders to protect their interests.

debit. (1) An increase in asset value or a decrease in the extent of liabilities.
(2) A subtraction of money from an account.

de Bono, Edward. A UK writer who developed the concept of LATERAL THINKING. His publications include *The Use of Lateral Thinking* (London: Jonathan Cape, 1967).

debt. An obligation to another, usually financial.

debt capital (loan capital). Money lent to a company on a long-term basis (at least one year) which must be repaid first if the company is liquidated. Interest is paid on debt capital on a regular basis and the lenders of such capital usually hold DEBENTURES in the firm.

debtor. One who owes a debt, usually financial.

debtors' ledger. *See* ACCOUNTS RECEIVABLE.

debt ratio. A FINANCIAL RATIO relating debt capital to total capital (i.e. both DEBT and CONTRIBUTED CAPITAL).

debug. The process of finding and eliminating errors and faults in development, especially of computer software. *See* BUG.

decelerating premium bonus. A BONUS scheme where the bonus rate payable goes down as more time is saved on the job.

decibel, adjusted. *See* DB(A).

decision analysis. A form of organization analysis suggested by Peter DRUCKER which examines the way in which decisions are made. The other two forms of analysis are RELATION ANALYSIS and ACTIVITIES ANALYSIS.

decision-band method. A technique used in JOB EVALUATION which grades jobs within a firm in terms of their decision levels. Higher value jobs are those which involve high-level decision-making; for example, under one system there are six levels of decision bands into which jobs are classified: (*i*) policy-making; (*ii*) programming; (*iii*) interpretative; (*iv*) routine; (*v*) automatic; and (*vi*) vegetative).

decision-mapping via optimum networks (DEMON). A marketing technique using NETWORK ANALYSIS to evaluate new product launches.

decision rules. Rules relating the choices which should be made to different types/values of expected outcome in using statistical methods to forecast the outcome of different decisions. For example, strategies can be developed to maximize the outcome or minimize the costs of any outcome etc. *See* BAYESIAN ANALYSIS.

decision support systems. Computer programs designed to aid management decision-making.

decision theory. Various mathematical techniques — such as game theory, risk analysis and sensitivity analysis — which are used in FORECASTING to explore the likely outcomes of different decision options.

decision tree. An aid to decision-making which is based on preparing a chart showing

the various options available and their consequences and subsequent decision choices.

declaration of solvency. When a company is wound up voluntarily, rather than to undertake bankruptcy proceedings, the directors are required to make a declaration of solvency which states that the debtors of the firm can be paid within 12 months of winding up. *See* WIND-UP.

dedicated automation. Automation in which special purpose equipment dedicated to one particular operation or process is used; for example, transfer lines in the automobile industry which are built to produce only one particular model. This contrasts with flexible automation in which the equipment can be reprogrammed for different operations, processes or product requirements.

deed. A document, suitably signed and sealed, which sets out a contract, bond or other legal arrangement.

deed of arrangement. A legal document which assigns property to a trustee who uses it to pay off creditors of an individual or organization.

deferred asset. Money receivable later than 12 months after the publication of a BALANCE SHEET.

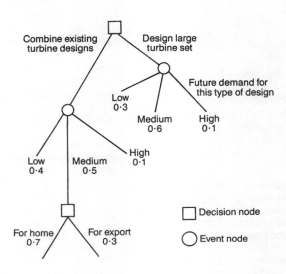

decision tree

deferred capital. *See* DEFERRED SHARE.

deferred charges. In accounting expenditure, charges written off over a period of time in instalments.

deferred compensation. A payment which will be made at some future date – for example, pensions for employees.

deferred liability. In accounting, an amount payable more than one year after the date of the BALANCE SHEET.

deferred share (deferred capital). A form of SECURITY on which a DIVIDEND is only paid after the ordinary shareholders have all received their dividends – the opposite of a PREFERENCE SHARE.

deferred taxation. An arrangement to pay tax which takes advantage of differences between profits in the time period for the balance sheet and for the tax period.

deficit financing (deficit spending). The financing of projects which cost more than the organization has available as cash or current assets and for which it therefore needs to borrow money.

deficit spending. *See* DEFICIT FINANCING.

deflation. A condition in which economic activity declines (often referred to as the economy slowing down) and the purchasing power is reduced. The opposite of INFLATION.

DEF131A. A UK Ministry of Defence procurement specification which sets out the procedures for acceptance sampling and quality assurance for firms wishing to supply them.

del credere agent. An agent who does not own the goods which he is selling directly but who undertakes some of the risk in the transaction by guaranteeing to pay the supplier even if the final purchaser does not pay. COMMISSION rates for del credere agents tend to be higher than for normal agents, reflecting the higher risk involved.

delegate. (1) A nominated representative of the views and interests of a group.
(2) To pass on authority and responsibility to someone else in an organization.

delegate conference (delegate meeting). A meeting whose members are DELEGATES representing larger numbers of people who, while being unable to attend in person, give their delegate a MANDATE to vote on their behalf.

delegate meeting. *See* DELEGATE CONFERENCE.

Delphi technique. A FORECASTING technique based upon canvassing the opinions of a panel of experts in the field being examined. Statements about the likely future are sent to members of the panel (who never meet fact-to-face) and they are invited to modify them based on their expert opinion and experience. The modified statements are then sent around a second time and further comments and modifications are invited; the process is repeated as often as necessary to achieve some consensus on the forecast.

demand. The requirement for goods or services in a market. Demand theory deals with relationships between demand and the price of goods.

demand analysis. The analysis of factors affecting levels and emergence of DEMAND in a market.

demand deposit. *See* AT CALL.

demand elasticity (elastic demand). In economics, the extent to which the demand for something varies with changes in its price. Inelastic demand is the condition when even major changes in price make little or no difference to the demand. The significance of demand elasticity to a business is that when demand is elastic, a rise in prices may result in falling revenues as a consequence of lost sales. *See* PRICE ELASTICITY.

demand inflation (demand pull). In economics, the condition in which prices rise because of increased demand which cannot be met. It contrasts with COST PUSH INFLATION in which prices rise because of an increase in costs which cannot be controlled.

demand pull. *See* DEMAND INFLATION.

demand pull innovation. When there is a demand for something − either in the market or as a social need − which triggers innovation. Its basis is the idea that 'necessity is the mother of invention'. *See* TECHNOLOGY PUSH.

demarcation dispute. In industrial relations, a dispute caused by disagreements over which group of workers should carry out particular types of work − for example, who should work new computer-based equipment in the printing industry − electricians or printers? Such disputes are particularly common in industries where traditionally many different craft unions have operated, each representing the interests of a particular craft or trade − such as in shipbuilding.

democratic leadership. *See* DEMOCRATIC MANAGEMENT.

democratic management (democratic leadership). A style of management which is based upon consultation and participation in the decision-making process − as opposed to AUTHORITARIAN MANAGEMENT in which a single manager takes all decisions. *See* PARTICIPATIVE MANAGEMENT.

DEMON. *See* DECISION MAPPING VIA OPTIMUM NETWORKS.

denationalization. *See* PRIVATIZATION.

Department of Education and Science (DES). A UK government department with responsibility for most aspects of education and training. The exceptions are in the field of vocational training where responsibility is taken on by the MANPOWER SERVICES COMMISSION.

Department of Employment (DoE). A UK government department with responsibility for managing the employment situation, both in terms of the conditions under which those in work are employed and in providing assistance to those seeking employment via training, subsidies to firms, information and advice etc.

Department of Energy. A UK government department with responsibility for the management of energy production and conservation and for developing policies for improving the pattern of energy management. In addition to providing information and advice, the department also funds a number of conservation schemes aimed at improving the ways in which energy is used in industry and commerce. Many of these schemes offer grants to firms to help them make such improvements.

Department of Health and Social Security (DHSS). A UK government department which has responsibility for health and welfare aspects, including the management of the National Health Service. The DHSS also manages the system of benefits paid to those out of work, including unemployment benefit, maternity benefit and sickness benefit.

Department of the Environment. A UK government department with responsibility for environmental matters, including the conservation and preservation of the natural environment. Its responsibilities cover various pieces of controlling legislation on pollution, the location and limitations on new industrial development, and the administration of relationships between national and local government.

Department of Trade and Industry (DTI). A UK government department with principal responsibility for matters pertaining to business and industry. Its prime areas of work are as follows: (*i*) overseas trade: setting and monitoring international trade policy and promoting UK interests in various international groups including the EUROPEAN COMMUNITY and the ORGANIZATION FOR ECONOMIC DEVELOPMENT; (*ii*) export promotion and particularly the operation of the British Overseas Trade Board; (*iii*) industrial policy and assistance, including regional support; (*iv*) competition and consumer affairs, including the establishment of competition policy and relations with the OFFICE OF FAIR TRADING and the MONOPOLIES AND MERGERS COMMISSION; (*v*) science, technology and research, including establishing policy in these areas, the provision of various forms of SUPPORT FOR INNOVATION, and the operation of several government laboratories and scientific stations, including the National Physical Laboratory, the National Engineering Laboratory, Warren Spring Laboratory, the Laboratory of the Government Chemist, and the National Weights and Measures Laboratory; (*vi*) financial services, company legislation, and regulation, including monitoring legislation on companies and operation of the Companies Registration Office, regulation of the insurance industry, regulation of radio frequencies and operation of the Patent Office; (*vii*) statistics, via the Business Statistics Office.

The department has its headquarters in London but operates a further seven regional offices in England and one each in Scotland, Wales and Northern Ireland. In total there are over 30 divisions of the DTI which cover the following areas.

Air: support for research and development, investment in projects and general activities affecting the aerospace industry.

Chemicals, textiles, paper, timber, miscellaneous manufacturing and service industries: sponsorship and support for research and development provision in a broad range of manufacturing and service industries.

Information technology: encouragement and support of the development and application of information technology in manufacturing and services, including the new areas of VALUE ADDED NETWORKS and tradeable information services.

Electronics applications: promotion of electronics applications in UK industry, including the operation of several programmes such as the MICROELECTRONICS APPLICATION PROJECT, the Optoelectronics Scheme and the Microelectronics Industry Support Programme (MISP) for specific and general support of the producers and users of electronics.

Mechanical engineering and manufacturing technology: encouragement of the application of new manufacturing technologies − computers, robotics etc − in the manufacturing industry, including the operation of specialist and general support schemes across a wide range of industries.

Minerals and metals: responsible for policy in these areas and particularly with the UK's iron and steel strategy for rationalization and harmonization with other European Community partners; also responsible for developments such as deep sea mining and waste management policy.

Shipbuilding and electrical engineering: general and specific support and research and development in these industries.

British National Space Centre: provides a national focus for space research and also represents the UK in the European Space Agency.

Posts and telecommunications: regulation and licensing in communications under the 1984 Telecommunications Act; represents UK interests in international projects and bodies such as the European Community's RACE programme and the efforts to provide agreed standards for the INTEGRATED SERVICES DIGITAL NETWORK.

Vehicles: sponsorship and support for the vehicle and components industries.

Alvey Directorate: established to promote research and development toward the so-called 'fifth-generation computer'; also responsible for links with international programmes such as the European Community's ESPRIT.

Quality and education: support of training and development of suitable skills for industry and the promotion of the communication between industry and the education system. Support includes the sponsorship of the ENGINEERING COUNCIL; promotion and awareness of good design practice including the funding of the DESIGN ADVISORY SCHEME and sponsorship of the DESIGN COUNCIL, and for quality matters via sponsorship for the BRITISH STANDARDS INSTITUTE and other bodies, and the provision of a Quality Advisory Scheme; represents the UK in international affairs related to establishing and developing standards for quality.

Research and technology policy: monitors and advises on technology and related policies and is responsible for co-ordinating overall research and development policy in the UK; operates the Teaching Company Scheme and sponsors various RESEARCH ASSOCIATIONS, the BRITISH TECHNOLOGY GROUP, and provides the secretariat for the various Technology Requirements Boards which advise the DTI on general policy for particular sectors in terms of research and development and technology support.

Research establishments: government-funded bodies such as the National Engineering Laboratory which provide a range of services including some contract research to industry.

General policy: co-ordination of policies within the DTI with those of other departments and exploring the implications of policies from outside; development of policies not covered elsewhere by a specific division.

Industrial financial appraisal: provision of financial appraisal and general financial accountancy advice to the DTI and particularly for assessing applications for financial assistance under the various DTI schemes.

Investment and development: responsible for various aspects of regional industrial policy on grants, ASSISTED AREA status, the CONTRACTS PREFERENCE SCHEMES, and for co-ordination on regional industrial policy with that of the European Community.

Regional offices: responsible for administration of the various regional offices of the DTI.

British Overseas Trade Board (BOTB): responsible for advising the government on matters of overseas trade and for directing the various export promotion activities. The BOTB is made up of members from the CONFEDERATION OF BRITISH INDUSTRY, the TRADES UNION CONGRESS, and from the DTI divisions, the Foreign and Commonwealth Office and the Export Credits Guarantee Department.

Overseas trade divisions: several divisions responsible for the promotion and protection of UK trading interests overseas. Services provided include the Projects and Exports Policy Division which supports major capital projects, the Fairs and Promotions Branch which supports UK presence at international trade fairs, the Exports Data Branch which provides export intelligence regarding opportunities and market conditions, and a variety of market specific branches which deal with different countries and the range of export support services (such as the Export Credits Guarantee Department) related to selling into them.

European commercial and industrial policy: responsible for dealing with aspects of policy which touch on the development of the European Community, such as trade agreements, some co-operative ventures (such as EUREKA) and the UK's obligations under various Community laws and directives.

International trade policy: responsible for external trade policy and for participation in the GENERAL AGREEMENT ON TARIFFS AND TRADE and relations with the UNITED NATIONS CONFERENCE ON TRADE AND DEVELOPMENT.

Consumer affairs: responsible for promoting the interests of the consumer in the UK and for maintaining the regulatory systems, such as the weights and measures legislation, product liability, advertising and other controls. Sponsors the National Consumer Council and its regional equivalents and co-ordinates with the OFFICE OF FAIR TRADING.

Companies: responsible for the administration of the 1985 COMPANIES ACT and related legislation concerning the formation and operation of companies within the UK.

Financial services: responsible for matters pertaining to the financial services sector and particularly for the administration of the FINANCIAL SERVICES ACT 1986.

Insolvency service: responsible for all aspects of insolvency administration under the various laws and procedures for winding up companies and dealing with individual bankruptcies. Under the Bankruptcy and Deeds of Arrangement Act 1976 it is responsible for the administration of the OFFICIAL RECEIVERS' service.

Insurance: responsible for administration of the Insurance Companies Act 1982 which covers the authorization and controls the operation of insurance companies.

Patent Office: responsible for matters concerning the protection of intellectual property.

Radio regulation: responsible for negotiation and allocation of frequencies within and outside the UK for radio and telecommunications and in particular for enforcing the Wireless and Telegraphy Acts.

dependency. *See* ACTIVITY ON NODE.

depletion. The amount by which a physical asset reduces — for example, minerals in a mine.

deposit. (1) A part payment for something which secures its ownership or from sale to another.

(2) The process of putting money into a bank or other financial institution.

(3) The initial outlay required to gain a futures position on the Stock Exchange.

deposit account. A bank account which pays interest to the depositor but which may impose restrictions on the speed, frequency or amount of withdrawals.

deposit administration fund. A PENSION scheme in which deposits made by employees are invested by an insurance company which manages the fund.

Deposit Protection Fund. Under the UK Banking Act 1979 a deposit protection fund was established in 1982 to provide a fund of between £5 and £6 million to protect depositors against bank failure. It is financed by contributions as a percentage of business by all major UK banks.

deposition. Written testimony given under oath. *See also* AFFIDAVIT.

depreciation. The decline in value of capital ASSETS over time − for example, as equipment wears out. A number of accounting procedures exist for calculating depreciation including STRAIGHT-LINE DEPRECIATION and REDUCING BALANCE METHODS. Tax allowances are made for depreciation and these are usually known as writing-down allowances, since the value of the asset is written down by a certain amount each year.

derived demand. *See* INDIRECT DEMAND.

DES. *See* DEPARTMENT OF EDUCATION AND SCIENCE.

Design Advisory Scheme. A scheme operated by the DEPARTMENT OF TRADE AND INDUSTRY to provide advice, consultancy and some financial support via grants and loans to firms wishing to improve their design management and performance.

Design Council. A UK organization established to promote the principles and practice of good design and its management within industry. It also operates the Design Advisory Service funded by the DEPARTMENT OF TRADE AND INDUSTRY, offering free design consultancy to firms employing between 60 and 1000 employees.

deskilling. The reduction of the range or level of skill required for the performance of a particular job.

desk research. Research which consists of reading and analysing data or information available from other sources rather than empirical research which requires collection of new information.

desktop computer. *See* PERSONAL COMPUTER.

desktop publishing. A form of document preparation system which involves a microcomputer with word processing and graphics software plus programs to enable different text and pictures to be assembled and laid out on the computer screen. When the page is ready for printing, a hard copy is produced on a high-quality LASER PRINTER.

Deutsche Bundesbank. The CENTRAL BANK in West Germany, linked to *Landes* banks in the 11 *Länder* which act as regional equivalents of the central bank.

Deutscher Gewerkshaftsbund (DGB). A federation of West German trade unions, equivalent to the TRADES UNION CONGRESS in the UK, and the negotiating partner of the BUNDESVEREIN DER DEUTSCHEN ARBEITGEBERVERBÄNDE (employers' federation association) in wage and other industrial relations issues at a national level.

devaluation. An instrument of national fiscal policy whereby a government chooses to reduce the value of its currency against others. This may be done for a variety of reasons − for example, it will help to make a country's exports more competitive. However, it also has negative effects, such as raising the cost of imported goods and raw materials.

development area. A special status afforded certain areas in the UK under the 1972 Industry Act which are designated as ASSISTED AREAS. They include parts of Scotland, Wales, Cornwall and northern England and in 1984 there were 42 such areas

Great Britain Assisted Areas as defined by the Department of Trade and Industry with effect from 29.11.84

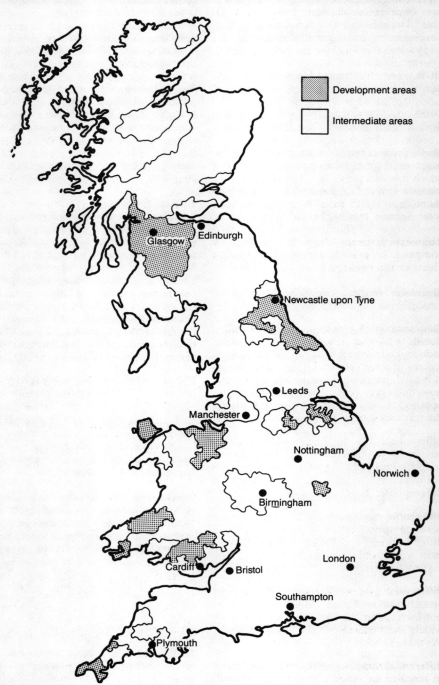

development areas

representing about 15 per cent of the nation's working population. Assistance available includes a 15 per cent regional development grant for capital expenditure and various forms of rent and rates relief.

DGB. *See* DEUTSCHE GEWERKSCHAFTS-BUND.

DHSS. *See* DEPARTMENT OF HEALTH AND SOCIAL SECURITY.

diadic product test. A market research technique used for fast-moving consumer goods which involves giving the respondent two or more samples of similar products and asking them to evaluate them − usually in blind tests. *See also* TRIADIC PRODUCT TEST.

diagnostic program (diagnostic routine). A computer program designed to find faults either in other systems or in itself.

diagnostic routine. *See* DIAGNOSTIC PRO-GRAM.

diary method. A technique used in organizational behaviour research which involves individuals involved in some process keeping a diary of what they spend their time doing. It is used, for example, in identifying exactly how managers really spend their time, as opposed to how they think they do or how the textbooks suggest they should.

differential. The established difference in pay levels for different groups of workers. Industrial relations disputes sometimes arise out of concern to preserve or eliminate such differentials.

differential costing. A method for choosing between options based on those costs which differ between options and excluding common costs which all options share. *See* MARGINAL COSTING.

differential piecework system. A range of PIECEWORK systems in which earnings do not increase at the same rate as output. A widely used example is the HALSEY BONUS SYSTEM.

differential sampling. A sampling technique in research in which a sample is chosen to highlight a particular feature.

differentiation. In organization theory, the process which an organization goes through when, in order to cope with an increasingly complex environment, it sets up various specialized functions. Although this provides the organization with specialist capabilities, it also poses problems of co-ordination between these groups. A full discussion of the advantages and problems in such a strategy is given in P. Lawrence and J. Lorsch, *Organization and Environment* (Cambridge, Mass.: Harvard University Press, 1967), and the subject is also well-covered in J. Child, *Organizations − A Guide to Theory and Practice* (2nd edn, London: Harper & Row, 1982).

digitizer. A device to convert images and pictures into electronic (digital) input suitable for manipulation in COMPUTER-AIDED DESIGN systems.

diminishing return. The principle in which a continuing increase in input to a system brings a declining increase in output. For example, the point at which putting more labour or machinery into a manufacturing process produces less than the cost of those inputs in the form of increased productivity.

DIN. A West German standard, issued by the Deutsche Institut für Normen, equivalent to the BRITISH STANDARD.

Diploma in Management Studies (DMS). A post-graduate/post-experience diploma in management validated in the UK by the COUNCIL FOR NATIONAL ACADEMIC AWARDS.

direct advertising (direct promotion). Advertising which involves leaflets, brochures etc, distributed direct to the audience rather than advertisements placed in publications or on television, cinema or other mass media.

direct broadcasting satellite (DBS). A mass communication system which involves broadcasting via specially-designed medium power (45−230 watts) satellites directly to individual home-receiving dish antennae.

direct cost (prime cost). (1) A cost which can be directly attributed to producing a product or service. *See* INDIRECT COST.

(2) *See* STANDARD COST.

direct costing. *See* MARGINAL COSTING.

direct expense. A direct cost which can be related to a particular expenditure. *See* STANDARD COST.

Direct Information Access Network for Europe. *See* EURONET DIANE.

directive interview (structured interview). An interview which involves asking the respondent a series of prepared questions, often in a prepared sequence, with the aim of directing the interviewee towards particular subjects.

directives. Within the EUROPEAN COMMUNITY the Council of Ministers and the European Commission have the power to make directives on issues affecting the Community as a whole and to which all member states must conform. The exact form in which they are implemented is left to the discretion and machinery of individual states.

direct labour. Those members of the workforce directly engaged in producing goods or services, as opposed to those carrying out supporting activities such as maintenance or staff functions. *See* INDIRECT LABOUR.

direct labour costs. Costs associated with DIRECT LABOUR.

direct mail advertising. A form of DIRECT ADVERTISING which involves sending material through the mail.

direct mail selling. A marketing technique in which the customer is approached directly via mail or COUPON ADVERTISING − as opposed to via retailers.

direct negative. An AMENDMENT to a motion in a formal meeting which involves stating the opposite − the direct negative − of that motion.

direct numerical control (distributed numerical control) (DNC). A form of numerical control in which several numerical control or computer numerical control machines are linked together under the overall control of a shop floor computer which is responsible for overall monitoring and scheduling of operations.

Director-General of Fair Trading. In the UK, the individual with responsibility for implementing the FAIR TRADING ACT 1973.

Directorates-General. *See* EUROPEAN COMMUNITY.

direct promotion. *See* DIRECT ADVERTISING.

direct response advertising (direct response promotion). Advertising which is designed to involve an instant response rather than a delayed one − for example, filling in a coupon and sending it off immediately after reading an advertisement.

direct response promotion. *See* DIRECT RESPONSE ADVERTISING.

direct selling. A form of sales which links the producer directly with the customer rather than via a shop or other medium.

direct tax. A tax levied directly on income or profits − as distinct from indirect taxes such as VALUE ADDED TAX.

Disabled Persons (Employment) Acts 1944, 1958. The main legislation in the UK covering the employment of disabled persons. The basic point is a requirement that all firms employing over 20 persons should employ some disabled persons and should also provide suitable training for them. It also provides for the establishment of a Disabled Persons Register which defines for employment purposes the status of disabled people.

disbursement. A cash payment.

disclosure of information by employers. The legal requirements on the part of employers to disclose information about their activities to trade unions for the purposes of COLLECTIVE BARGAINING.

discontinuous shift. Shiftwork which does not operate on a 24-hour-per-day basis.

discount. (1) A reduction in the price or cost of something.
(2) An amount of money deducted to compensate for interest which money could have earned up to the due date if it is

advanced against a BILL OF EXCHANGE or it is bought or sold.

discounted cash flow (DCF). A technique used in investment appraisal which allows the comparison of different project options in terms of their expected cash flow in the future, taking into account changes in the value of money over time.

discount house. A financial institution which purchases bills of exchange, promissory notes etc at a discount and sells them on. In the UK the name is particularly applied to the 12 members of the London Discount Houses Association. Their specialist role has two main features: (*i*) to make a market in various short-term financial instruments — such as Treasury bills, certificates of deposit or short-dated government stock; and (*ii*) to provide a channel through which the Bank of England can conduct its day-to-day operations on the money markets. Discount house funding is primarily of a short-term type whereas their assets are long-term; this means that they are vulnerable to interest rate shifts and require skilful financial management in their operations.

discount market. The business of DISCOUNT HOUSES.

disk. *See* FLOPPY DISK.

disk drive. A device to enable computers to read and write data onto a FLOPPY DISK or a HARD DISK.

diskette. *See* FLOPPY DISK.

disk operating system. *See* DOS.

displaced equipment. *See* DISPLACED PLANT.

displaced plant (displaced equipment). In accounting, plant which is taken out of use (displaced) earlier than planned — for example, because the technology involved has been displaced by a newer one. Such cases require special techniques to allow for DE-PRECIATION on the company's balance sheet.

display advertising. Advertising which attracts attention by some feature of its display

— size, colour, use of pictures etc — as distinct from basic classified advertising which simply supplies information about the product or service being offered.

dispute benefit. *See* STRIKE PAY.

disputes procedures. In industrial relations, agreements between employers and trade unions as to how industrial disputes should be handled.

dissatisfiers. *See* HERZBERG'S TWO-FACTOR THEORY.

distance learning. The range of techniques and technology to enable students to learn at a distance from their teachers rather than face-to-face. Examples include video, television, radio, written material, audio-visual etc and such materials may sometimes be augmented by some form of tutorial support. Correspondence courses were an early form of distance learning but the range and nature of packages currently available has expanded considerably. For example, in the UK distance learning includes study for a degree at the Open University or for the updating or acquisition of new skills via the Open Tech, and such packages may contain hardware such as robots or computers to be used in conjunction with television and radio programmes and written support material.

distributed numerical control. *See* DIRECT NUMERICAL CONTROL.

distributed processing. A computer system which links (via some form of network) a series of computers so that data-processing can be distributed throughout an organization but where communication of data between computers in the system is also possible.

distribution. (1) Mechanisms involved in moving goods or services from the point of production to the point of consumption.
(2) *See* FREQUENCY DISTRIBUTION.

distribution channels. The routes through which DISTRIBUTION of goods takes place.

distribution costs. Costs associated with distribution — transport, storage etc.

distribution mix. A range of approaches used by a firm to distribute its goods and or services.

distribution planning. A process of planning and optimizing distribution to make the best use of channels, transport options, storage options etc.

distributive trades. Wholesaling and retailing activities.

distributor. An individual or organization who has the right (sometimes exclusive) to sell goods or offer services on behalf of a producer in particular markets or geographical areas.

diversification. The process of moving beyond a company's basic activities into new fields via acquisition or by internal development.

dividend. A payment made to holders of shares or other securities, usually expressed as a percentage of the nominal value of the security held.

dividend cover. The extent to which a company chooses to invest its earnings (profits) rather than distribute them as dividends.

dividend yield. The amount a share yields in a dividend compared to its price on the stock market.

division of labour. A term coined by Adam Smith to describe the breaking down of work into a series of specialized tasks.

DMS. *See* DIPLOMA IN MANAGEMENT STUDIES.

DNC. *See* DIRECT NUMERICAL CONTROL.

documentary bill. A document accompanying a BILL OF EXCHANGE.

documentary credit (irrevocable documentary acceptance credit). An ACCEPTANCE CREDIT which is granted on production of suitable documentation.

DoE. *See* DEPARTMENT OF EMPLOYMENT.

dog. A term coined by the Boston Consulting Group to describe a product or product line which is unprofitable and has poor prospects. *See* BOSTON BOX.

dole, the. *See* UNEMPLOYMENT BENEFIT.

dominant element job evaluation. A JOB EVALUATION approach based on only the most important element against which all other elements are compared.

DOS (Disk Operating System). The computer program responsible for the management and control of operations involving reading and writing information onto floppy and hard disks. Various systems exist, among the best known being CP/M and MS/DOS.

dot matrix printer. A computer printer which generates characters by spraying ink through a matrix of tiny needles. The computer selects the pattern within the matrix which 'fires' ink at the paper to generate the required character. Dot matrix printers do not have as high a quality image as daisywheel or laser printers but are cheaper and faster.

double bond. A BOND which carries a penalty for failure to pay or deliver according to particular terms.

double day shift. A system of shiftwork based on two consecutive shifts during the daytime, from early morning to late evening.

double entry. A standard form of bookkeeping in which transactions are simultaneously entered twice, once as a debit to one account and again as a credit to the other so that the final totals of debits and credits always balance.

double taxation. A situation where a firm or individual becomes liable for tax on the same income in two or more countries or states simultaneously. Most countries operate double tax agreements to deal with this problem.

double time. An extra payment made at double the normal rate, usually for overtime or non-standard duties.

Dow Jones Index. The main index of share prices for the US stock market, published by Dow Jones and Co.

DP. *See* DATA PROCESSING.

DRAM (Dynamic Random Access Memory). A memory chip in a computer.

drawback (customs drawback). Where goods are imported and duty paid and then re-exported, either direct or as part of a manufactured product, the supplier can draw back the money.

drawee. *See* BILL OF EXCHANGE.

drawer. *See* BILL OF EXCHANGE.

Drucker, Peter. A US management writer, the author of 23 books and several hundred articles, including regular pieces for the *Financial Times* and the *Wall Street Journal*. His work covers a wide range of topics, but his main contributions are set out in two key books − *The Concept of the Corporation* (New York: John Day, 1946) (a study of General Motors used to illustrate how a large company operates) and *The Practice of Management* (London: Heinemann, 1954) (offering general guidelines for management, especially in the strategic field).

DTI. *See* DEPARTMENT OF TRADE AND INDUSTRY.

dumping. Exported goods which are sold below the price they cost in the country of manufacture.

duopoly. A market which is dominated by two firms. *See* MONOPOLY.

dutch auction. (1) An AUCTION in which the bidders are blind to each other's bids.
(2) A colloquial term for an attempt by a buyer to drive down suppliers' quotations by indicating that other bids are lower.

duty. A tax levied by a national government on imports.

duty-free. Goods which may be imported without paying DUTY.

Dynamic Random Access Memory. *See* DRAM.

E

E and OE (errors and omissions excepted). An abbreviation often found on bills or statements which attempts to cover errors or omissions in the document which are the fault of the issuer. The legality of the phrase is doubtful.

earliest event time. In NETWORK ANALYSIS, the earliest time at which an event in a network can take place.

earliest finish date. *See* EARLIEST FINISH TIME.

earliest finish time (earliest finish date). In NETWORK planning, the earliest time at which an activity can finish.

earliest start date. *See* EARLIEST START TIME.

earliest start time (earliest start date). In NETWORK planning, the earliest time at which an activity can start.

early shift. The morning shift in a three-shift system, or the earliest shift in other systems.

earned for ordinary. A financial term sometimes used to express profits. It is derived from the earnings of a company for its ordinary shareholders. *See* EARNINGS PER SHARE.

earned income. In INCOME TAX calculation, the various different types of income which might accrue to an individual by virtue of a profession, trade or vocation. It includes wages or salaries, pensions from previous employers, income from patent rights and all other income derived in some way from doing a job.

earning power. A FINANCIAL RATIO expressing the relationship between the net operating income of the firm and its operating assets.

earnings. The net profit of a firm after deductions for corporation tax, interest charges and dividends paid to preference shareholders.

earnings before interest and after tax (EBIAT). EARNINGS after CORPORATION TAX has been paid but before payment of interest charges and preference shareholders.

earnings before interest and tax (EBIT). The net profits before payment of any interest or tax.

earnings/dividend ratio. A FINANCIAL RATIO relating profits to dividends declared. It is often expressed as cover − that is, the number of times profits cover dividend payment.

earnings per share (EPS). A FINANCIAL RATIO which describes the earnings of a firm divided by the number of common stock shares. It provides a useful indicator of the financial performance of a firm.

earnings-related benefits. Benefits (including sickness and unemployment benefits) paid to an individual under the UK National Insurance Scheme which are related to the normal wage which he was getting, and usually also the contributions paid into the scheme before he became sick or unemployed. These benefits are paid at a higher rate than the standard flat rate payment.

earnings yield. A FINANCIAL RATIO relating the EARNINGS PER SHARE to the share price at a particular time; it gives some idea of how much an investor might get for his money.

easement. The right of a landowner to use another piece of land in a predefined way − for example, as a right of way. This right does not cover taking something away from the second piece of land − as in fishing or mining rights, for example.

EAT. *See* EMPLOYMENT APPEAL TRIBUNAL.

EBIAT. *See* EARNINGS BEFORE INTEREST AND AFTER TAX.

EBIT. *See* EARNINGS BEFORE INTEREST AND TAX.

EBQ. *See* ECONOMIC BATCH QUANTITY.

EC. *See* EUROPEAN COMMUNITY.

econometrics. A branch of economics specializing in quantitative (usually statistical) relationships between economic variables.

economic and monetary union. One of the basic elements necessary in setting up a COMMON MARKET. *See* EUROPEAN COMMUNITY.

Economic and Social Committee (ESC). A committee set up within the EUROPEAN COMMUNITY to ensure consultation between the Council of Ministers and the European Commission on the one hand and representatives of the economic and social structure of the Community on the other. Members of this latter group include farmers, businessmen etc. Member states submit lists of candidates to serve for a 4-year term on this committee which has 189 seats.

Economic and Social Research Council (ESRC; formerly the Social Science Research Council). A UK government-funded body which finances academic research and the dissemination into applications of the social and BEHAVIOURAL SCIENCES – economics, sociology, psychology, political science etc.

economic batch determination. *See* ECONOMIC BATCH QUANTITY.

economic batch quantity (economic batch determination; economic manufacturing quantity) (EBQ). The optimum size for a production batch in order to justify the cost of operating equipment, supplying materials, labour etc. It is calculated on the basis of a trade-off between amortized fixed costs (e.g. setting up of machines) and variable costs (e.g. stockholding) which vary with batch size. *See* JUST-IN-TIME PRODUCTION.

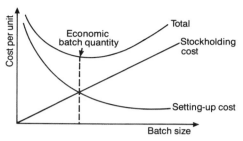

the concept of an optimum economic batch quantity at which unit cost is minimized in respect of setting-up costs and stock-holding costs

Economic Development Council ('little Neddy') (EDC). A tripartite committee (i.e. membership includes government, union and employer representation) in the UK serviced by the staff of the NATIONAL ECONOMIC DEVELOPMENT OFFICE which examines the problems and prospects of an industrial sector, initiates research, publishes discussion papers and carries out other activities aimed at promoting better awareness of the sector and improved performance within it. In the original 1964 Industrial Strategy 9 EDCs were set up and there are currently around 40.

economic indicator. A figure which provides some idea of how an economy is performing – for example, the rate of inflation, the exchange rate or the rate of growth.

economic life. The period over which an investment will yield a return.

economic lot size (ELS). *See* ECONOMIC ORDER QUANTITY.

economic man. In economic theory, an ideal human being who behaves in a totally rational fashion, who is perfectly informed and whose economic motivation when making decisions is towards maximizing utility.

economic manufacturing quantity. *See* ECONOMIC BATCH QUANTITY.

economic order quantity (EOQ) (economic lot size; optimum order quantity). In inventory control, the quantity of something which is regularly used and thus needs regular re-ordering. In order to minimize the costs of holding too much stock but at the same time ensuring that the the risk of running out of stock is also minimized, an EOQ is calculated.

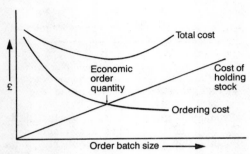

economic order quantity

economies of scale. The reduction in unit costs of producing an item as the scale of production is increased.

economies of scope. Those economic advantages which firms may obtain through being able to service a wide variety of different market demands. Although economies of scale favour large plants over small ones, it is possible to gain advantages in terms of flexibility and quality which may be important in helping a firm occupy a market niche. Such economies of scope depend upon efficient use of machinery and particularly high utilization rather than on scale of production.

ECGD. *See* EXPORT CREDIT GUARANTEE DEPARTMENT.

ECSC. European Coal and Steel Community. *See* EUROPEAN COMMUNITY.

ECU. European Currency Unit. *See* EUROPEAN COMMUNITY.

EDC. *See* ECONOMIC DEVELOPMENT COUNCIL.

EDF. European Development Fund. *See* EUROPEAN COMMUNITY.

EDP. The acronym for electronic data processing.

EE. Errors excepted. *See* E AND OE.

EEC. European Economic Community. *See* EUROPEAN COMMUNITY.

EETPU. *See* ELECTRICAL, ELECTRONIC, TELECOMMUNICATIONS AND PLUMBING UNION.

efficiency ratio. *See* ACTIVITY RATIO.

EFT. *See* ELECTRONIC FUNDS TRANSFER.

EFTA. *See* EUROPEAN FREE TRADE ASSOCIATION.

EFTPOS. *See* ELECTRONIC FUNDS TRANSFER AT POINT OF SALE.

EGM. *See* EXTRAORDINARY GENERAL MEETING.

EHO. *See* ENVIRONMENTAL HEALTH OFFICER.

EIB. European Investment Bank. *See* EUROPEAN COMMUNITY.

80:20 rule. *See* PARETO ANALYSIS.

einfache Gesellschaft (société simple) (Ger.: 'simple organization'). A form of partnership in Switzerland.

Einzelfirma (Ger.: 'single firm'). A form of company in West Germany.

EITB. *See* ENGINEERING INDUSTRY TRAINING BOARD.

elastic demand. *See* DEMAND ELASTICITY.

Electrical, Electronic, Telecommunications and Plumbing Union (EETPU). A major trade union in the UK representing the interests of the above groups. In recent years the EETPU has been involved in a number of controversial deals with employers including accepting single-union arrangements covering an entire firm, no-strike deals and, in the case of the newspaper industry, of redefining work traditionally carried out by printers on the grounds that, since it involved working with and maintaining computer equipment it was now classed as electrical and therefore their members could apply for jobs in this sector. This led to bitter conflict within the Trades Union Congress.

electronic funds transfer (EFT). The use of computer networks to execute financial transfers between banks and financial institutions directly.

electronic funds transfer at point of sale (EFTPOS). A computer-based linkage between retailers and banking, credit card firms and other financial institutions. As a transaction is completed so information about the sale is passed to the financial institution involved and the relevant accounts are automatically debited and credited.

electronic mail. Communication based on computer networks which allows users to send and receive, store and forward messages sent between terminals and to obtain HARD COPY for their records if necessary.

electronic office. *See* OFFICE AUTOMATION.

electronic time study systems. WORK STUDY tools enabling data collection and record storage and analysis by computer. Such systems are replacing the traditional stopwatch and enable observers to concentrate their attentions more fully on analysis rather than measurement.

element. In WORK STUDY, a discrete part of a specified job under study.

eligible bills. BILLS OF EXCHANGE which are issued by DISCOUNT HOUSES and which are generally of a short-dated nature.

ELS. (economic lot size). *See* ECONOMIC ORDER QUANTITY.

EMA. *See* ENGINEERS AND MANAGERS ASSOCIATION.

EMAS. *See* EMPLOYMENT MEDICAL ADVISORY SERVICE.

embargo. A form of prohibition of action. This might take the form of inhibiting trade between certain countries or in certain commodities, or in the form of information dissemination — for example, press releases with information about company plans are often embargoed until a particular date after which they may be used in publications.

embezzle. The act of stealing money or property entrusted to him or her by that employee.

emoluments. The total package offered to an employee in return for his or her work. This can include money, goods, travel or other benefits.

employee benefits. *See* FRINGE BENEFITS.

employee handbook. A booklet or leaflet given to an employee (usually in larger firms) which gives details of the firm and its practices. Apart from historical and financial performance information the handbook usually contains information on procedures for resolving problems encountered by the employee, and details of welfare and other provisions offered by the company.

employee participation. *See* PARTICIPATION.

employee relations. The various aspects of the relationship between employers and employees and procedures and sanctions available for dealing with problems which emerge in that relationship.

employee's contributory negligence. If, in a case for industrial injury compensation, it can be shown that the employee in question acted in a negligent fashion which contributed to his accident or to the seriousness of his injuries — for example, by failing to wear a safety helmet — the damages may be reduced.

employers' federation. An association of employers within a sector or country. Typical activities include negotiations with trade unions, lobbying government, providing advice and assistance to members and generally representing their interests. In some countries, such as West Germany, employers' federations are legally-constituted representatives in the negotiation process for wages and other industrial relations issues.

Employers' Liability Acts. Various pieces of legislation in the UK, the most recent being enacted in 1969, which indicate the extent to which the conditions under which employers are liable for compensating employees who sustain industrial injuries – for example, in the case of defective equipment. The acts also require them to insure against this possibility in order to guarantee that the employers will be able to pay such compensation and they must be able to provide a certificate of insurance to this effect.

employer strike insurance. The US equivalent of an INDEMNITY FUND.

Employment Acts 1980, 1982. Legislation in the UK covering a broad range of INDUSTRIAL RELATIONS questions, and introduced in part to try to curb and control the power of the TRADE UNIONS. Among the provisions of the 1980 act were the withdrawal of immunity from prosecution to trade unions for the consequences of industrial action, greater limitation of secondary picketing activity, and increased protection of individual workers in CLOSED SHOP organizations. The act also provided money for unions who wish to consult their members on key decisions via postal ballots. In the 1982 act the provision on making trade unions accountable in law for some of the consequences of industrial action were strengthened further, greater protection was offered to those employees not in a trade union and control was increased over issues such as compensation for unfair dismissal and the procedures and grounds for dismissing employees.

Employment Agencies Act 1973. UK legislation which covers the licensing and operation of EMPLOYMENT AGENCIES.

employment agency. An organization which acts as a BROKER between those seeking work and those seeking labour.

Employment and Training Act 1973. UK legislation which covers aspects of vocational training and, in particular, established the MANPOWER SERVICES COMMISSION as a statutory body with specific responsibilities in this field.

Employment Appeal Tribunal (EAT). A UK body set up to consider appeals regarding the verdicts of INDUSTRIAL TRIBUNALS.

employment costs. The total costs of employing someone, including remuneration, NATIONAL INSURANCE contributions, PENSIONS etc.

employment exchanges. The former name for offices where prospective employees would register for work. They are now known as JOB CENTRES and are operated by the MANPOWER SERVICES COMMISSION.

employment medical advisor. A doctor appointed to carry out medical examinations of particular groups of workers – such as those in dangerous jobs or young people – whose health may be affected by their job. The duties of such a doctor are set out in the Employment Medical Advisory Services Act 1972 and the HEALTH AND SAFETY AT WORK ACT 1974.

Employment Medical Advisory Service (EMAS). An organization set up after the HEALTH AND SAFETY AT WORK ACT 1974 as part of the Department of Employment to advise on matters concerning employee health at work.

Employment Protection Acts 1975, 1978. UK legislation concerning employee rights and protection against unfair dismissal etc.

Employment Service Division. The part of the MANPOWER SERVICES COMMISSION with responsibility for JOB CENTRES and other EMPLOYMENT AGENCIES operated by the government.

employment subsidy. A subsidy paid by the UK government intended to generate employment in particular regions, usually ASSISTED AREAS.

EMS. *See* EUROPEAN MONETARY SYSTEM.

encryption techniques. Techniques used in computer programming to improve the security of data against unauthorized access or duplication.

endogenous. An economics term meaning 'from within the system'.

endorsement. (1) The signing of a bill or INVOICE to indicate that it has been paid.

(2) The signing of a document to indicate transfer of ownership.

(3) The signing of a CONTRACT or any other document to indicate agreement with its contents or any changes which have been made in it.

endowment. An insurance policy in which money is payable at the end of a predetermined period – often on retirement.

end price support. Under the Common Agricultural Policy of the European Economic Community, the principle whereby prices of agricultural produce and commodities are guaranteed. *See* EUROPEAN COMMUNITY.

engineering change note (concession request form; engineering query note). A document which lists any changes or queries to the original design and accompanying drawings in a development project. This provides an up-to-date record of how the design has been altered during its development.

Engineering Council. A UK body set up in 1974 as a result of the FINNISTON REPORT. The Council took over functions originally discharged by the COUNCIL OF ENGINEERING INSTITUTIONS and other professional bodies representing the interests of professional engineers and in overseeing their training and establishing standards for their certification.

Engineering Employers' Federation. The major employers' federation in the UK for the engineering and related industries. Its local member organizations are the Engineering Employers' Associations.

Engineering Industry Training Board (EITB). One of the original TRAINING BOARDS set up by the UK government under the 1964 Industrial Training Act with responsibility for the engineering industries.

engineering query note. *See* ENGINEERING CHANGE NOTE.

Engineers and Managers Association (EMA). A UK trade union representing supervisory staff in the engineering industry.

English Estates. A UK government body set up to provide property development services for English regions. Most of its operations are concerned with ASSISTED AREAS and are similar to services provided by the Scottish and Welsh Development Agencies.

enterprise zones. Areas set up in the UK in the 1980s to promote industrial and commercial development. The first was in Swansea and there are now 25 located within inner cities and urban black spots. Enterprise zone status offers a range of financial incentives and regulatory relaxation to firms locating there.

entrepreneur. An individual who recognizes opportunities for new products or services and raises the money and organizes the wherewithal to produce and deliver them. The money may come from himself or from other sources. Entrepreneurs are essentially risk-takers who are generally associated with economic growth.

Environmental Health Officer (EHO). An officer responsible for monitoring and implementing the provisions of some aspects of the HEALTH AND SAFETY AT WORK ACT 1974 and other legislation pertaining to environmental health. For example, the conditions in factory kitchens and canteens fall under the EHO's area of responsibility.

EOC. *See* EQUAL OPPORTUNITIES COMMISSION.

EOQ. *See* ECONOMIC ORDER QUANTITY.

EPF. *See* EXCEPTED PROVIDENT FUND.

EPROM (Erasable Programmable Read Only Memory). A type of chip found in computers, usually used to carry software actually within the computer instead of on floppy disk or other storage medium which must be loaded in every time it is required.

EPS. *See* EARNINGS PER SHARE.

Equal Employment Opportunities Commission. The US equivalent of the EQUAL OPPORTUNITIES COMMISSION.

Equal Opportunities Commission (EOC). A body set up under the 1975 Sex Discrimination Act in the UK to monitor the availability of equal opportunities in employment for men and women and to research and advise on policy-making in this field.

Equal Pay Act 1970. UK legislation designed to provide for equal treatment of men and women in employment and in their CONDITIONS OF EMPLOYMENT.

equity. ORDINARY SHARES in a company.

equity capital (equity share capital). Capital raised by issuing shares or equity shares in a business.

equity dilution. If a company issues further shares after the original issue, the influence of the early shareholders will be reduced (i.e. their equity has been diluted).

equity share capital. *See* EQUITY CAPITAL.

equity shares. *See* ORDINARY SHARES.

equity stake. The ownership of a stake in a business based on holding shares − equity − in it.

equivalent pension benefit. If an employee has been a member of a CONTRACTED-OUT firm and leaves, he has the right to an equivalent pension benefit which entitles him to the equivalent amount of pension which he would have earned in the state scheme. He may receive this either by his former firm making a payment in lieu of his state pension contributions to the DEPARTMENT OF HEALTH AND SOCIAL SECURITY or by a certificate of assurance which he can take on to his next employer.

Erasable Programmable Read Only Memory. *See* EPROM.

ergonomics (human engineering; human factors engineering). The science of human/machine interaction which is concerned with identifying the principles of good equipment and systems design for ease of use and effective performance of tasks involving such equipment or systems.

errors and omission excepted. *See* E AND OE.

ESC. *See* ECONOMIC AND SOCIAL COMMITTEE; *see also* EUROPEAN COMMUNITY.

escalation clause. An agreement in a CONTRACT to allow for escalation in its price to accommodate increases in COSTS.

escape clause. A clause in a CONTRACT which allows either party to escape the terms and conditions of the contract under certain defined circumstances.

escrow (escrow agreement). Any arrangement in which a bond, deed or other document is adopted by two parties and given to a third for safekeeping to be surrendered only when some condition emerges; for example, an agreement to hold money from an employer pending a settlement of an industrial dispute by ARBITRATION. If the arbitration awards a pay increase, the money is used; if not, it is returned to the employer.

escrow agreement. *See* ESCROW.

ESF (European Social Fund). *See* EUROPEAN COMMUNITY.

ESPRIT (European Strategic Programme for Research and Development in Information Technology). A ten-year programme (1984−93) of collaborative research co-funded by the EUROPEAN COMMUNITY and organized in liaison with industry, national governments and the research community. Its main aim is to help provide the European information technology industry with the key components of the technology it needs to be competitive on world markets (especially Japan and the USA) within a decade.

ESRC. *See* ECONOMIC AND SOCIAL RESEARCH COUNCIL.

Ethernet. The proprietary name for a popular configuration of LOCAL AREA NETWORK.

ETUC. *See* EUROPEAN TRADE UNION CONGRESS.

ETUI. *See* EUROPEAN TRADE UNION INSTITUTE.

Euratom (European Atomic Energy Community). *See* EUROPEAN COMMUNITY.

EUREKA. An initiative taken by several European countries to stimulate high-technology research, orginally set up as a peaceful counter-measure to the US Strategic Defense Initiative ('Star Wars') programme. Countries backing the 1986 initiative included France, Italy, the UK, Sweden, West Germany and Austria.

Euorobond. A BOND which, as a consequence of the European Community's status as a monetary union, is negotiable in any of the member states of the Community.

Euroclear. A clearing house organization which acts as a central CLEARING BANK for EUROCURRENCY and EUROBOND transactions.

Eurocrat. A colloquial name for someone working for the European Commission.

Eurocurrency. Currency of one of the member states of the EUROPEAN COMMUNITY which is held outside the country to which it relates.

Eurodollars. A form of CREDIT in US dollars which circulates freely among European financial institutions as an alternative to their own national currencies. Markets and dealing also take place in other 'Eurocurrencies' such as Euromarks and Eurofrancs.

Euronet Diane (Direct Information Access Network for Europe). An information service established in 1980, Diane has a special transmission network (Euronet) linking all 12 EUROPEAN COMMUNITY countries, as well as Austria, Finland, Norway, Sweden and Switzerland; negotiations are in progress with Yugoslavia. Diane is composed of independent European computerized information services (known as 'hosts') which can give access to data bases and data banks on a wide variety of subjects (including business management, medicine, law, the environment, engineering, chemistry, and the social sciences).

European Coal and Steel Community (ECSC). *See* EUROPEAN COMMUNITY.

European Community (EC). A COMMON MARKET established in the 1950s among several European states and expanded to its present form where 12 countries (with a total population of 319 million people) share a number of common policies beyond those directly related to trade. Current member states are Belgium, West Germany, Denmark, Spain, France, the UK, Italy, Ireland, Greece, Luxembourg, the Netherlands and Portugal and it is expected that Cyprus will join in the near future. The EC currently accounts for about 30 per cent of all world trade.

The principal aims in early moves towards economic co-operation were to bring about some measure of post-war stability to both political and economic life within Europe and it is generally recognized that the first step along this road was the formation, with the signature in 1951 of the Treaty of Paris, of the European Coal and Steel Community (ECSC) which involved France, West Germany, Italy, Belgium, Luxembourg and the Netherlands. In 1957 the Treaty of Rome was signed by these six countries to establish formally a COMMON MARKET called the European Economic Community (EEC); in 1960 most of the remaining European states set up the EUROPEAN FREE TRADE ASSOCIATION. The Treaty of Rome covered basic items such as the establishment of a customs union, the dismantling of trade barriers between states and the foundations of common policies in the field of agriculture, transport, technology and external trade. It also covered the setting up of the European Atomic Energy Community (Euratom). These three organizations merged in 1965 under the Merger Treaty to become the European Community.

During subsequent years other states joined the Community: the UK, Ireland and Denmark in 1973, after several earlier applications, Greece in 1981, and Spain and Portugal in 1986.

The Community is run by the Council of Ministers which is made up of a representative from each of the 12 member states (in practice these are usually relevant cabinet ministers whose attendance depends on the issues being discussed). There is also the European Council which is made up of the heads of government of the member states and meets three times per year for largely informal discussion. Originally the intention was for all decisions to be made by either majority or unanimous vote but since the so-called 'Luxembourg Compromise' of 1966 individual member states have nominal power of veto over any decisions made; in practice this is still a function of political power so that the chances of a successful veto favour states like the UK. The presidency of the Council rotates every six months among member states.

The Council of Ministers acts on proposals made by the European Commission which is a policy-making and planning body with 17 members (Commissioners) whose duty is to act in the interest of the Community as a whole. Representation is based on at least one Commissioner for each member state with a second for larger states such as the UK, France and West Germany. Commissioners serve for a four-year period in office and each has responsibility for a particular portfolio; the presidency of the Commission is a rotating office, renewable after two years.

In order to improve liaison between the Council of Ministers and the European Commission a Committee of Permanent Representatives (COREPER) was established which involves an ambassador from each member state, based in Brussels. The role of the Committee is to prepare the ground for the meetings of the Council of Ministers and can be seen as analagous to senior civil servants such as Permanent Secretaries in the UK.

The Commission is answerable to the European Parliament, an elected assembly of 518 members who are elected for a 5-year period in their member countries. Distribution of seats is on the basis of size; 81 representatives each from France, West Germany, Italy and the UK; 60 from Spain; 25 from the Netherlands; 24 each from Belgium, Greece and Portugal; 15 from Denmark; 14 from Ireland; and 6 from Luxembourg. The Parliament is based for six months of the year in Strasbourg and six months in Luxembourg. Its role is intended to be supra-national although in practice

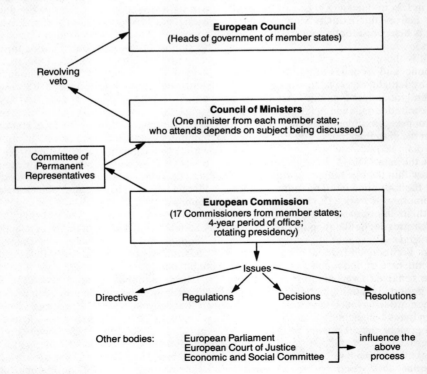

it reflects many of the political divisions of individual member states; it has no formal legislative power although it can exert an influence on this and on the financial and executive aspects of the Commission's work.

In terms of the legislative framework, the Commission can issue four levels of action: regulations, directives, decisions and resolutions (in each case after consultation with the Council of Ministers). Regulations, under the Treaty of Rome, have the status of law in the Community. Directives make a clear statement of the ends to be achieved but leave the means towards achieving those ends up to individual member states. Decisions are binding on the member states in question but may not apply to all states. Finally, resolutions are essentially a comment by the Commission on issues concerning the Community but are not binding on member states.

Disputes in European Community law are resolved by the 13-judge European Court of Justice which has the main responsibility of interpreting the Treaty of Rome; this body is based in Luxembourg. (This is not the same as the European Court of Human Rights, which is a separate body and meets in The Hague.)

Finally, there is a consultative body − the Economic and Social Committe − which must, by law, be consulted, although its recommendations need not be acted upon. The Committee is made up of various interest groups − employers, trade unionists etc − from the member states.

The diagram opposite sets out the basic nature of the relationship between these institutions within the Community.

The basic policies of the Community aim at promoting European co-operation and strength in international competition. The main features are as follows.

Free trade. There are no tariff or customs barriers between ten of the member states and in the case of Spain and Portugal, these will be removed over a seven-year transitional period. In addition, the Commission has been working at removing other non-tariff barriers such as health and safety standards between member states and hopes that all internal trade barriers within the Community will have been removed by 1992.

External tariff barriers. The Community has attempted to establish a common external tariff to protect against imports. (The policy towards members of the EUROPEAN FREE TRADE ASSOCIATION is slightly different favouring European neighbours over other competitor countries). In practice, this averages out at about 4.6 per cent as compared with the USA (4.3 per cent) and Japan (2.7 per cent), although these levels vary with different items and are subject to review at the GENERAL AGREEMENT ON TARRIFS AND TRADE.

Free movement of people within the Community. Since 1973 there has been relatively free movement for all citizens within the Community to seek work without the need for work permits and to obtain equal basic rights in the country to which they move. Agreement was reached on a European passport in 1985 which allows the bearer to pass freely within Community states.

Industry. A number of attempts have been made to develop and strengthen industry within the Community as a whole, although this has often proved difficult to reconcile with the interests of individual member states. Common policies exist in fields like steel, coal and textiles and attempts have been made to promote European co-operation in new technology fields through programmes such as ESPRIT (European Strategic Programme for Research and Development in Information Technology), RACE (Research into Advanced Communications for Europe) and FAST (Forecasting and Assessment in Science and Technology). In order to facilitate industrial investment the European Investment Bank (EIB) was established under the Treaty of Rome to provide loan finance for certain types of industrial project, and support for restructuring is available through the Coal and Steel Fund.

Agriculture. The Common Agricultural Policy (CAP) is the only fully-developed Community policy in full operation. It is a highly-complex arrangement with the broad intention of making the Community self-sufficient in agricultural produce; the main mechanism for achieving this has been the principle of intervention by the European Economic Community should the market prices fall below economically attractive levels. This has had the unfortunate effect of encouraging overproduction of some items, since the farmers are guaranteed a fixed price for their produce and has led to the creation of so-called 'butter' and 'beef mountains' and 'wine' and 'milk lakes'. These problems have led to a number of downward adjustments to production in areas like dairy produce which have concerned farmers in some member states. With the recent entry of countries strong in agriculture and favoured by good climatic conditions such as Spain there are likely to be further problems ahead for the CAP. *See* INTERVENTION PRICE.

Fisheries. Agreement was reached in 1983 in outline on a Common Fisheries Policy along similar lines to the CAP which places emphasis on conservation of stocks and aims to protect and strengthen the Community's fishing industry, if necessary at the expense of other fishing nations operating in European waters.

Social policy. Considerable efforts have been made by the Community to improve some of the problem areas within Europe, particularly in terms of areas hard hit by unemployment and urban decay. The European Social Fund (ESF) in particular spends a large budget on ventures designed to create jobs, improve training opportunities and provision, and to fight redundancy.

Regional policy. The Community established a Regional Fund in 1975 to help areas suffering from serious unemployment, poverty or economic decline.

Monetary policy. The European Monetary System (EMS) was established in 1979 to improve stability within the Community in the wake of the breakdown of the world monetary system based on the US dollar in the 1970s. This system (sometimes known as 'the snake') ties currencies to each other and limits the amount by which a currency can rise or fall against another; not all member states are linked in yet, but the process towards establishing full economic and monetary union is under way. Financing of the Community is by the automatic contribution from member states of revenues from all customs duties and all agricultural levies on goods entering the Community and up to 1.4 per cent of value added tax. All monies within the Community are handled in terms of European Currency Units (ECUs) which are approximately equivalent to US $1. The ECU replaced the European Unit of Account (EUA) in 1981.

Competition policy. This attempts to guarantee equal treatment throughout the Community for all firms and prohibits any form of direct state aid which restricts free competition.

Transport policy. This aims for the free movement of people and goods between member states.

Energy policy. A European Council meeting in Strasbourg in 1979 laid the foundations for a common energy policy aimed at ensuring a more rational use of scarce energy resources and this has led to a number of practical initiatives in the areas of research funding and in support of development of Community reserves of oil, coal and gas.

Development aid policy. Since 1961 the Community has operated a co-ordinated policy of development aid and support for Third World countries and it has a number of bilateral agreements with individual countries and with economic groupings among developing nations.

European Co-ordination Office. A branch of the UK DEPARTMENT OF TRADE AND INDUSTRY responsible for liaising with the EUROPEAN COMMUNITY.

European Court of Justice. *See* EUROPEAN COMMUNITY.

European Currency Unit (ECU). *See* EUROPEAN COMMUNITY.

European Economic Community (EEC). *See* EUROPEAN COMMUNITY.

European Free Trade Association (EFTA). An organization set up in 1959 as an alternative to the EUROPEAN COMMUNITY to facilitate tariff-free trade between European states. The main difference between the Community and EFTA is that the latter does not operate a COMMON EXTERNAL TARIFF. The members are Austria, Iceland, Norway, Sweden and Switzerland; Finland is an associate member. EFTA is governed by a Council with a small secretariat in Geneva.

European Investment Bank (EIB). *See* EUROPEAN COMMUNITY.

European Monetary System (EMS) ('the snake'). An agreement between major European countries to link the exchange rates for their currencies and, if necessary, to step in and provide support for a particular nation's currency should it come under attack in the currency markets. *See* EUROPEAN COMMUNITY.

European Parliament. *See* EUROPEAN COMMUNITY.

European Social Fund (ESF). *See* EUROPEAN COMMUNITY.

European Strategic Programme for Research and Development in Information Technology. *See* ESPRIT.

European Trades Union Congress (ETUC). An organization representing the interests of trade unions at European level to which national trade union confederations are affiliated.

European Trade Union Institute (ETUI). An organization based in Brussels and funded by trade unions of various European countries providing research and advice on matters affecting the interests of trade unions and their members.

European Unit of Account (EUA). *See* EUROPEAN COMMUNITY.

evaluated maintenance programme. A form of PLANNED MAINTENANCE which uses a historical analysis of previous performance and costs to develop future maintenance plans.

event. In NETWORK planning, a stage in a project.

excepted provident fund (EPF). A PENSION scheme which allows the total entitlement to be taken as a lump sum.

exceptional items (extraordinary items). Items appearing in a financial statement which are not a regular part of a firm's financial pattern — for example, one-off payments for redundancies or for writing-off of bad debts, or for income derived from extraordinary circumstances such as 'windfall profits'.

exception report. *See* MANAGEMENT BY EXCEPTION.

exchange control. An instrument of national economic policy which exerts control over the exchange of a currency for others — for example, by restricting the amount which can be exchanged at any time by an individual or organization.

exchange losses. Losses in a business due to fluctuations in EXCHANGE RATES.

exchange rate. The rate at which currencies of different countries are exchanged for each other.

excise duty (excise tax). A tax levied on goods sold within a country — as distinct from customs duty which covers goods imported into a country.

excise licence. A licence required by manufacturers and dealers to deal in items on which EXCISE DUTY is payable.

excise tax. *See* EXCISE DUTY.

ex-coupon. A SECURITY which excludes the right to the COUPON or interest rate.

ex-dividend. A SECURITY which excludes the right to a DIVIDEND on the SHARE.

executive director. A member of the board of directors of a firm who is employed full-time and takes executive responsibility for some function within the business — as opposed to a NON-EXECUTIVE DIRECTOR who is involved only in an advisory capacity and who is paid on a fee basis rather than full-time.

existing use value (current use value). The value of property based on the assumption that it continues to be used for its current purpose — as opposed to an alternative which may be more profitable — for example, the use of agricultural land for industrial development.

exogenous. An economics term meaning 'from outside the system'.

expectancy theory. *See* MOTIVATION.

expected monetary value. In DECISION THEORY, the outcome of different decision options can be compared by calculating the expected monetary value of each as based on the probability of their representing the final outcome. This gives a useful way of choosing between options and applying decision rules about preferred outcomes.

expenditure tax. *See* INDIRECT TAX.

experience curve (experience effect). A concept, particularly associated with the Boston Consulting Group, which argues that the unit costs of producing an item fall as a firm acquires experience in its manufacture. This effect is due to several factors including economies of scale in all aspects of producing and selling the product – purchasing, research and development, administration, sales etc – and what has been termed the 'experience effect', which is a generally-observed phenomenon whereby the costs of producing fall by about 30 per cent every time the total (cumulative) number of units produced doubles. The equation governing the shape of the experience curve can be expressed as $Yn = an^{-b}$, where Yn is the total cost of producing the nth product, a is the cost of the first unit produced and b is the learning rate. *See* LEARNING CURVE.

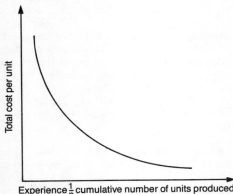

experience curve

experience effect. *See* EXPERIENCE CURVE.

expert system. *See* ARTIFICIAL INTELLIGENCE.

expert witness. A technically skilled and experienced person in a particular field who may be called to give evidence in courts of law, public enquiries, inquests and other examination processes.

exploratory forecasting. *See* FORECASTING.

exponential smoothing. A statistical technique used in FORECASTING.

export agent. An agent who acts on behalf of exporters in another country.

Export Credit Guarantee Department (ECGD). A part of the UK DEPARTMENT OF TRADE AND INDUSTRY, responsible for administering the Export Credit Guarantee Scheme under which exporting firms can be guaranteed payment for their goods so that they are able to obtain finance etc required in advance of actual production.

Export Data Branch. A branch of the DEPARTMENT OF TRADE AND INDUSTRY.

export finance house. A FINANCE HOUSE which specializes in arranging finance for exports.

export house (export merchant house). An organization which assists the export of goods, either as an export merchant or as an agent. In the former, the goods are purchased and the export house becomes a dealer, selling in the export market. In the latter, the export house acts as an agent on behalf of the manufacturer.

Export Intelligence Service. A branch of the DEPARTMENT OF TRADE AND INDUSTRY.

export leasing. An arrangement which involves a leasing company buying an item in one country and then leasing it to an importer in another.

Export Licensing Branch. A branch of the DEPARTMENT OF TRADE AND INDUSTRY.

export merchant house. *See* EXPORT HOUSE.

Export Planning and Development Division. A branch of the DEPARTMENT OF TRADE AND INDUSTRY.

Export Services Division. A branch of the DEPARTMENT OF TRADE AND INDUSTRY.

export subsidy. Financial or other support given by governments to assist the export of goods produced by manufacturers in their country. Such actions act in restraint of free trade and may provoke an importing country to impose some form of tariff barrier to protect its own manufacturers. *See* DUMPING..

ex-ship. Goods supplied by sea where the buyer must pay for collection from the ship.

extensive factors. *See* EXTRINSIC REWARDS.

external storage. Storage devices for computer data which are not part of the processing unit — for example, floppy disks.

extractive industries. Industries which obtain products by exploiting natural resources — mining, oil and gas etc.

extraordinary general meeting (EGM). A GENERAL MEETING of SHAREHOLDERS called to discuss a specific issue as distinct from the ANNUAL GENERAL MEETING.

extraordinary items. *See* EXCEPTIONAL ITEMS.

extrinsic rewards (extensive factors). Various kinds of external rewards offered to an employee — salary, bonuses, FRINGE BENEFITS, travel etc — as distinct from the internal rewards of MOTIVATION.

ex-warehouse. Goods supplied direct from a company's warehouse rather than via a retailer. The buyer is responsible for any costs associated with collection.

ex-works. Goods supplied direct from the factory or works rather than via a retailer. The buyer is responsible for any costs associated with collection.

F

face value (nominal value; par value). The amount, excluding interest, due on maturity to a holder of a BOND or SECURITY.

facsimile transmission (FAX). A method of sending documents between locations which involves converting their images into electronic data, transmitting this over a telecommunications or other form of network and then converting it back to images on paper. The devices used resemble photocopiers into which documents are fed and from which facsimiles of the originals are produced at the destination.

FACT. *See* FACTOR ANALYTIC CHART TECHNIQUE.

factor. A form of trade in which an agent sells a stock of goods on behalf of someone else — a principal. The agent receives a commission on goods sold but the pincipal bears the risk of a lack of sales.

factor analysis. A statistical technique used to identify and isolate significant combinations of factors with a high degree of CORRELATION from within a large set of data.

factor analytic chart technique (FACT). A form of JOB EVALUATION.

factor comparison. A form of JOB EVALUATION scheme in which identified factors are used as a basis for comparison — such as skills required, responsibility involved in a job etc. A series of BENCHMARK jobs are rated according to the extent to which the factors chosen are involved, and other jobs to be evaluated can then be compared with the benchmark.

Factories Act 1961. Legislation, now largely superseded by the HEALTH AND SAFETY AT WORK ACT 1974, which set out various requirements on health, welfare, safety etc of factories in the UK.

factor inputs. *See* FACTOR OF PRODUCTION.

factor of production (factor inputs). In economics, an input to production — such as capital, labour or land.

factor prices. The price of factor inputs to a production process.

factor rating. *See* JOB EVALUATION.

factory agreement. A form of agreement after COLLECTIVE BARGAINING in industrial relations which covers all the employees in a factory, as opposed to sector or national agreements or agreements concluded with workers in a particular part of the plant.

Factory Inspectorate (Health and Safety Inspectorate). A body of people trained and commissioned to implement the provisions of the FACTORIES ACT 1961 and the HEALTH AND SAFETY AT WORK ACT 1974. Her Majesty's inspectors are responsible to the HEALTH AND SAFETY EXECUTIVE.

Fair Trading Act 1973. UK legislation covering issues connected with fair trading practice — including coverage on MONOPOLIES and MERGERS, and preservation of free competition. Among provisions of the legislation was the setting up of the office of DIRECTOR-GENERAL OF FAIR TRADING, the establishment of a permanent body — the OFFICE OF FAIR TRADING, the setting up of the CONSUMER PROTECTION ADVISORY COMMITTEE, and the strengthening of the MONOPOLIES AND MERGERS COMMISSION.

Fair Wages Resolution 1946. UK legislation which requires government to press for fair wages and CONDITIONS OF EMPLOYMENT to be offered by all contractors for public works and supplies, and to include a fair wages clause to that effect in all their CONTRACTS.

false market. A market in which either buyers or sellers act on false information; for example, buying at inflated prices because the buyers have been led to believe that goods are scarce.

Family Expenditure Survey. Statistics collected by the DEPARTMENT OF EMPLOYMENT on the expenditure of households in the UK and used to calculate the RETAIL PRICE INDEX.

father of chapel. A CONVENOR or SHOP STEWARD in the printing industry.

fat work. Work in which it is relatively easy to earn bonuses. *See* LEAN WORK.

FAX. *See* FACSIMILE TRANSMISSION.

Fayol, Henri. An early management writer associated with the school of formal organization theory which essentially argues that effective organizations depend on formal structural principles. In particular these are specialization, a clear chain of command (the scalar principle) unity of command (i.e. employees report to one boss), clearly identified spans of control, vertical communication, line and staff division of managerial labour and minimum authority levels (keeping hierarchies short and manageable). Good accounts of his work and thinking can be found in D. Pugh et al (eds), *Writers on Organizations* (3rd edn, Harmondsworth: Penguin, 1983) and J. Child, *Organizations – A Guide to Theory and Practice* (2nd edn, London: Harper & Row, 1982).

featherbedding. (1) Restrictive labour practices.
(2) Economic conditions which provide an easy environment – a 'feather bed' – in which companies can make profits, for example, by low levels of tax regulation.

Federal Communications Commission. The US regulatory agency responsible for telecommunications.

Federal Funds. Deposits by banks within the US FEDERAL RESERVE SYSTEM.

Federal Funds rate. The rate at which funds are traded between US financial institutions, which in practice gives the key to prevailing US interest rates.

Federal Reserve System. A part of the US banking system in which the 12 Federal Reserve Banks co-ordinated by the Federal Reserve Board act as the US equivalent of the Bank of England (i.e. as a CENTRAL BANK).

Federation of Medium and Small Employers. A UK employers' federation serving the interests of smaller firms.

feedback. A principle in control theory which is often applied in management and organizational behaviour. In feedback control information about the output of a system is fed back to the controller where it is compared with the output required. Should there be a difference suitable control action can be taken to bring the system back to the desired output performance. *See* CYBERNETICS.

fiduciary. An arrangement or relationship which is based on mutual trust.

field research. A type of research common in marketing, in which data is collected (via questionnaire, interview etc) from those involved in the 'field' being studied (e.g. the marketplace in MARKET RESEARCH). It is the opposite of DESK RESEARCH which involves using information and materials at second-hand – in books, videos, reports etc.

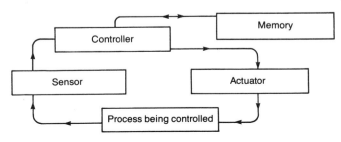

feedback

field warehouse. A warehouse operated by a warehousing company on the premises of another firm which is involved in producing goods which are stored in the warehouse.

FIFO. *See* FIRST IN, FIRST OUT.

fifth generation computer. In 1984 Japan announced the intention of building a 'fifth generation' computer by the 1990s and this led to major programmes in response by the UK (the ALVEY DIRECTORATE), the EUROPEAN COMMUNITY (ESPRIT), and the USA. Fifth generation refers to the next generation of computers which are expected to make use of very advanced integrated circuits of high density, novel computer architectures (expecially based on what is called parallel processing as opposed to the present sequential approach) which will give high operating speeds, sophisticated man−machine interfaces (such as speech recognition and synthesis) which will make computers much easier to use and advanced software employing many of the principles of ARTIFICIAL INTELLIGENCE to begin to make computers able to 'think' for themselves.

FII. *See* FRANKED INVESTMENT INCOME.

FILO. First in, last out. *See* LAST IN, FIRST OUT.

final dividend. A final DIVIDEND (as distinct from an interim dividend) paid to shareholders on a company's profits in a given financial year.

Finance Act. In the UK, the final form of legislation covering the conditions for taxes, allowances etc which are put forward by the Chancellor of the Exchequer in his budget each financial year.

Finance Bill. In the UK, the draft of the FINANCE ACT which is put up for discussion and debate both in the House of Commons and the House of Lords prior to being given Royal Assent.

Finance Corporation for Industry. A UK organization set up in 1945 to provide investment capital to British industry in the post-war period. The money came mostly from the larger banks and financial institutions. *See* INVESTORS IN INDUSTRY.

Finance for Industry. A UK body set up in 1973 after the merger of the INDUSTRIAL AND COMMERCIAL FINANCE CORPORATION and the FINANCE CORPORATION FOR INDUSTRY to provide medium-term loans to industry. It changed its name in 1982 to INVESTORS IN INDUSTRY and in 1986 to 3i.

finance house. Any organization which lends money.

Finance Houses Association. The representative body in London of the major UK FINANCE HOUSES.

financial models. Simulation (usually computer-based) of financial aspects of a company's business.

financial ratios. Ratios between items on an organization's BALANCE SHEET or FINANCIAL STATEMENT which give useful information about some aspect of its performance and which provide the basis for comparison between different organizations.

Financial Services Act 1986. UK legislation introduced to monitor and regulate the financial services industry, especially in the wake of the BIG BANG on the London Stock Exchange. In particular, it set up the SECURITIES AND INVESTMENTS BOARD (SIB) as a regulatory agency to supervise the provisions of the Act and to report to the DEPARTMENT OF TRADE AND INDUSTRY; in this it did not replace the various voluntary watchdog bodies of the Stock Exchange but took on a supervisory role over them. The SIB is modelled on the US Securities and Exchange Commission which is a federal statutory body charged with policing financial matters.

financial statement. A statement which gives information about the financial performance of a firm or organization. These can take many forms but the most common are BALANCE SHEETS or PROFIT AND LOSS ACCOUNTS.

Financial Times. A UK-based daily newspaper covering all news but with a strong financial and business emphasis and containing considerable detail on markets, company performance etc. It is printed on distinctively coloured paper which gives it its nickname of the 'Pink 'un'.

Financial Times—Actuaries All-Share Index (All—Share Index). A broadly-based index covering 730 UK industrial, commercial and financial companies at 31 December 1986.

Financial Times Industrial Ordinary Share Index (FT Industrial Ordinary Index; 30 Share Index). An index covering 30 leading UK industrial and commercial companies. This is the UK index most commonly used in financial comment by the media.

Financial Times—Stock Exchange 100 Index (FT—SE 100). A computerized stock exchange index launched in 1984 in the UK (3 January 1984 = 1000). It is a weighted arithmetic index based on the minute-by-minute share price movements of 100 of the most highly capitalized companies listed on the UK Stock Exchange, and covers around 70 per cent of the total equity market by capitalization.

Unlike the FINANCIAL TIMES INDUSTRIAL ORDINARY SHARE INDEX, which is calculated mechanically every hour to give a picture of how the market's leading stocks are moving, the FT—SE 100 is calculated and updated continuously by computer. A key factor is that the index is 'real time' (i.e. it is calculated almost instantaneously). The computer operates at 1-minute intervals: for 60 seconds it monitors the price changes which are being continuously collected from the MARKET MAKERS and keyed into terminals, then it recalculates the index in approximately 2 seconds.

financial year. The period of 12 months chosen by a company over which its ACCOUNTS will run.

finished goods. INVENTORY (stock) made up of finished products waiting to be sold.

Finniston Report. A report of the enquiry into the engineering profession, chaired by Sir Monty Finniston, to examine the status, training and general role of engineers in the UK. The report, published as *Engineering our Future* (London: HMSO Cmnd 7794, 1974), made a number of recommendations including the setting up of the ENGINEERING COUNCIL.

firefighting. *See* MANAGEMENT BY CRISIS.

firmware. Computer software which has been programmed on a memory chip and is resident in the computer — as opposed to on magnetic tape or FLOPPY DISK where it needs to be loaded before it can be run by the machine.

first-day premium. The gain where shares appreciate between the day of issue and the day on which dealing commences.

first in, last out (FILO). *See* LAST IN, FIRST OUT.

first line. A term used, particularly of supervisory or maintenance management personnel, to describe those who are directly connected with and responsible for keeping production running on the shop floor.

fiscal year. The FINANCIAL YEAR of a government. In the UK this runs from April to April and in the USA from July to June.

fixed asset. An asset — usually property, plant or equipment — which will be used by a firm over a long-term period — a minimum of one year — and which is not a CURRENT ASSET.

fixed charge (fixed expense). A recurring LIABILITY, such as regular rental or interest payments.

fixed cost. A cost incurred in producing goods or services which is independent (i.e. it remains fixed) of the amount produced. Examples would be the rental of premises for production or offices, or the rates payable on them.

fixed expense. *See* FIXED CHARGE.

fixed-interest security. A SECURITY of BOND which offers a guaranteed interest payment and which usually has a fixed term before it matures. An example of a fixed-interest security would be GOVERNMENT SECURITIES.

fixed-shift system. A shiftwork system where each team of workers always works the same shift.

flag of convenience. A merchant shipping flag flown by a ship registered in a country other than that of the owners in order to obtain tax or cost advantages.

flat rate. The rate of interest on a loan or in the purchase of an item by some form of credit system which does not take into account the fact that the sum to be repaid is reducing. Interest rates are quoted as a percentage based on the original sum involved and thus appear lower than the actual rate which will be paid. In the UK consumer credit law requires that the full rate actually paid − known as the ANNUAL PERCENTAGE RATE (APR) − is quoted in any advertisement or contract.

flat rate (benefits and contributions). Every worker and employer in the UK must contribute to the NATIONAL INSURANCE fund. This provides − under the terms of a variety of pieces of legislation − for the payment of a range of benefits should anything affect the employee's ability to work, such as sickness, industrial injury or being made redundant. The basic rates of contributions into the scheme and benefits payable by the scheme are fixed and are known as flat rates − as distinct from other forms which may be related to particular indices − such as EARNINGS-RELATED BENEFIT.

flat-rate pension scheme. See PENSION.

flexible manning (flexible working practices). Alternative arrangements in work organization which permit a greater degree of flexibility within an organization in its use of labour along one or more dimensions. Among relevant kinds of flexibilty are FLEXIBLE WORKING HOURS, levels of manning and skill levels (where flexibility is concerned with moving workers around a plant to provide cover for the various operating requirements of machinery), trade union practices (where flexibility relates to removing some of the rigidities of demarcation between trades) and in payment systems.

flexible manufacturing system. An arrangement of computer-controlled machine tools and transport and handling systems which operates as an integrated system under the supervisory control of a larger computer. Such systems began to emerge in the 1980s and offer considerable improvements in the speed with which batch production goods can be made and reductions in the amount of working capital tied up in the work-in-progress inventory. In particular they hold out the prospect of smaller firms being able to compete on the basis of ECONOMIES OF SCOPE.

flexible working hours (flexitime; variable working hours). An increasingly common arrangement whereby employees can choose their working times during the day provided the total number of hours worked over a period is the same as specified on their CONTRACT OF EMPLOYMENT. Most schemes operate a CORE TIME system which specifies certain hours (usually 10am to 3pm) during which employees must be present, but outside of this time employees may choose the hours they work. In many cases, extra time worked under such a scheme (up to a certain limit) may earn an equivalent holiday.

flexible working practices. See FLEXIBLE MANNING.

flexitime. See FLEXIBLE WORKING HOURS.

float. (1) In network planning, time which can be added to the duration of an activity without affecting the overall project duration.
(2) To offer securities for sale for the first time.
(3) A small amount of cash held for giving change etc.
(4) To allow a currency to find its own exchange rate against others (rather than by fixing it by CENTRAL BANK intervention at a chosen level).

floating assets. See CURRENT ASSETS.

floating charge. The surrender of rights of ownership of property (e.g. the title deeds of a house) when the property is used as COLLATERAL for a loan. The charge remains in effect until the loan is repaid, although the property can still be used.

floating labour. Part of the national or regional workforce (usually unskilled) which has no stable employment but which moves around both in terms of job category and geographical location on a short-term basis.

floating point operations per second. *See* FLOPS.

floppy disk (minifloppy; diskette). A small magnetic disk on which data can be stored in a computer system. Two sizes dominate − 5.25 inches and 3.5 inches in diameter. It differs from a HARD DISK in that it can be removed from the DISK DRIVE.

flops (floating point operations per second). The measure of the power and speed of a computer.

flotation. The process of launching a new issue of SECURITIES.

flow production (continuous production). Continuous production in which raw materials are fed in at one end of the process and finished products emerge at the other having passed through in an uninterrupted flow through the process. It differs from batch production in which the flow is interrupted as the components move from stage to stage. Examples of continuous flow production include the manufacture of petrochemicals, sugar, steel and other commodity products.

flyback timing (snapback timing). A technique used in WORK STUDY where a stopwatch is used to time each element of a job and then zeroed.

flying pickets. A group of pickets who are mobile and can be moved quickly to a particular site to concentrate pressure on a large multi-location firm and counter the attempts of the firm to maintain production by switching operations between multiple sites. The concept originated in the 1974 UK miners' strike but has been curbed to some extent by the provisions of the EMPLOYMENT ACTS 1980, 1982.

FOB. *See* FREE ON BOARD.

Follet, Mary Parker. A UK management writer and researcher of the 1930s, and a member of the Classical Management School. She was particularly interested in the question of how conflicts are resolved in organizations and coined the term 'the law of the situation' in which she attempted to depersonalize the sources of conflict. 'If orders are simply part of the situation, the question of someone giving and someone receiving does not come up. Both accept the orders given by the situation.' This rational model is outlined in her book *Creative Experience* (London: Longmans, 1924), and a review of her work can be found in D. Pugh et al (eds) *Writers on Organizations* (3rd edn, Harmondsworth: Penguin, 1986).

FOR. *See* FREE ON RAIL.

forecasting. Attempts to describe what will happen in the future. These can be either qualitative − using techniques like the DELPHI TECHNIQUE, the SCENARIO WRITING APPROACH − or quantitative − using TIME SERIES FORECASTING, trend extrapolation etc. Forecasting can be applied to many areas in business (e.g. marketing, technology, sales, production capacity and demand etc).

foreclosure. If money has been lent on the basis of a MORTGAGE, the lender can foreclose on the loan by taking steps to acquire ownership of the property on which the mortgage is based unless the debt is repaid.

foreign exchange. Foreign currencies.

foreign exchange market. A market in which currencies are traded. This is usually a notional rather than a physical meeting place since most financial transactions in foreign exchange are now conducted on a worldwide basis via telephone or electronic means.

foreman (charge hand). A SUPERVISOR (usually a leading worker) responsible for planning and overseeing the work of a group of workers.

foreshift. The morning shift in a three-shift system.

form letter. A WORD PROCESSING term for a letter sent to different people with only the name and address and some other particulars changed to give it the appearance of being personally written. The computer automatically inserts a new name and address etc each time the letter is printed. It is often used in conjunction with a MAIL MERGE facility.

Formula Translation. *See* FORTRAN.

FORTRAN (Formula Translation). A high-level computer language especially suitable for engineering work.

Fortune. A US magazine covering aspects of business and industry. It maintains a monitoring profile on the Fortune 500, a list of the top firms in the USA and their performance over time.

forward. Relating to the future – as in forward planning or forward deliveries.

forward contract. A contract which indicates that goods or commodities will be delivered at some future date – either exactly specified (an outright forward contract) or one chosen by the buyer or seller (an option forward contract). FUTURES CONTRACTS are a special case of forward contract since the buyers/sellers are speculating on price changes in the intervening period and have no intention of actually making or taking delivery of the items covered by the contract.

forward cover. Foreign currency bought in advance to cover a future obligation.

forward integration. The extension of a company's business operations further down along the production and distribution chain – for example, from manufacturing into retailing.

forward market (terminal market). A market dealing in FUTURES CONTRACTS. Two basic items are traded – interest rate and currency – on special exchanges in London, New York, Chicago etc, and two types of trading dominate – HEDGING and full trading.

forward pass. In PROJECT NETWORK TECHNIQUES, the calculation of earliest start and finish times for activities and events.

forward price. A price agreed for the buying or selling of goods or commodities for delivery at some future date.

forward rate. An exchange rate agreed for buying or selling currencies at some future date.

fourth generation language. A class of high-level computer languages which emerged in the mid-1980s as tools to enhance software productivity and reliability. One of the key characteristics of fourth generation languages is their modular structure which enables programs written in them to be checked and tested easily.

franchise. A business in which exclusive rights are purchased for selling goods or services under a specified trade name and within a specified geographical area. The franchisor supplies the product or teaches the service to the franchisee who then sells it, paying in return a fee and/or royalty on the sales. Examples include fast food restaurants, instant print services etc and well-known names include Kentucky Fried Chicken, McDonalds, The British School of Motoring and Budget Vehicle Rental.

franked investment income (FII). Income received by a UK company as a dividend from another company and on which ADVANCE CORPORATION TAX has already been paid.

free alongside ship. In international trade, a CONTRACT in which goods are delivered alongside a ship nominated by the buyer. The cost of this delivery is met by the seller, but the loading onto the ship is the buyer's responsibility.

free enterprise. A system of management and organization of business which operates without government intervention or control.

free float. In NETWORK planning, the time for which an activity can be delayed without delaying any subsequent activity.

free on board (FOB). In international trade, a CONTRACT in which goods are delivered and loaded direct onto a ship nominated by the buyer. The cost of this delivery is met by the seller, and the buyer thus has his goods free on board.

free on rail (FOR). In international trade, a CONTRACT in which goods are delivered and loaded direct onto a railway truck. The cost of this delivery is met by the seller, and the buyer thus has his goods free on rail.

free port. A port which allows goods to be temporarily imported and held within the port area without paying duty – providing they are re-exported later. Free ports provide a way of encouraging economic development around port regions since they require considerable support from the local infrastructure and provide a range of employment.

free trade. An economic policy based on trade between nations free of taxes, DUTIES or TARIFF BARRIERS.

free trade area (free trade zone). An agreement between nations to encourage free trade between them by removing TARIFF BARRIERS. It is similar to a COMMON MARKET but does not involve the erection of tariff barriers against non-members.

free trade zone. *See* FREE TRADE AREA.

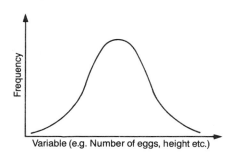

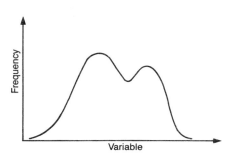

examples of frequency distributions

frequency distribution. In statistics, the frequency of occurence of given values in a set of results. Examples of frequency distributions are given above.

friendly society. An organization in the UK which is set up for the benefit of its members, according to the terms of the Friendly Societies Act 1897. One of the main provisions of this act is that friendly societies cannot make a profit but instead must pay the benefits to members.

fringe benefits (employee benefits). Rewards to employees beyond their basic remuneration package – such as free or subsidized food or travel, special low-interest mortgage rates, special price access to a company's products etc.

frozen asset. An asset which is not readily convertible into cash or which can only be sold at a great loss in value. An example would be money trapped in a foreign country with some form of EXCHANGE CONTROL.

FT Industrial Ordinary Index. *See* FINANCIAL TIMES INDUSTRIAL ORDINARY INDEX.

FT–SE 100 Index. *See* FINANCIAL TIMES STOCK EXCHANGE 100 INDEX.

full cost. *See* ABSORPTION COSTING.

full-line strategy. *See* BROAD-LINE STRATEGY.

functional organization. An organization structure based on dividing tasks to be done into a number of discrete functional areas – for example, research and development, marketing, production, quality control etc – and giving these areas autonomy under a line manager. *See* LINE MANAGEMENT.

funding statement. A statement in the ACCOUNTS of an organization which, together with the BALANCE SHEET and the PROFIT AND LOSS ACCOUNT, shows the sources of a company's funds and the ways in which they are used. It is of particular value in showing the current position rather than that shown on a historical basis.

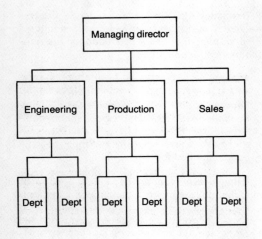

functional organization

futures contract. A FORWARD CONTRACT to buy or sell SECURITIES, COMMODITIES, currency etc at some future date at a price agreed at the present date.

futures market. *See* FORWARD MARKET.

future shock. A phrase coined by the US writer Alvin Toffler in a book of the same name, published in 1971, which deals with the increasingly rapid pace of change in the environment and our growing inability to adapt at the same rate.

G

game theory. A theory which applies to situations which involve conflicts of interest between different parties, and which attempts to model them mathematically and predict outcomes and indicate optimal strategies.

Gantt chart. A system, invented by Henry Gantt, a US engineer, which represents graphically the progress of a project over time on the basis of actual versus planned performance.

Gantt task and bonus payment system. A PAYMENT-BY-RESULTS system, developed by Henry Gantt, which involves setting STANDARD TIMES for producing one unit of output. A guaranteed minimum wage is calculated on the basis of hours worked per week divided by this standard time which gives a weekly standard number of units which a worker can produce. Bonuses for producing more are calculated on the basis of standard time multiplied by standard hourly rate multiplied by 120 per cent of the actual number of units produced.

gap analysis. A strategic management technique which examines a company's markets and competition in a systematic fashion to identify product gaps into which the company can position itself in the future.

garbage in, garbage out. *See* GIGO.

gatekeeper. An individual in an organization who acts as an informal communication focus, collecting information from a variety of sources external to the company and passing

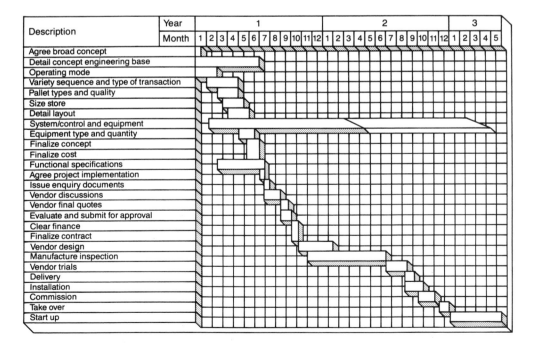

example of a Gantt chart

it on to individuals within the company to whom it will be relevant. A good description of the role of gatekeepers can be found in T.J. Allen, *Managing the Flow of Technology* (Cambridge, Mass.: MIT Press, 1977).

gateway. Telecommunications equipment or software designed to interface with some form of information or communications network — for example, into a VIEWDATA system.

GATT. *See* GENERAL AGREEMENT ON TARIFFS AND TRADE.

Gaussian distribution. A PROBABILITY DISTRIBUTION, named after the German mathematician Karl Friedrich Gauss. *See* NORMAL DISTRIBUTION.

GDP. *See* GROSS DOMESTIC PRODUCT.

gearing (leverage). The extent to which a company is financed by debt capital. It is usually expressed as a ratio — for example, debt capital to equity.

General Agreement on Tariffs and Trade (GATT). An international treaty which covers the terms under which international trade takes place, with particular reference to import duties and exchange controls. Regular meetings are held to renegotiate these terms and the GATT has a permanent headquarters in Geneva. At these meetings (the last was in Uruguay in 1986) a number of bilateral agreements are worked out between countries. The GATT has four main elements: (*i*) agreement on MOST FAVOURED NATION STATUS; (*ii*) detailed rules on the conduct of international trade; (*iii*) procedural matters; and (*iv*) special provision for trade with developing countries. There are now over 90 countries signatory to the GATT accounting for around 75 per cent of world trade.

General and Municipal Workers Union (GMWU). The major UK trade union representing public sector workers.

General Index of Retail Prices. *See* RETAIL PRICE INDEX.

general manager. A senior manager with responsibilities for policy and planning across the whole range of an organization, rather than for a specific functional area.

general meeting. A meeting which all members and shareholders of a company are invited to attend. *See* ANNUAL GENERAL MEETING; EXTRAORDINARY GENERAL MEETING.

general strike. Strike action called by several trade unions simultaneously. It often refers specifically to the 1926 strikes in the UK which were called to support the miners and which involved most key unions in a long battle with employers and the government.

generic competitive strategy. Broad company strategies identified by Michael Porter which affect the success of the business in terms of overall cost leadership, focus and market differentiation. He identifies three generic strategies — differentiated, undifferentiated and concentrated — in his textbook, *Competitive Strategy: Techniques for Analysing Industries and Competitors* (New York: Collier Macmillan, 1980).

Gesellschaft mit beschränkter Haftung (GmbH) (Ger.: 'company with limited liability'). The West German equivalent of a UK private limited company. As with other forms of company in Germany, the terms under which a GmbH is set up are legally prescribed, requiring a minimum of DM 20,000 CONTRIBUTED CAPITAL, but unlike an AKTIENGESELLSCHAFT the firm does not require a supervisory board unless the number of employees exceeds 500. GmbH is also a form of company in Switzerland and Austria, again with legally specified requirements for the amount of contributed capital involved.

GIGO (garbage in, garbage out). In computing, the point that the output of a system depends on what is put into it.

gilt-edged stock (gilts). Government stocks which are considered as extremely safe investments because their interest and repayment is guaranteed by the government. *See* BLUE CHIP.

gilts. *See* GILT-EDGED STOCK.

Gilbreth, Frank and Gilbreth, Lilian. US management scientists active in the 1920s who carried out much of the original work on MOTION STUDY and contributed to the development of the principles and practice of scientific management.

giro. A credit transfer system between banks in Europe.

Girobank. Banking services offered by the UK Post Office.

Glacier Project. A long-term research project carried out in the Glacier Metal Company in the UK by researchers from the Tavistock Institute in London. The researchers were led by Elliot Jacques and the work was actively supported from within the firm by Wilfred Brown, then the chairman and managing director. The project ran from 1948 until 1965 and examined a number of organizational and human relations issues; significantly the purpose of the work was to develop practical outputs and in particular the project led to some of the earliest UK experiments with employee PARTICIPATION. A useful summary of the project is given in E. Jacques and W. Brown, *Glacier Project Papers* (London: Heinemann, 1971).

GMWU. *See* GENERAL AND MUNICIPAL WORKERS UNION.

GNP. *See* GROSS NATIONAL PRODUCT.

golden handcuffs. A payment made to an employee as an inducement to him to remain with the organization because of his value to it.

golden handshake. A payment made, usually to a senior executive, on leaving a company, especially when the departure is involuntary — for example, in the aftermath of a take-over or boardroom battle. The size of the payment is usually large, hence the adjective golden.

golden hello. A payment made to induce a prospective employee to join a firm.

golden parachute. A bonus payment which directors of a firm agree to pay themselves in the event of losing a take-over battle. The payment is so-called because one likely consequence of such a battle would be that they would be made redundant.

gold standard. A system of monetary organization under which the value of a country's money is legally defined as a fixed quantity of gold, and domestic currency takes the form of gold coin and/or notes convertible on demand into gold at legally determined rates. Originally all major trading nations backed up their national currencies with gold; this meant that it was theoretically possible to exchange a one pound note, for example, for its equivalent in gold. With economic recession and the rapidly fluctuating value of currencies, it became increasingly difficult to tie currencies to the value of gold and the gold standard was progressively abandoned, in most cases in the 1920s and 1930s. The UK finally abandoned it in 1932.

goods. In economics, anything which a company produces for sale — physical products, services etc.

goods in process. *See* WORK IN PROGRESS.

goods received note. A document issued by a firm on receipt of a delivery which sets out what goods and how many items have been delivered.

goods returned note. A document issued by a firm on receipt of goods which it originally supplied and which have been returned because of faults, wrong type or quantity etc.

goodwill. The intangible set of factors which develop in a business such as customer loyalty, reputation, special expertise etc. When the business is sold it is often the practice to put a value on such goodwill and it may appear as an INTANGIBLE ASSET in the accounts of a firm.

Gosbank USSR. The CENTRAL BANK of the USSR.

go-slow. Industrial action in which employees work more slowly than normal but do not actually stop work or go on strike. *See also* WORK-TO-RULE.

government broker. A STOCKBROKER appointed to deal in government securities.

government securities (government stock). Securities issued by a government.

government stock. *See* GOVERNMENT SECURITIES.

Gozinto chart (assembly chart). A chart which indicates the way in which complete assemblies are built up. It details the sequence in which components go into subassemblies and how these in turn are made up into complete assemblies.

graded hourly rates. A form of payment system where employees are paid according to their MERIT RATINGS.

gratuity (tip). A payment given to someone as a gift over and above the cost of the service which they have performed.

graveyard shift. Night shift.

greenfield site. A completely new industrial development in a new area, as opposed to being built within an existing facility. Because of the relative ease of escaping from traditional practices the term is sometimes extended to cover progressive union and personnel policies.

greenmail. A colloquial term for the process of buying shares in a company and then forcing the directors to buy them at a higher price under threat of take-over.

Green Paper. A UK government publication which sets out proposed legislation and is intended to stimulate discussion of these proposals before the publication of a WHITE PAPER which details actual legislation passed by Parliament. Green Papers are so-called because they are issued with a green cover.

grey market. A market on which securities are traded before official dealing commences.

grid organizational development. *See* MANAGERIAL GRID.

grievance interview. A part of a GRIEVANCE PROCEDURE.

grievance procedure. A procedure laid down by a company for dealing with complaints or grievances of employees. Such procedures are often negotiated by TRADE UNIONS in order to secure the rights of individual employees.

gross domestic product (GDP). In economics, the total value of business activity — production, investments, services, property etc — within a domestic economy.

gross investment. The total of all the investment expenditures in an economy or firm.

gross margin. *See* GROSS PROFIT.

gross national product (GNP). In economics, the total value of business activity — production, investments (both nationally and abroad), services, property — of a country. Both GNP and GROSS DOMESTIC PRODUCT give an indication of the relative worth of a country.

gross profit (gross margin). A figure representing the revenue from sales of a product or service minus the cost of its production. No other costs or taxes are deducted at this stage in the accounts.

gross profit margin. A FINANCIAL RATIO derived from the GROSS PROFIT for a given item over time, divided by the sales revenue from that item, expressed as a percentage.

group appraisal. A PERFORMANCE APPRAISAL carried out by a group of employees' superiors.

group dynamics. In organizational behaviour, the patterns of behaviour — including formation, leadership, norm-setting, conflict etc — of groups and the individuals within them.

group incentive payment. An incentive payment based on the performance of a work group rather than an individual. *See* PAYMENT-BY-RESULTS.

Group of Ten. A name given to the richest nations (of which there are actually 11:

Belgium, Canada, France, Italy, Japan, the Netherlands, Sweden, Switzerland, the UK, the USA, and West Germany) in the world and which all belong to the INTERNATIONAL MONETARY FUND and which meet regularly to co-ordinate economic policies. In recent years smaller groups – the Group of Five (France, Japan, the UK, the USA and West Germany) and the Group of Seven (Canada, France, Italy, Japan, the UK, the USA and West Germany) are examples – have also begun to meet regularly and to influence policy.

group production. *See* GROUP TECHNOLOGY.

group relief. A tax arrangement for companies within a larger group whereby tax liabilities can be transferred between them so as to reduce the overall tax burden on the group. Thus if one member company makes a loss and another a profit, the loss can be transferred to the profitable company so as to reduce the tax payable.

group technology (group production). An arrangement of machines in batch production such that all the machines required to make a particular product are grouped together – as opposed to arrangements which group similar kinds of machines together and the products are required to pass through all stages sequentially.

group training. A variety of training techniques and approaches based on GROUP DYNAMICS. Examples include COVERDALE TRAINING and T-GROUPS (LABORATORY TRAINING).

grupu. Japanese industrial groups. *See* ZAI-BATSU.

guarantee. A legal promise given by a manufacturer that in the event of defects in a product within a defined period after purchase, they will be made good or the product replaced.

guarantee company (company limited by guarantee). A REGISTERED COMPANY in the UK in which members guarantee to pay up to a declared limited liability to meet the company's debts if it is liquidated.

guaranteed bond. A BOND in which the interest due is guaranteed by another firm to the company issuing the bond. Often within a large group the guarantee is given by the parent company.

guaranteed stock. A SECURITY in which another agency (often a government) guarantees that DIVIDENDS will be paid.

guaranteed week. An agreed number of hours per week for which a worker is paid as long as he is available for work – even if there is no work for him to do.

guarantor. One who gives a GUARANTEE.

guide price. In the EUROPEAN COMMUNITY under the Common Agricultural Policy, the equivalent of a TARGET PRICE for beef and veal. The guide price acts both as a target price and as a guage for deciding on import control and intervention buying. *See* INTERVENTION PRICE.

H

hacker. A colloquial term for an individual who specializes in breaching computer security and accessing systems and data to which he is not entitled.

halo effect. A phenomenon in which the perception about one thing influences the perception about other related things. For example, in an ATTITUDE SURVEY strong negative attitudes towards a superior might also influence statements made about other aspects of the workplace.

Halsey bonus system. A form of PAYMENT-BY-RESULTS scheme which includes a bonus element for improving on-target performance. However, the bonus payable is not related to the degree to which performance is exceeded, as with a conventional incentive bonus scheme.

hammering. In the Stock Exchange, a public announcement that a member cannot pay his debts. The name derives from the old practice of banging the rostrum three times before making such an announcement.

hard copy. A permanent record − usually a computer printout − of data stored on the computer, as distinct from other forms of information storage such as tape or FLOPPY DISK which are stored electronically or in a computer memory.

hard currency. A national currency generally recognized as strong, stable and easily convertible. Examples include Swiss francs or German Deutschemarks.

hard disk. A computer storage device which consists of a magnetic disk held in a protective casing and which has the advantage of a high capacity in comparison with FLOPPY DISKS. It is sometimes known as a Winchester, named after a major manufacturer of hard disks.

hardening. Increasing, usually of prices.

hard loan. (1) A loan that is repayable in HARD CURRENCY, often extended to countries with SOFT CURRENCIES.

(2) A loan with high interest, short payback or other stringent criteria.

hardware. The physical components of a system. The term is mainly used in the context of computer systems where it refers to physical parts such as the central processing unit, the screen, disk drives, printer and other peripherals. The programs which run on the machine are known as SOFTWARE.

Harvard Business Review. A US academic journal, published by the Harvard Business School which deals with analysis of business organization and performance.

HaSaWA. *See* HEALTH AND SAFETY AT WORK ACT 1974.

Hawthorne effect. When the act of studying behaviour changes that behaviour. *See* HAWTHORNE EXPERIMENTS.

Hawthorne experiments (Hawthorne studies). A series of experiments carried out under the leadership of Elton Mayo between 1927 and 1932 in the behavioural sciences which led to the emergence of the Human Relations School of Management Thinking. The Hawthorne plant of the Western Electric Company was the subject of experiments to determine the influence of physical factors in the environment − such as heating or lighting − on ouput and productivity. Results showed that these factors had little effect but that the interpersonal relationships between workers − and, indeed, the very act of management being seen to take an interest in them − were very influential. The results were widely published and a good summary can be found in F. Roethlisberger and W. Dickson, *Management and the Worker* (Cambridge, Mass.: Harvard University Press, 1939).

Hawthorne studies. *See* HAWTHORNE EX-PERIMENTS.

headhunter. An individual specializing in recruiting specialist and high-level personnel by approaching them, and, in many cases, inducing them to leave their present employment.

Health and Safety at Work Act 1974 (HaSaWA). A UK law passed in 1974 to update and rationalize earlier legislation (such as the Factories Act 1961) covering working conditions, safety procedures and employee welfare in factories in the UK. It was essentially a piece of enabling legislation and in many areas gave general aims rather than setting specific standards; some of these have subsequently been developed into codes of practice.

Health and Safety Commission (HSC). An organization set up to oversee the operation of the HEALTH AND SAFETY AT WORK ACT 1974 and specifically to monitor the activities of the HEALTH AND SAFETY EXECUTIVE. The Commission has up to nine members appointed by the Secretary of State for Industry and also has the responsibility of advising on the development of safety and related legislation.

Health and Safety Executive (HSE). An organization set up to implement the HEALTH AND SAFETY AT WORK ACT 1974 and to enforce the regulations covering safety in all branches of industry and commerce in the UK. The HSE has three members and a large staff of inspectors, many of whom were previously employed enforcing legislation under earlier separate acts in the field such as the Alkali Act, the Factories Act, the Mines and Quarries Act etc.

Health and Safety Inspectorate. *See* FACTORY INSPECTORATE.

hedge. (1) To protect against loss or failure in the future (usually financial).
(2) In trading, the practice of reducing the risk of existing commitments (e.g. in the commodity or currency markets) by buying into the futures market for those items.

Herzberg's two factor theory. A theory of MOTIVATION developed by Frederick Herzberg, a US psychologist. It was based on an analysis of JOB SATISFACTION and especially a study of 200 accountants and engineers in which he found 2 classes of factors which were influential. Satisfaction was due to a class of factors he termed 'motivators' which included achievement, recognition, job content, responsibiltiy and opportunities for advancement. Dissatisfaction was due to concerns with the general conditions and procedures at work − termed 'hygiene factors' − which included administrative policy, physical working conditions, working relationships, salary and supervision. Herzberg's original work is described in his book *Work*

Determinants of job satisfaction
Motivators

> Achievement
> Recognition
> Work itself
> Responsibility
> Advancement

Higher order needs
Intrinsic factors

Presence = Job satisfaction
Absence ≠ Job dissatisfaction
Absence = Lack of job satisfaction

Determinants of job dissatisfaction
Hygiene factors

> Company policy and administration
> Supervision
> Salary
> Interpersonal relations
> Working conditions

Lower order needs
Extrinsic factors

Presence ≠ Job satisfaction
Presence = No job dissatisfaction
Absence = Job dissatisfaction

Herzberg's two factor theory

and the Nature of Man (New York: Staples Press, 1968). This 'two factor' theory of motivation was taken up by a number of other workers, notably W. Paul and K. Robertson in the UK who used it in a major study of ICI (published as *Job Enrichment and Employee Motivation* (Epping: Gower Press, 1970)). Work of this kind led to emphasis being placed less on extensive factors and more on intrinsic motivation via different approaches to JOB ENRICHMENT.

heuristics. Simple rules of thumb which have been acquired by experience and which provide a useful approach to solving problems. Identifying and recording heuristics is a major task in developing systems involving ARTIFICIAL INTELLIGENCE.

hidden agenda. Items not appearing on the formal agenda of a meeting but which nevertheless influence the way in which that meeting progresses.

hierarchy. An orderly arrangement of positions in an organization on the basis of increasing responsibility and authority as one moves towards the top. This provides the basis for the classical pyramidal structure of many organizations.

hierarchy of needs. A popular concept originated by the US psychologist Abraham Maslow to explain human MOTIVATION. In essence, the theory suggests that Man is driven to try and satisfy various needs arranged in a hierarchy, moving from the very basic to a high level. These are usually grouped into five classes: (*i*) physiological − food, drink, sleep etc; (*ii*) safety needs − shelter, stability, security etc; (*iii*) belonging needs − love, family, friendship etc; (*iv*) esteem − respect of others in a family or a group etc; (*v*) self-actualization − personal development.

The implications of the theory for management is that lower order needs must be satisfied before any incentive based on high-level needs will have an effect. So, for example, a more satisfying job will not motivate an employee who is concerned about the fact that his wages are not sufficient to pay the rent or to feed his family. Maslow's views remain a popular explanation of motivation although they are now considered a

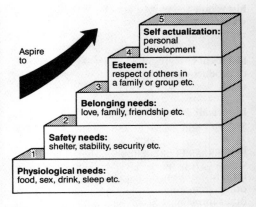

the hierarchy of needs

little simplistic among behavioural researchers. However, they are described in detail in several books, perhaps the best being Maslow's own *Motivation and Personality* (2nd edn, New York: Harper & Row, 1970).

high-level language. A computer language which allows the user to program instructions for the computer in a series of logical statements which approximate to human language and which make it easy to work with the computer. It differs from low-level or machine code language in which the actual instructions which control the computer need to be represented and which is based on binary numbers. High-level languages exist for many general and specific applications and examples include FORTRAN, ALGOL, COBOL, BASIC, PASCAL and LOGO; in each case the languages are translated within the computer into machine language by an interpreter or compiler.

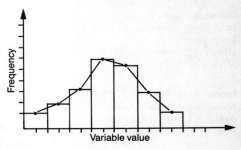

a histogram

histogram (column diagram). A diagram in which a FREQUENCY DISTRIBUTION can be represented.

historical cost. In accounting, the actual cost of producing an item at the time it was produced.

historical cost accounting. An accounting system based on HISTORICAL COSTS.

holding company (holding group; parent company). (1) A company which carries out little or no business itself but which controls other companies in which it has shares or other forms of security.
(2) In UK tax law, a company which holds shares or securities in companies which are 90 per cent subsidiaries of it.

holding group. See HOLDING COMPANY.

horizontal integration. The extension of a company's business into other areas which involve it in producing the same product or service (or developments of it) across a broader front – either selling into different markets or by acquiring or amalgamating with a competing company in the same business.

horizontal merger. A MERGER between two firms within the same sector with similar profiles of activity within that sector.

host computer. In distributed computer systems, especially those used in industrial control such as DIRECT NUMERICAL CONTROL, the central computer to which all other processors and computers communicate and refer.

house journal. A newspaper, magazine or newsletter produced by an organization to keep its members and employees informed about the performance of the company and other developments.

house style. The image which a company presents of itself in written material in its dealings both internally and externally.

House style may be formally specified to cover the way in which news and other information is written up and published.

HSC. See HEALTH AND SAFETY COMMISSION.

HSE. See HEALTH AND SAFETY EXECUTIVE.

human asset accounting (human resource accounting). A concept which involves various attempts at expressing the contribution or value given to a firm by its employees. Examples of measures include capitalizing, recruiting and training costs, current replacement costs, opportunity costs and net present value of future salaries of the businesses' future earnings directly related to its human resources. Pioneering work in this area was done by Rensis LIKERT in the USA and is described in his book *The Human Organization: its Management and Value* (New York: McGraw-Hill, 1967).

human engineering. See ERGONOMICS.

human factors engineering. See ERGONOMICS.

Human Relations School of Management Thinking. An influential school of management thought which grew out of the results of the HAWTHORNE EXPERIMENTS. It emphasizes the importance of human relations – between employees and management, within work groups etc – and the need to obtain satisfactory fulfilment of these needs in organizations. Among the most influential of the many researchers in this school were Elton Mayo (who led the Hawthorne team), Kurt LEWIN, whose work laid the foundations for modern ORGANIZATION DEVELOPMENT work, and Douglas MACGREGOR, who developed the idea of THEORY X AND THEORY Y approaches to management.

human resource accounting. See HUMAN ASSET ACCOUNTING.

hygiene factors. See HERZBERG'S TWO FACTOR THEORY.

I

IBRD (International Bank for Reconstruction and Development). *See* WORLD BANK.

IBRO. *See* INTERNATIONAL BANKING RESEARCH ORGANIZATION.

ICFC. *See* INDUSTRIAL AND COMMERCIAL FINANCE CORPORATION.

icons. Pictures displayed on a computer screen to represent various functions which can be performed in a program – for example, a filing cabinet might represent filing operations or a waste basket the deletion of data – developed for use on USER-FRIENDLY computer systems.

ICOR. *See* INCREMENTAL CAPITAL OUTPUT RATIO.

IDA. *See* INTERNATIONAL DEVELOPMENT ASSOCIATION.

IDC. *See* INDUSTRIAL DEVELOPMENT CERTIFICATE.

IDD. The abbreviation for International Direct Dialling in telecommunications.

idle time. *See* MACHINE IDLE TIME.

IE. *See* INFERENCE ENGINE.

IFC. *See* INTERNATIONAL FINANCE CORPORATION.

IGES. *See* INITIAL GRAPHICS EXCHANGE STANDARD.

III. *See* INVESTORS IN INDUSTRY.

IKBS. *See* INTELLIGENT KNOWLEDGE-BASED SYSTEMS.

illegal contracts. Certain classes of CONTRACT which are not legally binding. Examples include those between firms in countries at war with each other, those which involve committing a crime or

hindering the course of justice, those which would act in restraint of trade (such as a merger not sanctioned by the MONOPOLIES AND MERGERS COMMISSION in the UK) and those involving some form of conflict of interest.

ILO. *See* INTERNATIONAL LABOUR OFFICE.

IMF. (1) *See* INTERNATIONAL METALWORKERS FEDERATION.
(2) *See* INTERNATIONAL MONETARY FUND.

immediate annuity rate. The rate at which an ENDOWMENT assurance policy can be converted to a PENSION on maturity.

impact day. The day on which new shares are issued to the public.

impact testing. A technique for measuring the effectiveness – the impact – of ADVERTISING.

imperfect market. In economics, a market in which there are constraints on its free operation – for example, when there are few buyers and many sellers, or barriers to entry or when products and/or services offered for sale are not homogenous.

impingement pay. A payment made to employees who work on through their normal holiday break.

import duty. A DUTY charged on goods or services imported into a country.

import licence. A licence obtained by an importer (necessary for certain countries and certain classes of goods) for the government of the country into which the goods are to be imported.

import penetration. The degree to which a country's domestic markets are satisfied by imported goods or services as opposed to those produced indigenously.

imposed date. In NETWORK planning, the time by which an activity must take place.

imprest (imprest system). A cash advance or loan used in PETTY CASH transactions, where a FLOAT is given to the person responsible and at the end of a period he provides details of expenditure against that float which is then made up again to its original level and the process repeated.

imprest system. *See* IMPREST.

improshare. A form of PAYMENT-BY-RESULTS scheme.

improvement curve. *See* LEARNING CURVE.

imputed costs. Costs which must be paid by a firm, irrespective of the size or number or type of business transactions which it makes (e.g. paying interest on money borrowed).

incentive bonus. *See* PAYMENT-BY-RESULTS.

incentive bonus schemes. *See* BONUS SCHEMES.

incentive engineer. *See* INDUSTRIAL ENGINEER.

incentive payment. *See* PAYMENT-BY-RESULTS.

incentive scheme. *See* PAYMENT-BY-RESULTS.

incestuous share dealing. Dealing in securities between individuals or firms which have some connection − for example, companies within the same group. Such dealing may be carried out to take advantage of inside information or to secure tax benefits; it is illegal under the Stock Exchange rules.

income and expenditure statement. A PROFIT AND LOSS ACCOUNT used by organizations which are non-profit-making (such as charities) to indicate the financial state of their operations.

income benefit insurance policy. A form of LIFE INSURANCE which allows for the payment of a guaranteed income to the dependants of the policyholder should he die before retirement.

income bond. A SECURITY which pays interest only when the company makes a profit.

income elasticity of demand. In economics, the relationship between the amount of purchasing power of people and the level of demand for goods or services. *See* DEMAND ELASTICITY.

income fund. An investment made with the purpose of providing income rather than capital growth.

incomes policy. The various forms of government control of the pay negotiation process used to keep wage increases under control and hence reduce the risk of inflation. For example, this can be achieved by recommending or fixing limits for pay increases in a period or by penalizing those who exceed these limits.

income statement. The US equivalent of a PROFIT AND LOSS ACCOUNT.

income tax. A tax levied by a government on individuals living in a country based on their income less various forms of allowance. Most income tax systems involve multiple rates of some kind so that those earning more are taxed proportionately higher. In the UK income tax is levied according to six schedules covering different ways of obtaining income. These are: (*i*) income from property; (*ii*) income from commercial woodlands; (*iii*) income from interest and annuities payable out of public revenue; (*iv*) income from professional or trade activities, from businesses and from other sources of profits; (*v*) income from employment deducted at source via a PAY AS YOU EARN scheme; and (*vi*) income from dividends subject to higher rates of tax.

in-company training. Training provided within a firm rather than at an external venue, though the trainers involved may be brought in from outside.

incorporated company. *See* PARTNERSHIP.

incremental capital output ratio (ICOR). A form of CAPITAL OUTPUT RATIO which is calculated on an incremental basis − for example, on a month-by-month basis the amount of the capital input is compared with the output of goods or services in a firm.

incremental costing. *See* MARGINAL COSTING.

incremental payment system. A payment system based on employees receiving regular increments along a scale.

indemnify. To provide protection against legal proceedings.

indemnity fund (employer strike insurance). A form of protection against the costs of INDUSTRIAL DISPUTES which is provided by employers paying into a special fund.

indenture. (1) In the UK, a CONTRACT between an employer and an apprentice.
(2) In the USA, a contract between a corporation and its bondholders.

index linking. Mechanisms for allowing for the effects of changes in the value of money — for example due to inflation — by linking investments, pensions etc to an index which reflects these changes.

index method. A FORECASTING technique which links the change in something — for example, potential sales of a new product — to an index which will at least give an indication of the trends involved — such as population growth.

indicative planning. A form of planning which is based on agreeing targets.

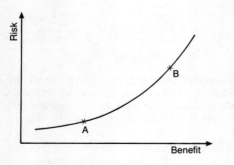

an indifference curve (whilst the benefit at point B is greater than that at point A, so is the risk; the investor is thus indifferent as to which position he is faced with)

indifference curve. A charted curve linking benefit to risk in any venture. For any point on the curve the level of benefit is only reached by taking a certain risk. The investor is thus indifferent to where a proposal stands on the curve.

indirect costs (burden). Costs which are not directly connected with the production of a particular product or service.

indirect demand (derived demand). A demand for a product or service which is not directly consumed but instead forms an input to another product or service — for example, components for an assembled product like a washing machine.

indirect labour. Employees not directly connected with the production of goods or services. In practice this includes a large number of essential workers (e.g. in maintenance) without whom production could not take place.

indirect materials costs. Costs related to those materials not directly used in the production of a product.

indirect tax (expenditure tax). A tax levied not on income or profits but on goods or services purchased — for example, VALUE ADDED TAX, or Customs and Excise DUTY.

individual training methods. Training approaches based on individual as opposed to group development.

induction course (induction training). A course given to new employees on joining a firm to introduce them to the company, its organization and procedures etc.

induction training. *See* INDUCTION COURSE..

industrial accident. In the UK, an accident which takes place at work and entails a minimum of three days' absence from work. Such industrial accidents are covered by legislation under the HEALTH AND SAFETY AT WORK ACT 1974.

industrial action. The various kinds of response made by employees, usually organized by their TRADE UNION, to action by employers. Industrial action can take the form of a complete stoppage of production (a STRIKE), a slowing down (GO-SLOW or WORK-TO-RULE), a restriction on overtime or flexibility (OVERTIME BAN) or other.

Industrial and Commercial Finance Corporation (ICFC). A UK development finance company formed in 1946 by the Bank of England and the London and Scottish clearing banks, at the insistence of the government, to fill one of the gaps in the UK capital market. The company advances capital on equity and debt terms to small companies in amounts too large or too long-term for bank lending but too small to be raised by a public issue of securities, and it also assists with management advice. In 1983 it merged with Finance for Industry to form INVESTORS IN INDUSTRY, and changed its name in 1986 to 3i.

Industrial Common Ownership Act 1976. UK legislation setting out the framework under which various forms of CO-OPERATIVE can operate.

industrial democracy. Attempts to increase the level of participation by employees in the decision-making, planning and management of firms in which they work. It has been particularly developed in West Germany under the CO-DETERMINATION legislation, but in the UK the proposals published in the BULLOCK REPORT, while much discussed, have not been widely implemented.

Industrial Development Act 1982. UK legislation extending the powers originally granted to the DEPARTMENT OF TRADE AND INDUSTRY under the INDUSTRY ACT 1972 in respect of deciding on ASSISTED AREA status.

industrial development certificate (IDC). A certificate issued by the DEPARTMENT OF TRADE AND INDUSTRY in the UK for planning applications for industrial activities. Exceptions are made for firms operating in special status areas such as ASSISTED AREAS.

industrial diseases. A range of diseases and illnesses which are caused by some aspect of work or its environment − for example, asbestosis, silicosis, dermatitis etc.

industrial dispute. A dispute between employers and employees, the latter usually represented by their TRADE UNIONS.

industrial engineer (incentive engineer). An individual specializing in the area of WORK STUDY and METHOD STUDY, but who often is also involved in related fields like production control. *See also* ERGONOMICS.

industrial espionage. The stealing of secret or confidential information by one firm from another.

Industrial Health and Safety Centre. A UK agency set up by the DEPARTMENT OF EMPLOYMENT providing guidance on health and safety-related questions.

Industrial Injuries Advisory Committee. A UK committee serving the DEPARTMENT OF HEALTH AND SOCIAL SECURITY which advises on payment of benefits due as a result of industrial injuries, accidents and diseases.

Industrial Injuries Fund. A UK fund, administered by the DEPARTMENT OF HEALTH AND SOCIAL SECURITY, which provides the resources for payments to the victims of industrial injuries. Its work is guided by the INDUSTRIAL INJURIES ADVISORY COMMITTEE and its resources are drawn from both taxes and employer/employee contributions. Its disbursement is covered by various pieces of legislation in the NATIONAL INSURANCE ACTS.

Industrial Location Advisory Service. A service offered by the DEPARTMENT OF TRADE AND INDUSTRY in the UK to enable firms to relocate, especially in areas with ASSISTED AREA status.

industrial market research. MARKET RESEARCH aimed at identifying and exploring the market for industrial as opposed to consumer goods.

industrial park (business park). A property development aimed at industrial users and offering suitable facilities for such use.

industrial property rights. *See* PATENT.

industrial relations (labour relations). Issues raised by the relationship between employers and employees, usually via the TRADE UNION representation of the latter. *See also* EMPLOYEE RELATIONS.

Industrial Relations Act 1971. Legislation introduced in the UK in an attempt to rationalize and strengthen much fragmentary earlier legislation on INDUSTRIAL RELATIONS. The act was repealed by the Labour government in 1974 and replaced by the TRADE UNION AND LABOUR RELATIONS ACT which was itself repealed, and many of the provisions of the Industrial Relations Act were restored by the EMPLOYMENT ACTS 1980, 1982.

Industrial Safety Advisory Council. A UK committee reporting to the DEPARTMENT OF EMPLOYMENT on matters pertaining to industrial safety.

Industrial Society. An independent body in the UK concerned with promoting the image of industry and providing advice and training on aspects of personnel development at all levels. It was granted a Royal Charter in 1985.

industrial trade union (industry union). A TRADE UNION which is empowered to represent all the workers in an industry. It is common in countries like West Germany where, for example, all workers in a steelworks are represented by IG Metall, the metalworkers union, even though there may be electricians, plumbers or supervisors etc in the workforce. In the UK the more common pattern is one of MULTI-UNIONISM in which representation is by skill or craft grouping so that one site may have several unions involved.

Industrial Training Act 1964. Legislation which covers the area of manpower planning and training in the UK and which resulted in the setting up of a number of statutory INDUSTRIAL TRAINING BOARDS for particular sectors of the economy.

Industrial Training Boards (ITBs). A number of statutory bodies set up in the UK under the INDUSTRIAL TRAINING ACT 1964 responsible for education and training provisions within various industrial sectors. Each board is made up of employers' and employees' representatives plus specialist government assessors. Following changes in the administration of the act there are now only six ITBs left which are still statutory bodies although others exist as private ventures.

industrial tribunals. UK organizations originally set up under the INDUSTRIAL TRAINING ACT 1964 to hear appeals pertaining to levies imposed on employers. They were subsequently expanded to cover a variety of employment-related cases — such as those concerning equal opportunities or dismissal. There are currently 27 of these in England and Wales. They are usually chaired by a qualified solicitor or barrister and have two lay members, one nominated by the CONFEDERATION OF BRITISH INDUSTRY and the other by the TRADES UNION CONGRESS. One feature of industrial tribunals is that they do not have the same strict laws of evidence as other courts, so employees can plead their own case rather than requiring a solicitor to plead on their behalf. Around 80 per cent of the cases heard are concerned with some form of UNFAIR DISMISSAL.

Industry Act 1972. A major piece of industrial policy legislation in the UK. It covers several issues, including the provision for investment in new plant and equipment (Section 8) and the setting up of regional development support for special areas, generally designated ASSISTED AREAS.

industry agreement. *See* INDSUTRY-WIDE AGREEMENT.

industry union. *See* INDUSTRIAL TRADE UNION.

industry-wide agreement (industry agreement). An agreement in INDUSTRIAL RELATIONS which covers an entire branch of industry as opposed to a single site.

industry-wide bargaining. A process of COLLECTIVE BARGAINING which takes place at a national level between employers and trade union representatives of an industry and may lead to an INDUSTRY-WIDE AGREEMENT.

inertia selling. Selling which requires the potential consumer to make an active statement rejecting the goods he has been offered otherwise it is assumed that he has bought them and he will be invoiced accordingly. It often involves sending unsolicited goods to someone by mail in the hope that the receiver will not bother to return them.

inference engine (IE). A computer program used in expert systems and other applications of ARTIFICIAL INTELLIGENCE. IE works out the rules on which to base its reasoning and judgments. *See* INTELLIGENT KNOWLEDGE-BASED SYSTEMS.

inflation. In economics, the condition in which prices rise to reflect rising incomes which in turn pushes up the demand for greater purchasing power, eventually leading to increased prices. Such an upward spiral (sometimes called overheating of the economy) does not mean that an individual's purchasing power is increased but it does mean that he pays significantly higher prices (inflated prices) than before; in conditions of inflation there is a rise in unemployment as labour becomes too costly.

inflation accounting. Accounting procedures which attempt to take the diminishing value of money over time into account — for example, CURRENT COST ACCOUNTING.

information science. The science underpinning the storage, retrieval and management of information within organizations.

information technology (IT). The convergent group of technologies concerned with the storage/retrieval, processing and communication of information. The main contributing branches are computing, microelectronics and telecommunications but others include optoelectronics, office equipment technology, systems theory and artifical intelligence theory and practice.

Information Technology Centres (ITeCs). UK centres funded by the DEPARTMENT OF TRADE AND INDUSTRY and the MANPOWER SERVICES COMMISSION to provide training and experience opportunities for young people in the area of INFORMATION TECHNOLOGY.

information theory. A theory, largely mathematically based, that deals with the process of communicating information.

infrastructure. The network of supporting services which underpins an industry or industrial society, such as roads, communications or utilities (water gas, electricity etc).

Initial Graphics Exchange Standard (IGES). A widely-recognized standard for transferring data between two COMPUTER-AIDED DESIGN systems.

injury benefit. A benefit paid to an employee in the UK who has sustained an industrial injury and is unable to work. The money to pay for this benefit comes from the INDUSTRIAL INJURIES FUND.

Inland Revenue. The UK government organization responsible for the collection and assessment of income tax.

innovation. To make something new. Usually taken to mean technological innovation which can be defined as the technical, organizational and commercial steps which are involved in the introduction of new manufactured products to the marketplace and of new manufacturing processes to the factory or of new working technologies into the production and delivery of services.

innovation warrant. A document issued in the UK to provide partial protection to innovators for inventions. It is a low-cost, short-term alternative to patenting which offers some help to the individual inventor who may not have the resources to file a full PATENT application.

input device. Any device which provides data input to a computer — such as a keyboard, bar code reader or touch screen.

input/output analysis. A statistically-based technique used particularly in economics and marketing in which tables of inputs to and outputs from a system — for example, an industry — are produced which show the changing nature of their relationship over time.

in-service training. Training carried out while in employment, with the aim of developing skills or enhancing experience which will be useful in that employment in the future.

insider dealing. *See* INSIDER TRADING.

insider trading (insider dealing). The practice of dealing in securities by those who have some form of privileged 'inside' information (e.g. members of the board of a company or their relatives who trade in the shares of that company). This knowledge could be used, for example, to sell shares before the public is told of poor performance by the company. The practice is illegal and is controlled by statutory bodies in most countries (the SECURITIES AND EXCHANGE COMMISSION in the USA and under the provisions of the FINANCIAL SERVICES ACT 1986 in the UK, for example).

insolvency. The inability to pay debts. This is not the same as being BANKRUPT, since the latter refers to the legal status of an individual after court proceedings.

Insolvency Act 1986. UK legislation covering and strengthening existing legal provision in the field of company liquidation and winding up. It is administered by the DEPARTMENT OF TRADE AND INDUSTRY and covers issues like the disqualification and personal liability of directors.

inspection. *See* QUALITY CONTROL.

Institute of Directors. A UK body which represents the interests of senior executives in manufacturing, service and public sector organizations.

Institute of Patentees and Inventors. A UK organization, established in 1919, which represents the interests of inventors and provides advice and support in the area of intellectual property rights and their protection.

Institute of Personnel Management (IPM). A UK professional body for personnel managers, trainers and others involved in the human resource aspects of business.

institutions. In financial circles, organizations with considerable purchasing power for securities – such as major pension funds – which exert a strong influence on the Stock Exchange.

in-store promotion. A form of SALES PROMOTION which takes place within a retail outlet rather than via advertising or other routes.

insurance. A form of protection taken out in case of an event happening – for example, damage or loss of an item, inability to work due to injury etc – in the future.

Insurance and Companies Department. A branch of the DEPARTMENT OF TRADE AND INDUSTRY.

insurance broker. An individual or organization acting as a go-between arranging INSURANCE of various kinds between insurance companies and those requiring insurance.

insurance company. An organization dealing in INSURANCE

insurance underwriter. An individual or organization concerned with arranging INSURANCE, though not necessarily providing it directly.

intangible assets. Assets which are not of a physical nature – such as equipment or cash – but nevertheless have a value and appear on a BALANCE SHEET (e.g. GOODWILL, PATENTS, TRADEMARKS and COPYRIGHT).

integral job evaluation. A form of JOB EVALUATION which treats jobs as complete entities rather than attempting to break them down in analytical elements. Comparisons are then made between these integral jobs.

Integrated Services Digital Network (ISDN). An advanced high-capacity telecommunications network standard which enables the carriage of a wide range of traffic including data, text, image and broadcast signals. It is expected to be installed in developed nations such as the USA and the countries of western Europe by the late 1990s.

integrated software package. A type of software applications package in which several different applications are provided in such a way that output from one can be used as input to another. For example, a spreadsheet can be used to calculate a forecast which is then inserted into a document being prepared on a word processing program within the same package.

integration. The process of bringing functional units in an organization closer together. The opposite of DIFFERENTIATION.

intelligence test. See PSYCHOLOGICAL TESTING.

intelligent knowledge-based systems (IKBS). A branch of ARTIFICIAL INTELLIGENCE which aims to develop computer-based systems which approximate to some aspect of human intelligence – for example, in their ability to reason or learn.

intelligent terminal. A computer terminal which has some form of internal information processing capability which means that it can work on a stand-alone basis or be linked into a network where it communicates with a central processing unit.

interaction matrix. A matrix used in various kinds of exploratory work to examine interconnections between things and to display them graphically. In FORECASTING it is known as a CROSS-IMPACT MATRIX.

interactive skills (interpersonal skills). The class of individual skills associated with interacting with other people – in a group, in an interview, in dealing with customers etc.

interactive video. A system which combines video technology (usually a videodisk because of its greater storage capability and faster access time) with computer control. In such a system instead of watching in a sequential fashion, the viewer can move around the programme to suit particular requirements. Thus in a tourist enquiry system, for example, a user could ask about holiday destinations and would then be able to move instantly to that section of the disk which held information on the particular destination he wanted rather than all possible ones. Once there, he could view in video film format, a variety of details about it – hotels, amenities, transport arrangements etc. Its particular strength lies in the fact that the information stored is not data but video images. In training, such systems allow for 'tailoring' of standard video packages to suit individual needs.

interbank rate. The rate at which international banks place deposits with each other.

Interbank Sterling Market. A market in the City of London which specializes in movements of sterling. Participants include the major UK banks, ACCEPTING HOUSES, DISCOUNT HOUSES and overseas banks. Its main role is to provide short-term (less than three-month) deposit facilities.

intercompany comparisons (interfirm comparisons). Comparisons made between firms on a number of dimensions to ascertain how well firms perform relative to each other and to identify areas for improvement or development.

interest. A payment made in return for allowing an individual or organization the use of capital. Interest is payable at an agreed INTEREST RATE over time.

interest cover. A measure of the extent to which INTEREST payments can be met out of profits, usually calculated by taking interest due over a period and relating it to profits before tax and interest have been paid.

interest rate. The percentage of the total sum loaned which will be added to it as INTEREST.

interface. (1) The point of contact between two or more things.
(2) In computing, the man–machine interface is that between the computer system and the user.
(3) The boundaries between two or more organizational functions – such as manufacturing and marketing.

interference pay. A payment paid to an employee in a PAYMENT-BY-RESULTS scheme when his work has been interrupted by other work, causing interference with his achievement of those results.

interfirm comparisons. *See* INTERCOMPANY COMPARISONS.

interim dividend. A DIVIDEND paid during the course of a financial year in addition to that due at the end after the company's accounts are complete.

intermediary holdings. *See* NOMINEE HOLDINGS.

intermediate area. A status conferred on a region by the DEPARTMENT OF TRADE AND INDUSTRY under the general class of ASSISTED AREA. Such areas receive some development support, notably grants and tax allowances. There were 57 intermediate areas in 1985 covering around 20 per cent of the UK working population.

intermediate goods. Goods which are used as an input to another manufacturing process. For example, steel is made into pressings by one manufacturer and these represent intermediate goods for a final user such as a car assembler.

internal audit. The process of reviewing on a regular basis some aspect of a company's operations or organization. Most common is a financial audit but other types include manpower audit, technology audit, social audit, innovation audit and energy audit.

internal memory. In computer systems, the amount of memory which the machine itself possesses and which gives an indication of the size of program it will be able to execute.

internal rate of return (actuarial rate of return). In techniques such as DISCOUNTED CASH FLOW which attempt to take into account the changing value of money over time, projects must be compared with the rate of interest applying in the outside world. One way of doing this is to calculate a rate of return on the project itself and to compare this internal rate with external rates of return. The figure can also be used in other calculations such as NET PRESENT VALUE.

Internal Revenue Service (IRS). The US equivalent of the UK INLAND REVENUE, the federal body responsible for the assessment and collection of income tax.

International Banking Research Organization (IBRO). A research body funded by major banks to conduct research into banking and related financial matters.

International Brotherhood of Teamsters, Chauffeurs, Warehousemen and Helpers of America (Teamsters Union). One of the oldest, largest and most powerful trade unions in North America, founded in 1903.

International Chamber of Commerce. An organization, based in France, which co-ordinates the activities of CHAMBERS OF COMMERCE in various countries.

International Court of Justice. A United Nations body established in 1946 in The Hague to deal with arbitration in matters of international law.

International Development Association (IDA). A specialized agency of the United Nations affiliated to the WORLD BANK, founded in 1960 with the aim of providing investment finance for developing nations. Its headquarters are in Washington, DC.

International Finance Corporation (IFC). A specialized agency of the United Nations affiliated to the WORLD BANK, founded in 1956 with the aim of stimulating private sector investment in developing countries. Its headquarters are in Washington, DC.

International Labour Office (ILO). An international organization founded in 1919 and a specialized agency of the United Nations since 1946 with headquarters in Geneva. It is concerned with aspects of employment, such as training, work organization, equal opportunity and working conditions throughout the world. The structure of the ILO is tripartite, with its main boards consisting of representatives from governments, trade unions and employers in member states of the United Nations.

International Metalworkers' Federation (IMF). A trade union federation based in Geneva which co-ordinates trade union activities in the metalworking and related industries on a world-wide basis.

International Monetary Fund (IMF). An international organization set up in 1945 by the United Nations as a consequence of the Bretton Woods meeting on international finance and development in 1944. Its aims are similar to those of the WORLD BANK in terms of supporting economic development and international trade and promoting stability in currency exchange rates on a world-wide basis. Member states (there are currently about 100) pay in a quota of money (proportional to national economic wealth) which is available for lending − often with strict conditions − to developing nations. Each member state has a seat on the main governing board.

International Standard Classification of Occupations (ISCO). A system of occupation classification developed by the INTERNATIONAL LABOUR OFFICE.

International Telecommunications Union (ITU). An international organization founded in 1865 and a specialized agency of the United Nations since 1947 with headquarters in Geneva. It is repsonsible for the co-ordination of policies, standards etc in the field of telecommunications.

interpersonal skills. *See* INTERACTIVE SKILLS.

interpreter. A computer program which interprets HIGH-LEVEL LANGUAGE instructions into MACHINE CODE instructions.

intervention. In ORGANIZATION DEVELOPMENT work, an action taken to bring about some form of change. Such intervention may be structural or involve some change in the organization process − in the way in which things are done or in which the organization CULTURE operates.

intervention price. In the EUROPEAN COMMUNITY under the Common Agricultural Policy, the price at which national intervention agencies are obliged to buy up agricultural commodities which are offered to them. This price is fixed at 12−20 per cent below the TARGET PRICE for wheat, barley, maize and rye, at 10 per cent below the GUIDE PRICE for beef and veal and at 103 per cent of the basic price for pork.

intrafirm comparisons. Comparisons made between different departments or groups within a company on a number of dimensions to ascertain how well the departments or groups perform relative to each other and to identify areas for improvement or development. *See also* INTERCOMPANY COMPARISONS.

intrapreneurship. A name coined to describe the process of generating new business ventures within an existing company − usually large − often involving a break with the bureaucratic traditions of the parent firm. The name originated in the Xerox Corporation in the USA but has been widely used to describe such internal innovation within large firms.

in-tray exercise. A training exercise where an individual is given the role of a manager and required to make decisions about various items which are presented to him as the contents of a fictitious in-tray. This simulates one aspect of the typical business of management − dealing with memos, complaints, enquiries and other forms of paperwork.

intrinsic rewards. Rewards which are internal to the employee − such as job satisfaction or self-actualization, rather than external such as pay or FRINGE BENEFITS. *See* EXTRINSIC REWARDS.

inventory (stock). The various forms of material held by a company at any time − raw materials, partly-finished products (work in progress) and finished goods awaiting despatch. In accounting the term is used to describe the costs of such materials.

inventory control. *See* STOCK CONTROL.

inventory management. *See* STOCK CONTROL.

inventory turnover. *See* STOCK TURNOVER.

investment. The spending of CAPITAL on something − securities, property etc − in order to increase its value or to generate an income (in the form of DIVIDENDS etc) over a period of time. In businesses investment is made in the ASSETS of a firm which will contribute towards its ability to make a profit and repay the investors.

investment appraisal. The process of examining different opportunities and proposals for INVESTMENT and for comparing between them. For example, a company may wish to ascertain whether to spend its CAPITAL on a new plant and the process of investment appraisal would enable it to assess the costs and benefits of this compared to putting the money into an interest-earning account. Various techniques exist for investment appraisal, from simple comparisons to complex financial accounting techniques.

investment bank. A bank in the USA which specializes in handling investments in securities. The bank makes a large purchase and then sells on the securities in smaller units. These functions are carried out by a MERCHANT BANK in the UK.

investment trust. A public listed company in the UK whose function is to invest in other organizations. It raises CAPITAL in a manner similar to other companies and usually invests the proceeds in a wide range of other organizations to spread risk. An investment trust frequently raises part of its capital in the form of DEBENTURE stocks or loan stock as well as ORDINARY SHARES and can thus obtain the benefits of GEARING. Investment trusts put their capital into both equities and gilt-edged securities and now constitute a leading example of an institutional investor in the UK along with others such as pension funds and insurance companies. There are around 300 investment trusts in the UK and their invested funds greatly exceed those managed by UNIT TRUSTS despite the greater public knowledge of the latter.

Investors in Industry (3i). A UK organization funded by the major clearing banks and financial institutions in the UK to provide funds for industrial development, especially for medium-term (up to 15-year) loans. It was formed in 1973 out of a merger between the INDUSTRIAL AND COMMERCIAL FINANCE CORPORATION and the FINANCE CORPORATION FOR INDUSTRY under the name Finance for Industry. In 1982 it changed its name to Investors in Industry, and in 1986 to 3i.

invisible exports and imports. A class of items in a nation's balance of payments current account which are not physical goods but services such as banking or insurance or payments/receipts such as profits or interest.

invisible hand. A phrase coined by Adam Smith in 1776 which enshrines the doctrine of self-interest in economic behaviour, the principle being that individuals will be led in pursuit of that self-interest as if by an invisible hand to seek the best good for all. It is used as an argument in support of free trade policies and against government intervention.

invisible import. *See* INVISIBLE EXPORTS AND IMPORTS.

invisible trade. *See* INVISIBLE EXPORTS AND IMPORTS.

invoice. A document requesting payment which sets out the goods or services supplied and their price.

IPM. *See* INSTITUTE OF PERSONNEL MANAGMENT.

irrevocable documentary acceptance credit. *See* DOCUMENTARY CREDIT.

IRS. *See* INTERNAL REVENUE SERVICE.

ISCO. *See* INTERNATIONAL STANDARD CLASSIFICATION OF OCCUPATIONS.

ISDN. *See* INTEGRATED SERVICES DIGITAL NETWORK.

islands of automation. A philosophy in automation where a firm does not attempt to change the whole factory in one move but builds up gradually by installing 'islands' of new technology within the overall 'sea' of existing technology. Such an incremental approach is lower in cost and allows for easier progress along the LEARNING CURVE associated with new technologies and protects against the possibility of depending too much on a single new system with which the firm has no experience. The danger in an islands of automation approach is that the islands must be carefully planned as part of a longer-term integration strategy, otherwise there may be problems of incompatibility at a later stage.

ISO. *See* INTERNATIONAL STANDARDS ORGANIZATION.

issue by tender. A SECURITIES issue in which potential investors are invited to TENDER for them and they are then sold to the highest bidder.

issued capital (share capital). The value represented by the face value of all the shares or other securities issued by a firm.

issuing house. An organization which specializes in arranging for the issuing of

SECURITIES on behalf of a firm. This role may often by played by a MERCHANT BANK.

issue price. The price at which a SECURITY is offered for sale.

IT. *See* INFORMATION TECHNOLOGY.

ITBs. *See* INDUSTRIAL TRAINING BOARDS.

ITeCs. *See* INFORMATION TECHNOLOGY CENTRES.

ITU. *See* INTERNATIONAL TELECOMMUNICATIONS UNION.

J

JIT. *See* JUST-IN-TIME PRODUCTION.

job analysis. A systematic examination of aspects and components of an individual's job, usually for the purposes of JOB EVALUATION.

jobber. A firm or individual dealing in SECURITIES. A jobber differs from a STOCK-BROKER in that the former actually owns the securities bought whereas the latter acts only as an agent arranging sales and purchase on behalf of others. Since the BIG BANG in the London Stock Exchange the distinction between these two roles has become blurred and is rapidly disappearing.

jobber's turn. The margin of profit obtained (turned) by a jobber in buying securities at one price and selling at a higher one.

jobbing. (1) Carrying out small pieces of work for various different customers or an individual or firm operating in this fashion (e.g. jobbing carpenter, jobbing foundry etc).
(2) Trading in securities by a stock JOBBER.

job card. A document attached to an item being produced in a batch production process which details the work to be done at that particular stage. A copy of the card is held by the PRODUCTION CONTROL department to enable them to keep track of what is going on on the shop floor.

job centre. An EMPLOYMENT EXCHANGE (agency) in the UK operated by the MAN-POWER SERVICES COMMISSION responsible for all aspects of identifying employment needs on the part of employers, advertising vacancies, interviewing potential applicants and introducing them to prospective employers. In addition, the job centres manage a number of programmes designed to help the unemployed, and provide advice and training in the process of job hunting and career development.

job costing. A process of cost allocation in production calculated on the basis of the cost spread over each different job. Relevant costs are charged to specific products so that at the end of the production process it is possible to arrive at a total cost for each product or batch of products. *See* UNIT COST.

job cycle. A set of operations needed to complete a particular job task by an employee.

job description. A written description of the scope, responsibilities, expectations etc of an individual's job.

job design. Activities associated with the analysis of the tasks to be performed and the responsibilities carried within a particular job, and deciding between the various alternatives available to carry that job out.

job enlargement. A technique to motivate employees in which additional tasks are assigned to workers in an attempt to make the overall job more interesting and varied. Such a process may also involve some element of training to carry out the new tasks.

job enrichment. A technique to motivate employees involving changing aspects of the job or tasks within it to make it more satisfying to the employee.

job evaluation. A system of comparing jobs based on an analysis of factors such as content, complexity, duration, experience required etc. It is used as a basis of setting up payment systems, for example. There are several types of job evaluation, some of which are based on proprietary systems. The main classes are: (*i*) ANALYTIC JOB EVALUATION; (*ii*) DOMINANT ELEMENT JOB EVALUATION; (*iii*) INTEGRAL JOB EVALUATION; (*iv*) JOB FACTOR COMPARISON; (*v*) JOB GRADING; (*vi*) JOB RANKING; (*vii*) POINTS RANKING; (*viii*) PROFILING SYSTEMS; and (*ix*) time span analysis.

job factor comparison. A form of JOB EVALUATION based on comparing component factors within the job under study.

job grading. A form of JOB EVALUATION which involves grading different types of job according to their component elements, complexity, skills required etc.

job mobility. See LABOUR MOBILITY.

job ranking. A form of JOB EVALUATION similar to JOB GRADING.

job rotation. A process of individual training and development by moving around between different jobs to gain experience and understand different perspectives within a company. Job rotation can also be used on a smaller scale within a working group to offer some measure of JOB ENRICHMENT.

job satisfaction. The degree to which an employee is satisfied with the job he does – in terms of its general content and conditions, and particularly with its motivational or INTRINSIC REWARDS.

job sharing. A practice in which two or more individuals share a single job, each doing it for part of the time and receiving part of the remuneration for it.

joint consultation. Arrangements in which employees and employers can discuss issues of concern where there is some measure of consultation by management, although there may be only limited scope for negotiating the outcome of management decisions – as distinct from COLLECTIVE BARGAINING.

joint costs. Costs involved in the simultaneous production of two or more goods or services. They are often found where one raw material is made into several different products – for example, in oil refining – where the costs of producing particular fractions cannot be separated from each other.

joint demand. The demand for products normally used together, where an increase in demand for one product leads to an increase in demand for the other – for example, graphite and wood for the production of pencils.

joint stock bank. See COMMERCIAL BANK.

joint stock company. A form of LIMITED LIABILITY COMPANY where the liability is limited to the nominal value of shares issued.

joint venture. A project or company in which two or more individuals or organizations participate, agreeing to share the risks and benefits according to some agreed formula.

journal. See DAY BOOK.

journeyman. A skilled craftsman. The term derives from the fact that such a craftsman was independent rather than employed by a firm and often journeyed around seeking work for his skills.

judgment creditor. A CREDITOR who has secured a court order stating that he is owed money by a judgment debtor. If a judgment debtor fails to pay on this court order, his assets may be seized and sold to recover the debt.

judgment debtor. See JUDGMENT CREDITOR.

junk bonds. High-risk; high-yield BONDS issued by companies, mainly in the USA, often to finance a merger or takeover.

just-in-time production (JIT). An approach to management originally developed in Japan which emphasizes very low inventories, frequent deliveries by suppliers, operator involvement and quality awareness. JIT also encompasses a philosophy of production organization and management within the firm, based on reducing inventory and batch sizes which involves a problem-solving approach to those bottlenecks which prevent the smooth flow of work through the factory. A good description of JIT applied in Japan and in a Western context is given in R. Schonberger, *Japanese Manufacturing Techniques: Nine Hidden Lessons in Simplicity* (New York: Free Press and Macmillan, 1982). *See also* KANBAN.

K

K. *See* KILOBYTES.

kanban. A form of inventory control developed at the Toyota company in Japan which provides the basis for the JUST-IN-TIME approach to production, which involves only calling for parts as they are needed in the production process. The word literally means 'visible card', although kanban systems using squares painted on the factory floor or any other form of token can equally well be employed. The principle is essentially one of 'pull' through production rather than the traditional approach of 'push' from stocks through the system.

KD. *See* KNOCKED DOWN.

Kelly repertory grid. A technique based on construct theory in psychology which is used to obtain opinions. It is particularly used in market research. The basis of the technique is to ask the respondent to explain why two attributes − for example, characteristics of a new product − are similar to each other and different from a third.

Kennedy Round. A major trade agreement initiated by John F. Kennedy in the mid-1960s which covered general tariff reductions between the then 58 members of the GENERAL AGREEMENT ON TARIFFS AND TRADE; it was subsequently extended to a wider range of countries.

Kepner−Tregoe method. A form of systematic problem-solving and retrospective problem analysis developed by the US management consultants Kepner−Tregoe.

key factors (key points). In JOB ANALYSIS, factors of particular importance in the performance of work.

key operation. In WORK STUDY, the longest operation in a series of simultaneous tasks which must be completed before work can move on to the next stage.

key points. *See* KEY FACTORS.

key results analysis. *See* KEY TASK ANALYSIS.

key task. The main task associated with a particular operation which determines the time taken for the whole job.

key task analysis (key results analysis). A training approach which involves analysing key tasks and levels of performance required in carrying them out.

Key Workers Scheme. A UK government scheme operated by the DEPARTMENT OF EMPLOYMENT to assist employers to transfer employees with particular characteristics − such as specialist skills − to new plants in ASSISTED AREAS.

KG. *See* KOMMANDITGESELLSCHAFT.

KGaA. *See* KOMMANDITGESELLSCHAFT AUF AKTIEN.

kickback. A bribe or inducement given to someone in return for their assistance in influencing the course of a business decision − for example, the awarding of a contract.

kilobytes (K). The measure of the memory capacity of a computer, equal to 1024 bytes of information. Very roughly, 2 pages of A4 text represents around 1K of information.

kinaesthetics. The study of human movements. It is used in MOTION STUDY and WORK STUDY.

knocked down (KD). Products supplied or shipped in kit form. Often the term COMPLETELY KNOCKED DOWN is used.

Kommanditgesellschaft (KG). A firm in West Germany involving a limited partnership. It is also found in Austria and Switzerland (where it may also be known as a société en commandite).

Kommanditgesellschaft auf Aktien (KGaA). A firm in West Germany involving a limited partnership with some shares issued.

Kondratiev long wave. A form of cyclic activity in economics originally noted by the Russian economist Nikolai Kondratiev. He found that there were 'long waves' in economic development of boom and recession running roughly every 45−50 years. The boom side corresponded to major technological innovations − such as the invention of steam power, the spread of the railways, the spread of electrical power, the automobile − and the recession side with the widespread use of these innovations to reduce costs. A good description of long waves appears in C. Freeman et al, *Unemployment and Technical Innovation: A Study of Long Waves and Economic Development* (London: Frances Pinter, 1982). *See* BUSINESS CYCLES.

L

laboratory training (T-group). A form of GROUP DYNAMICS training in which content is relatively unstructured, although carefully controlled by the trainer. The emphasis of this training is on participants learning from their own experience as they form a group, begin to adopt its norms and experience and try to resolve conflicts which develop. The training is designed to develop participants' interpersonal skills over a period of time through regular meetings in which the relationships between group members are analysed.

labour hour rate. The hourly rate of pay.

labour-intensive. A firm or process which relies mainly on labour rather than on technology to produce its goods or services.

labour law. The body of law covering legislation about INDUSTRIAL RELATIONS.

labour market. The pattern of supply and demand for different kinds of labour, both skilled and unskilled.

labour mobility (job mobility). (1) The extent to which workers are prepared or able to move geographical location in search of work.
(2) In the context of FLEXIBLE MANNING, the degree to which workers are prepared or able to move between different jobs and tasks in the same firm.

labour-only subcontracting. Subcontracting based on hiring labour from someone else rather than buying goods or services.

labour relations. *See* INDUSTRIAL RELATIONS.

labour stability index. An index sometimes used to express LABOUR TURNOVER which relates the number of employees who recently joined the firm (up to a year ago) to the number who were employed in the previous year.

labour turnover. The number of workers entering and leaving employment in a firm over a given time period, usually one year, expressed as a percentage of the total labour force.

ladder activities. In project NETWORKS, overlapping or interdependent activities.

ladder logic (ladder programming). A simplified form of computer programming using a small vocabulary of logical symbols. It is used for relatively small programs on devices such as machine controllers (e.g. some CNC machine tools) where the range of information processing involved is small.

ladder programming. *See* LADDER LOGIC.

laissez-faire. A form of economic policy which allows forces in the market to operate freely without government intervention.

lame duck. A colloquial term for an individual or organization which performs consistently badly and relies on or is seeking some form of government subsidy. The term was originally used to describe an individual who had been HAMMERED OUT of the Stock Exchange.

LAN. *See* LOCAL AREA NETWORK.

Landsorganisationen Danmark. A Danish trade union federation; the equivalent of the TRADES UNION CONGRESS in the UK.

Landsorganisationen Norge. A Norwegian trade union federation; the equivalent of the TRADES UNION CONGRESS in the UK.

laser printer. A high-speed, high-quality computer printer.

laser scanning. A process of CHARACTER RECOGNITION in which the characters to be read are BAR CODES and the reader is a device based upon a laser. The information is read into a small computer which can convert it to recognizable text which can be output to a printer. One of the main advantages of laser scanning over LIGHT PENS and other readers is the speed and accuracy with which it works. The system is widely used in retailing at supermarket checkouts and in warehousing to keep track of INVENTORY movements.

last bag system. See TWO-BIN SYSTEM.

last in, first out (LIFO) (first in, last out). A principle in INDUSTRIAL RELATIONS used when negotiating redundancies in which those employees who have been in the firm longest are the last to be made redundant. The term is also used to describe the usage of materials on the same basis.

lateral thinking. A concept developed by the UK writer Edward de Bono which offers an alternative approach to looking at and solving problems. It utilizes a number of techniques based on research into creativity and human information-processing and is particularly useful for complex, open-ended problems for which there may be no single correct answer. The concept is described in a number of de Bono's books, including *Lateral Thinking for Management* (Harmondsworth: Penguin, 1982).

latest allowable time. See LATEST EVENT TIME.

latest event time (latest allowable time). In NETWORK planning, the latest time at which an event can take place before the entire project is delayed.

Latin square design. An approach to the design of research experiments which involves treating research data to two different experiments, the results of which are plotted against each other. This offers a more efficient use of data and also gives some indication of the relative strengths and weaknesses of each experiment and of support or otherwise for the hypotheses being tested. The name comes from a diagram sometimes used to display the experiments and data relative to one another. The technique is particularly used in MARKET RESEARCH.

law of the situation. See FOLLETT, MARY PARKER.

Law Reform (Contributory Negligence) Act 1945. UK legislation which supports an employee's claim for damages, albeit at a reduced level, for injuries received at work where it can be proved that there was some element of EMPLOYEE'S CONTRIBUTORY NEGLIGENCE. In other words, the employee receives less than full damages because he was partly to blame.

lay day. In shipping, a day allowed in port without paying harbour charges.

lay off. To suspend employees from work. This action is usually taken because of lack of work or inability to produce due to problems other than labour disputes − for example, breakdown of machinery or delays in receiving incoming components. Lay-offs can often result from labour disputes further upstream or downstream in the supply chain − for example, strikes at a car builder may lead to lay-offs at component suppliers unable to deliver their goods − or vice versa.

LDC. See LESS-DEVELOPED COUNTRY.

leadership. The characteristics and behaviour of individuals who are responsible for leading groups within organizations and the field of studies of those factors. Early studies, such as those by Kurt LEWIN identified different approaches, ranging from laissez-faire, through authoritarian to democratic, and suggested that the more democratic styles were more effective. Later work in the 1960s, such as that coming out of the Michigan Survey Research Center (based on large-sample surveys), identified several two-dimensional models which located style on a spectrum ranging from employee-centred to production-centred. This was also supported by Robert Blake and Jane Mouton's work developing the MANAGERIAL GRID, which presented concern for people on the y-axis and concern for the production or task on the x-axis. Each was scaled on a nine-point scale and, through interview and questionnaire research, a managerial style could be plotted.

Rensis LIKERT's work developed from the Michigan studies and identified four management systems, ranging from exploitative/authoritarian through benevolent/authoritative and consultative to full participative management. More recent research has focused on a number of themes and has indicated that there is no single leadership style which is effective under all circumstances. Rather, a contingency model is required in which the properties of effective leadership depend on the circumstances in question. A number of books cover the subject well, including F. Fiedler, *A Theory of Leadership Effectiveness* (New York: McGraw-Hill, 1973), and an overview can be found in C. Handy, *Understanding Organizations* (Harmondsworth: Penguin, 1976).

leading indicator. A measure of economic activity which moves ahead of the general upward or downward trend and gives a rough guide to the way in which markets are moving.

lead/lag method. A FORECASTING technique, often used in MARKET RESEARCH, which makes use of TREND EXTRAPOLATION not of the subject under study but of factors related to it which are likely to have an influence on it.

lead rate. A BONUS or premium payment due to an employee when using extra skills or exercising extra responsibility.

lead time (door-to-door time). The time taken to complete an activity − for example, to respond to a customer order by supplying a finished product or to develop a new product and move through research and development to actual production.

lean work. In PAYMENT-BY-RESULTS systems, work at which bonus levels are low. By contrast, FAT WORK is work where it is easy to earn high bonuses.

learning curve (improvement curve). The rate of progress made by an individual or organization in acquiring new skills, absorbing new technological capability etc. In general, the more experience in doing something which an individual or organization has, the faster or better it is able to perform − for example, the ability to produce to better and more consistent quality, or to make improvements. In the case of operator performance this learning effect is often expressed as a logarithmic relationship. One

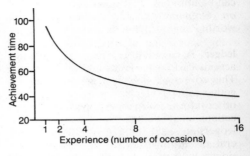

a learning curve

implication of this is that after a certain point − the learning plateau − it becomes difficult to make further improvements without some form of external input − for example, new educational inputs.

learning plateau. *See* LEARNING CURVE.

lease. An arrangement whereby the owner of something − land, transport, property etc − makes over its use to someone else for a specified period of time but retains ownership. The former is known as the lessor and the latter the lessee. In many cases after a certain time the lessee does take over ownership. For this reason leasing is used as a route to the purchase of some items (such as cars) since it has tax and other advantages over conventional instalment payment systems (such as hire purchase) or outright purchase.

leaseback. When a holder of a LEASE sells it and then buys it back on new terms. The term usually applies to long-term items like land or property, rather than short-term items like cars.

least squares method. A mathematical technique used in REGRESSION ANALYSIS to identify the best fit for a line through a set of data plotted on a graph.

Leavitt, Harold. A US psychologist and management writer who carried out research in various fields, including work on the pattern of communication in organizations. One of his most famous books is *Managerial Psychology* (4th edn, Chicago: University of Chicago Press, 1978). A review of his work can be found in D. Pugh et al (eds), *Writers on Organizations* (3rd edn, Harmondsworth: Penguin 1986).

ledger. A complete record of all the transactions carried by an individual or a firm. This covers all debit and credit notes, together with payments and discounts, and any other information about the financial transactions of the firm. In practice, several ledgers are often maintained, usually a general or nominal ledger and various subsidiary ledgers, such as those for debtors or creditors.

legal reserve. Under European Community law it is a requirement on banks, insurance companies and other classes of financial institution that they keep some money (usually a proportion of profits) in a special reserve fund to protect creditors and depositors against financial losses should the company run into difficulties or collapse. The terms of this legal reserve system are set out in the Fourth DIRECTIVE on company law. The UK has not subscribed to its provisions and the system is not used there.

legal tender. Money which is legally acceptable in payment of public and private debts.

lender of last resort. A role played by a CENTRAL BANK in a country which involves it acting as a banker to other banks within the national system; in the unlikely event of their coming under pressure, they can obtain loans and support from the central bank.

less-developed country (LDC). A name sometimes given to countries involved in international trade which are generally considered to be part of the the Third World and are relatively immature in terms of industrial development.

letter-box company. A company registered in name in a country with advantageous tax laws − for example, the Cayman Islands − although its actual operations take place in a high-tax country.

letter of credit. A document issued by a bank or financial institution which guarantees credit up to a stated amount. This can be used by the borrower to draw BILLS OF EXCHANGE against, or to arrange other transactions which are then effectively backed by the bank or institution issuing the letter of credit.

letter of hypothecation. Documentation required by a bank when it takes collateral for a loan based on goods or property as evidence of its LIEN to those items.

letters patent. Documentation given to an individual or organization when awarded a PATENT on an invention.

LE Trust. *See* LOCAL ENTERPRISE AGENCY.

Lewin, Kurt. A US management researcher and writer and one of the key figures in the HUMAN RELATIONS SCHOOL OF MANAGMENT THINKING. His influential work includes studies of LEADERSHIP, where he identified three different styles − autocratic, democratic and laissez-faire. His work is described in D. Pugh et al (eds), *Writers on Organizations* (3rd edn, Harmondsworth: Penguin, 1986).

liability. Various forms of debt or obligation owed. Two main types of liability exist − current and secured. Current liabilities are debts which must be settled within a 12-month period, whereas secured liabilities are debts which are secured against some form of asset which guarantees their payment in the long term.

licence. A permit to do something − for example, to use a PATENT granted to someone else − to produce or sell goods or offer services originally produced by someone else, or to import or export items which are subject to government control of some sort.

licensed deposit taker. A bank or financial institution licensed by the Bank of England to take deposits and operate as a bank.

lien. The right of a seller to hold on to goods which he is selling until payment has been received.

lieu bonus. *See* LIEU PAYMENT.

lieu days (days off in lieu). Days taken as holiday in lieu of overtime worked.

lieu payment (lieu bonus). If an employee is not able to join a PAYMENT-BY-RESULTS scheme, he may be entitled to lieu pay, in lieu of the BONUS he would otherwise have earned. *See also* MAKE-UP PAY.

life cycle. *See* PRODUCT LIFE CYCLE.

life cycle costing. The costing of an asset over its entire life cycle.

life insurance. INSURANCE taken out on a person's life so that if they die unexpectedly during the period of the policy, a payment will be made to specified beneficiaries.

LIFO. *See* LAST IN, FIRST OUT.

light pen. A device which allows entry of data into a computer system by scanning light and dark areas on a surface. It is used in BAR CODE reading, in STOCK CONTROL and other activities.

Likert, Rensis. A US management researcher and writer who has made a number of major contributions to management study, including the development of the LIKERT SCALES, while carrying out survey-based work at the Survey Research Center in Michigan. His work also covers the question of the use of human resources in an organization where, he argues, effective usage depends on individuals belonging to efficient groups with high levels of skill and performance. In organizational terms, this led to the idea of 'linked-pin' management structures in which semi-autonomous groups are linked together by their managers into an organizational structure − rather than the traditional hierarchy. He developed the concept of HUMAN ASSET ACCOUNTING and his ideas are described in books such as *The Human Organization: its Management and Value* (New York: McGraw-Hill, 1967) and *New Patterns of Management* (New York: McGraw-Hill, 1961).

Likert scales. Scales often used in questionnaires and surveys which allow the respondent to indicate the degree of agreement or disagreement with a set of statements. This allows them greater choice than a simple either/or choice, and allows a wider range of opinion or attitude to be examined. The idea originated with Rensis LIKERT in work at the Survey Research Center at the University of Michigan.

limited liability company. A company in which the LIABILITY of its shareholders is limited in some way − usually by the value of the issued shares, but sometimes by GUARANTEE. *See* PRIVATE COMPANY; PUBLIC LIMITED COMPANY.

linear programming. A technique used in OPERATIONAL RESEARCH to assist decision-making, enabling different solutions to be developed for different outcomes. It is based on identifying an objective variable and then finding solutions which maximize or minimize this factor − for example, finding the least cost or shortest route solution to a problem.

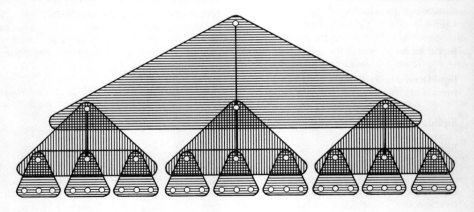

Likert's linked-pin model of management reporting

line balancing. Various techniques in MASS PRODUCTION based on a flow line used to ensure that the production line remains balanced while coping with product variations being made along the line.

line functions. See LINE MANAGEMENT.

line management (line functions). A type of management associated with taking executive responsibility for a particular functional area — production, marketing, design, quality control etc — within an organization. It gives rise to the traditional pyramid model of management — as opposed to a MATRIX ORGANIZATION or other structure. In many ways line management is similar to the organizational principles of the military, where there is a line of responsibility running down from the commander-in-chief to the private soldier. The same principles of limited and clearly defined areas of responsibility, the idea of a chain of command and the concept of developed responsibility for particular functions apply in a business organization. In addition, there are some supporting and co-ordinating functions which would be carried out by staff officers and personnel in the military and such staff management and functions also apply in organizations — for example, providing central data processing or research and testing facilities for all line areas.

line of credit. The extent of CREDIT made available to an individual or organization.

linked-pin management. An approach to organization structuring originated by Rensis Likert.

liquid assets. See ASSET; CURRENT ASSETS.

liquidated damages. DAMAGES arising from a breach of CONTRACT.

liquidation. The legal process of formally closing down a company, which involves liquidating its assets to obtain cash to pay off its debts. See WIND-UP.

liquidator. A person appointed in the UK to oversee the winding up of a company. See WIND-UP.

liquidity. The ease with which a firm can obtain cash — either from a bank or by converting ASSETS into cash.

liquidity ratio. See CASH RATIO.

liquid ratio. A FINANCIAL RATIO which gives an indication of the LIQUIDITY of a firm. It is calculated by taking the ratio of CURRENT ASSETS to CURRENT LIABILITIES minus the value of stocks. It has the advantage over a CURRENT RATIO in that by excluding stocks (which may vary over time in the extent to which they can be readily sold) it gives a more accurate picture of the liquidity of a firm.

LISP. A high-level computer language used particularly in expert systems and ARTIFICIAL INTELLIGENCE work. It takes its name from LISt Processing language, since it is designed to handle text statements rather than numerical processing.

listed company. A company whose shares are listed on the Stock Exchange.

listed securities. SECURITIES which are listed on the Stock Exchange.

list price. The price manufacturers establish for the sale of their products. Retailers may alter this by discounting — as in 'x% off list price' — in an attempt to attract customers.

list renting. A business based on selling or renting access to information, such as names and addresses of people and/or organizations, for the purposes of ADVERTISING, DIRECT MAIL SELLING etc.

little Neddy. See ECONOMIC DEVELOPMENT COUNCIL; NATIONAL ECONOMIC DEVELOPMENT OFFICE.

livery company. An organization in the City of London which is descended from the mediaeval craft guilds and which exists now largely for ceremonial purposes. Examples include the Haberdashers, Goldsmiths, and Fishmongers.

Lloyd's. An organization based in the City of London, founded in the 17th century,

which offers a variety of forms of INSUR-
ANCE through its SYNDICATES, which are
listed as Lloyd's Brokers and Underwriters.
Syndicates offer insurance cover for almost
anything except in the area of life assurance,
but Lloyd's is particularly famous for its
marine insurance and a large proportion of
the world's shipping is insured there.

loan capital. *See* DEBT CAPITAL.

loan guarantee scheme. A form of UK
government support for small and new
businesses which involves the state guaranteeing a loan from a bank; in the event of
failure of the business, the government will
repay the loan.

loan shark. A colloquial term for an individual who loans money at very high and de-
ceptive rates of interest to people who are
not fully aware of the commitments into
which they are entering.

local. *See* LOCAL UNION.

local area network (LAN). A computer network which allows communication of data
within a local area (e.g. a building) between
all nodes in the network. A number of different configurations exist, including the
star, the wheel and the ring, and each allows
(in theory) any items of information technology to be connected – computers,
printers, fax machines etc.

local authority deposit market. A source of
funds in the UK for local authorities to
finance their operations. Although technically they grant unsecured loans, local
authorities are generally regarded as low-
risk borrowers.

Local Enterprise Agency (LE Trust). A UK
agency established to encourage and support
new small businesses by providing a range of
advice and services, including finance and
resources. There are some 200 LE Trusts in
the UK and they receive support from local
government and various industrial and commercial sponsors who may support with cash
or in kind.

Local Enterprise Development Unit. An
agency which provides a variety of small

business support in Northern Ireland; it is
similar to the Scottish and Welsh development agencies.

local union (local). The US equivalent of a
TRADE UNION branch.

lock-in. A situation in which an individual or
organization is prevented from acting freely
in business transaction. For example, firms
can become locked in to a particular supplier – say of computer equipment – and be
unable to buy from other suppliers because
such equipment would be incompatible, and
abandoning the original supplier's equipment would be too costly. Consequently the
firm must continue to depend on the original
supplier.

lockout. A response sometimes made by
employers during INDUSTRIAL ACTION which
involves them closing or restricting access to
a plant, thus locking out the workers or
those members of the workforce in dispute.

LOGO. A high-level computer language.

logo. A logotype incorporating the name,
trademark, or, especially, the identifying
symbol of an organization. Logos are used
extensively in advertising and publicity
material.

long-dated stocks. SECURITIES, particularly
government stocks, which are offered on a
redeemable basis over a long time period –
usually beyond ten years.

long lease. A LEASE with an unexpired term
of more than 50 years.

long-term liabilities. LIABILITIES which do
not have to be met until a specified time in
the long-term future, usually beyond three
years.

loose rate. In a PIECEWORK payment system,
a rate for the job which allows relatively easy
earning of bonuses.

loss leader. (1) In marketing, a product or
service which is sold at, or even below, its
cost price as an incentive to customers to buy

other products or to use other services offered by the firm.

(2) In retailing, items offered at low prices to attract customers into a shop.

Luddite. An individual who resists the introduction of new technology. The name derives from the Luddites, a group of 19th-century textile workers who rioted and smashed new machinery which they saw as a threat to their traditional craft skills.

lump labour. Labour which offers itself for hire on a LABOUR-ONLY SUBCONTRACTING basis; it is particularly common in the building industry.

Lutine bell. The famous bell at LLOYD'S which is sounded prior to reporting good or bad news of major significance. One stroke means bad news — such as the loss of a ship — and two strokes mean good news.

M

McClelland, David. A US psychologist who developed a theory of MOTIVATION based on the idea of the need for achievement (nAch). He found that people who were generally seen as high achievers worked hard to accomplish goals and structured their work to help them in this by choosing tasks of moderate risk with a high probability of success, which offered regular opportunities for feedback on performance to tell the individual how well he was doing in his working towards that goal. The theory is described in his book, *The Achieving Society* (New York: Van Nostrand Rheinhold, 1961).

MacGregor, Douglas. A US psychologist and researcher and a member of the HUMAN RELATIONS SCHOOL OF MANAGEMENT THINKING. He developed a view of MOTIVATION based on the concept of THEORY X AND THEORY Y which expressed two different ways in which managers view subordinates and which influence their behaviour in trying to motivate them. Theory X assumes money to be the key motivator and that people's natural state is one which dislikes work. Thus, in order to achieve organizational goals they need to be controlled and coerced; further, because they do not wish to take on responsibility, work should be broken down into small tasks which are easily monitored. Theory X provides the basis for some PAYMENT-BY-RESULTS schemes.

Theory Y derives from the human relations view and assumes that people are motivated by work, can exercise self-direction and control, will accept responsibility and have higher-order needs than money. This view leads to managerial approaches to employee motivation which go beyond simple payment by results – such as MEASURED DAYWORK or other time-related payment systems. MacGregor's work is described in his book, *The Human Side of Enterprise* (New York: McGraw-Hill, 1960).

machine ancillary time. Non-productive time when a machine is being serviced, cleaned, set up etc. It differs from downtime in that this is a planned stoppage of the machine.

machine code. The operating level set of instructions of a computer, expressed in binary numbers. This is the lowest level computer language.

machine downtime. Time when a machine is not producing due to breakdown or other unplanned stoppage factors.

machine idle time (idle time). Time when a machine is not producing due to lack of material or operators.

machine loading. In production planning, the planning of work such that machines are used as efficiently as possible (i.e. they are loaded with the optimum amount of work).

magnetic character reader (MCR; magnetic ink character reader). A CHARACTER RECOGNITION system which uses special ink containing magnetic particles which can be read by suitable machinery. It is used in banks to read cheques, for example.

magnetic ink character reader (MICR). *See* MAGNETIC CHARACTER READER.

mail merge. A facility offered by many WORD PROCESSING software packages which allows a list of names and addresses held on a DATA BASE to be used in conjunction with a FORM LETTER or document. Each time it is printed a new name and address is inserted so that the final document appears as if produced individually.

mainframe. A large computer system for multi-user applications or very complex problems (such as weather forecasting or expert systems) which require large amounts of processing power.

mainstream corporation tax. *See* CORPORA-TION TAX.

maintenance shift. A special shift laid on specifically for the purposes of maintaining a plant at times when it is not in production.

make-or-buy decision. An approach sometimes used in COSTING which calculates whether it would be cheaper for a firm to buy in components or services from a subcontractor rather than carry the costs of producing them in-house.

make-up pay. An element in a PAYMENT-BY-RESULTS scheme which involves extra payments made to those employees who fail to earn enough to achieve an agreed minimum wage.

make-work. Work done in order to keep employees or machinery occupied rather than because there is a demand for it.

managed costs. Costs in a project over which management has some measure of control, as opposed to those which are inevitably incurred once the decision to go ahead has been made.

managed fund. *See* PENSION.

management accounting. Accounting concerned with supporting management decision-making through the provision of regular information and analysis of financial performance and the operations open to a firm. It includes techniques for recording, classifying and analysing costs and the development of financial planning and control mechanisms.

management audit. An AUDIT concerned with aspects of management in an organization – such as MANAGEMENT SUCCESSION, training and PERFORMANCE APPRAISAL.

management buyout. The purchase of a firm by its managers from the original shareholders. It is often used when the original owners wish to sell a firm but when the managers believe it can be made into a profitable and going concern.

management by crisis (crisis management; firefighting). An approach to management which focuses on solving short-term problems as they arise, if necessary by mobilizing extra resources to deal with them. This management style has a number of disadvantages, including the fact that it only addresses immediate short-term problems rather than long-term objectives, that it may treat symptoms of more fundamental problems rather than getting to their cause and that it may divert resources away from other areas in which they are needed, creating a new set of problems there.

management by exception. An approach to management in which senior managers are called in only to make decisions under exceptional circumstances which fall outside a previously agreed plan. The responsibility for day-to-day decision-making is delegated to subordinates.

management by objectives (MBO). A management technique which involves a manager and subordinate agreeing individual subordinate goals. A form of PERFORMANCE APPRAISAL, it aims to quantify executive performance and improve motivation, as the subordinate 'owns' the goals set.

management development. A form of management training for improved job performance and succession which stresses the personal development of the manager by both work experience and formal training inputs of various kinds.

management information systems (MIS). Information systems, usually computer-based, which provide management with the necessary information for decision-making on various aspects of the business.

management ratios. Quantitative ratios between aspects of a company's performance which give management information for control purposes. These are usually recorded continuously over time so that control action can be taken and its effects monitored. Examples include sales to stocks, direct to indirect labour. Management ratios are also used in INTERCOMPANY COMPARISONS, where they can highlight strengths and weaknesses between firms in a sector. The line between management ratios and FINANCIAL RATIOS is blurred, although the

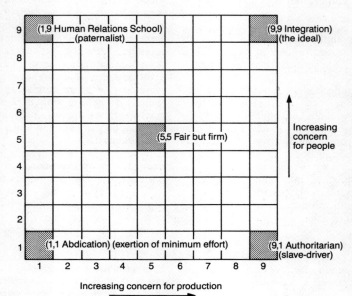

the managerial grid

former extend beyond purely financial indicators about the firm into areas such as manpower or resource provision and performance.

management science. The application of quantitative methods in management problem-solving. *See also* OPERATIONAL RESEARCH.

management services. A group of services provided to management, such as WORK STUDY, ORGANIZATION AND METHODS and DATA PROCESSING.

management style. The overall approach taken by management in discharging its functions of decision-making, motivation, communication etc. Styles vary from authoritarian to participative. Some research has suggested that the most successful managers are those who are able to vary their style to suit different situations, groups of employees etc.

management succession (succession planning). The process of ensuring that suitably trained and experienced young managers are available to succeed those currently in senior positions.

Management Today. A widely-read UK publication covering general management issues, published in association with the BRITISH INSTITUTE OF MANAGEMENT.

management union. A trade union concerned with the interests of white-collar managerial workers.

managerial grid. A concept developed by Robert Blake and Jane Mouton used in management and organizational development work. It provides a way of measuring managerial behaviour along two dimensions which express concern for the task and concern for the people. A 9:9 score would indicate a high degree of concern for both. *See* LEADERSHIP.

mandate. Voting instructions given to a delegated representative by those he represents at a meeting or conference. *See* BLOCK VOTE; CARD VOTE.

manpower analysis. In MANPOWER PLANNING, a process which involves analysing the pattern of employment in a company in terms of various factors — for example, age distribution, skills distribution, length of service of employees etc.

manpower planning. A process of analysing the future employment requirements of a firm and the development of plans to ensure an adequate supply of suitably trained manpower to meet those needs. A number of techniques may be used, including ratio trend forecasting (which extrapolates requirements from the existing pattern of employment within the firm) and theoretical requirements forecasting (which is used for new situations, such as starting up a new plant).

manpower ratios. MANAGEMENT RATIOS which cover manpower-related issues such as wage costs, sales per employee, added value per employee etc.

Manpower Services Commission (MSC). A body set up in the UK in 1972 linked to the DEPARTMENT OF EMPLOYMENT to assume responsibility for a variety of employment-related issues such as training and retraining, selection and information provision about manpower needs and resources. The particular issues covered are set out in the Employment and Training Act 1973. The Commission is made up of ten commissioners, all of whom are appointed by the Secretary of State for Employment to whom they report. Membership is on a tripartite basis, with employers and unions providing three representatives each, local government two, and the final two places are filled by an educational specialist and the chairman.

manual workers. *See* BLUE-COLLAR WORKERS.

manufacturing automation protocol (MAP). A standard protocol developed by General Motors to enable different factory automation systems to communicate with each other. Based on the seven-layer model for OPEN SYSTEMS INTERCONNECTION, MAP is not tied to any particular equipment supplier but permits any system to be integrated with any other. It is widely supported as the *de facto* standard for communication in factory automation.

manufacturing resources planning (MRP2). A system of production management developed by the Oliver Wight Company in the USA. It extends the concept of MATERIALS REQUIREMENTS PLANNING by introducing the idea of a MASTER PRODUCTION SCHEDULE, which is generated by a mixture of forecasting of sales demand and actual customer orders. From this master schedule a materials requirements plan and a capacity requirements plan are generated and used in connection with the BILL OF MATERIALS to produce orders for materials. MRP2 differs

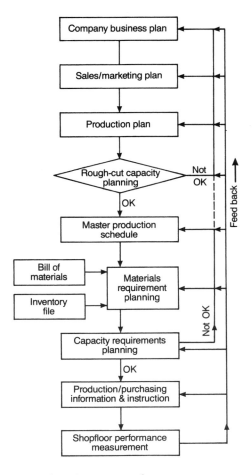

a manufacturing resources plan

from MATERIALS REQUIREMENTS PLANNING in its strategic nature, taking into account the entire operational resource base of the company.

MAP. (1) *See* MANUFACTURING AUTOMATION PROTOCOL.
(2) *See* MASTER ACTIVITY PROGRAMMING.
(3) *See* MICROELECTRONICS APPLICATION PROJECT.

marginal cost. The extra cost of producing an additional item on top of those already produced.

marginal costing (direct costing; incremental costing; variable costing). An approach to costing which separates costs into two categories — fixed and variable. Fixed costs are those which remain constant over time; variable costs include all those which vary over time or in relation to output.

marginal cost pricing. *See* MARGINAL PRICING.

marginal pricing (marginal cost pricing). A method of establishing the price of products based on marginal costing which has the advantage in that it allows for future cost variations. Products may be sold at a price that covers only fixed costs or fixed costs plus part of the marginal costs.

margin of safety. *See* BREAK-EVEN CHART.

mark-down. A price reduction used in retailing to move stock more quickly — for example, in clearance sales where the stock needs to be moved to allow more space for new lines.

market assessment. A systematic identification and evaluation of the factors which affect the present and future markets for a company's goods or services.

market capitalization. The total value of a LISTED COMPANY's shares as indicated on the stock market.

marketing. The range of activities involved in identifying demand for goods or services and providing the facilities and channels for their efficient distribution and sale. A good textbook which outlines the general principles is M. Baker, *Marketing — Theory and Practice* (2nd edn, London: Macmillan, 1983).

marketing boards. UK organizations set up to facilitate distribution and standardization of quality and prices. Their main purpose is to regulate marketing and encourage efficiency of production; they are mainly found in agricultural sectors such as milk or potatoes.

marketing budget. Part of an overall budget appropriation earmarked for marketing expenditure, covering items like advertising, sales promotions and the costs of the sales team.

marketing expense to sales ratio. A ratio indicating the efficiency of marketing by relating the expense of marketing to the value of sales generated for the company.

marketing mix. Methods used to market a product (e.g. price, distribution channels, quality, advertising etc). It is sometimes referred to as 'the four Ps' — product, price, position (in the market) and place.

market maker. A UK Stock Exchange firm which commits itself to always being ready to deal in a range of stocks in which it is registered.

market niche strategy. A marketing strategy which aims to identify small gaps or niches in the market and then provide suitable products or services to exploit them. It is a useful strategy for smaller firms competing with large firms in mature markets.

market price. The price at which SECURITIES are bought or sold on the stock market.

market push. Pressure from a company's market which forces it to follow a particular course of action.

market research. A branch of marketing which covers the various techniques and procedures for identifying and quantifying the market for goods or services. Market research also examines the effectiveness of marketing tools such as advertising or sales promotions, and attempts to understand the influential factors which determine buyer behaviour.

market segmentation. The breakdown of a market into a number of differentiated segments based on factors like price, quality, delivery, performance etc. Markets are segmented in an attempt to find chunks which are small enough to become the subject of a niche strategy but large enough to provide a viable business opportunity for the firm.

market share. An indication of the amount of the total market which a firm's sales of goods or services represent. It is usually expressed as a percentage of the total market sales during a period.

mark-up. The level of increase in price a retailer makes over the wholesale price of items he is selling.

Marshall plan. A post-war programme of US aid to western European countries to assist in economic reconstruction, proposed by George Marshall, the then US Secretary of State, set up in 1947.

Maslow's hierarchy of needs. *See* HIER-ARCHY OF NEEDS.

mass production. Production in high volumes based on standardization of the product and production process. It was first developed in the motor vehicle industry by Henry Ford and others, following the ideas of SCIENTIFIC MANAGEMENT set out by Frederick TAYLOR and employing special-purpose machinery to enable the products to be assembled in as near continuous fashion as possible. Mass production is best suited to those products which vary little in design or specification over large volumes, so that once set up, machinery does not need more than minor modifications.

master activity programming (MAP). A procedure used in organizing office systems which involves observation of current activities and the development from these of control standards.

master budget. The main financial budget for a firm from which various sectional budgets are derived.

master clerical data (MCD). A WORK MEASUREMENT system based on METHODS TIME MEASUREMENT, used for clerical work.

Master of Business Administration (MBA). A widely-recognized degree in management.

Master of Public Administration (MPA). A US accountancy qualification.

master production schedule (MPS). A production schedule that indicates which products will be made using which sequence of operations, which raw materials, which human resources, and so on. It is used as the basis of several production planning systems.

master standard data (MSD). A form of PREDETERMINED MOTION-TIME SYSTEM.

material control. A MATERIAL MANAGE-MENT function responsible for the acquisition of components and raw materials in accordance with purchase orders and production requirements.

material control schedule. A delivery request issued by MATERIAL CONTROL in accordance with a blanket order. The schedule is normally for some long-term period (e.g. three months) with varying degrees of firmness (i.e. the period over which indicated requirements will not change).

materials handling. The range of technologies and techniques used in the storage and movement of components, sub-assemblies and products around a factory.

materials management. The range of techniques and methods used to optimize the use and flow of materials through a factory. It includes STOCK CONTROL, warehousing, materials handling, purchasing and distribution.

materials requirements planning (MRP). A technique which takes a forecast of anticipated sales over time and produces a breakdown of the total materials requirements — raw materials, components, sub-assemblies etc — for meeting those targets. From such information a series of activities — purchase orders, sub-contract orders, in-house production of components orders etc — can be initiated. The weaknesses of MRP are that it is only as good as the forecast and, since it involves a large number of variables, can take a long time to produce. For this reason, most MRP systems are now computer-based. Many systems now offer a degree of 'closing the loop' to improve on the information base by bringing in other production information apart from the initial sales forecasts. *See* MANUFACTURING RESOURCES PLANNING.

maternity rights. Women in the UK with a specified period of continuous employment have the right (most recently reaffirmed under the 1985 Social Security Act) not to be dismissed if they become pregnant, although they may be given other suitable work if their pregnancy prevents them doing their normal job. Providing they work up to 11 weeks before the baby is due they are entitled to Statutory Maternity Pay (payable on a 2-tier basis) equivalent to 90 per cent of normal pay for a 6-week period at the higher rate and a lower rate beyond that for a further 12 weeks. In addition, they may return to work 29 weeks after the birth providing that 21 days' notice is given both before the absence and before the return to work. To qualify for maternity rights a woman must have worked either for 2 years (104 weeks) continuous service at a minimum of 16 hours per week or 5 years if working between 8 and 16 weeks per year.

matrix organization. An organization structure, often used in project management, in which employees are responsible to two supervisors. Typically, the first supervisor will be a line manager to whom the employee would normally report, and the second a project leader to whom he also reports for the duration of the project. Matrix organization is most suited to situations where there is a requirement for putting multi-function or multi-discipline teams together to work on specific projects — such

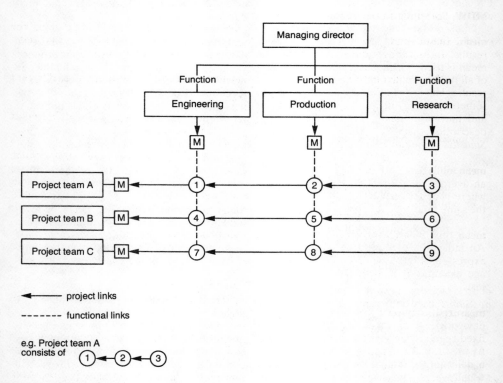

a matrix organization

as in research and development, product development, consultancy or major building projects.

maximax. *See* DECISION RULES.

maximin. *See* DECISION RULES.

maximum/minimum control A STOCK CONTROL system which involves re-ordering up to a maximum level whenever stocks drop to a preset minimum level.

maximum working area. In ERGONOMICS, the space over which a worker makes movements to carry out a task (e.g. reaching for tools).

MBA. *See* MASTER OF BUSINESS ADMINISTRATION.

MBO. *See* MANAGEMENT BY OBJECTIVES.

MCD. *See* MASTER CLERICAL DATA.

MDW. *See* MEASURED DAYWORK.

mean. In statistics, the average of a set of results. In most cases the simple arithmetic mean is used, which is calculated as the sum of all the results divided by number of sets of results. However, other forms of means are sometimes used, including geometric mean and harmonic mean. For a more detailed description see A. Plews, *Introductory Statistics* (London: Heinemann, 1970).

mean audit date. A fixed date for an audit of an average shop in a group of retail shops where it is not possible to audit them all at the same time.

mean time before/between failure (MTBF). An indication of the reliability of a system expressed in the time taken before an average example of it has failed in a previous test.

measured daywork (MDW) (controlled daywork). A payment system based on a fixed regular wage rather than on PAYMENT BY RESULTS. The wage is paid on the basis of a daily target rate of productivity which is usually set by some form of WORK MEASUREMENT technique.

mechanical aptitude tests (mechanical comprehension tests). Selection tests used to establish the level of a subject's mechanical understanding and ability.

mechanical comprehension tests. *See* MECHANICAL APTITUDE TESTS.

mechanistic organization. In their pioneering work on organization structures, Tom Burns and George Stalker found two forms which were suitable under different conditions – mechanistic and ORGANIC. Mechanistic organization structures are based on a bureaucratic model (i.e. one involving high division of tasks and allocation of clear responsibility and vertical hierarchies) and are appropriate for activites such as production with high levels of predictability requiring a high degree of control.

media analysis. A form of analysis used in advertising to determine the success of different channels or media in reaching particular audience segments.

median. In statistics, the middle value (or group of values) in a FREQUENCY DISTRIBUTION.

media research. The testing out of different channels in advertising.

media testing. The testing out of different channels in advertising.

medium-term liabilities. LIABILITIES which must be met within the medium term (usually a maximum of three years) but which do not appear as CURRENT LIABILITIES on a BALANCE SHEET.

member bank. A US COMMERCIAL BANK; the equivalent of a CLEARING BANK in the UK.

memo–motion study. A technique used in WORK STUDY based on the analysis of a film taken of work on a sampling basis.

memorandum of association. In the UK, a document setting out the basic reasons for establishing a company and identifying the amount and type of share capital involved. *See* ARTICLES OF ASSOCIATION.

menu-driven. In computing, programs which offer the user a choice on screen from which he can select the option for the task he requires.

merchandise balance. The balance of payments in a country, based only on physical goods imported or exported (i.e. excluding INVISIBLE EXPORTS AND IMPORTS).

merchandising. In MARKETING, the process of distributing and displaying a product to encourage sales.

merchant bank. A UK bank which specializes in longer-term and higher-risk lending than a CLEARING BANK. Merchant banks also offer a range of specialist services, including acting as ISSUING HOUSES or ACCEPTING HOUSES, and as financial advisors, especially on large-scale ventures such as a new company launch or a merger.

merger. A mutually-agreed joining together of two or more firms, as distinct from a TAKEOVER. Mergers are covered by the UK FAIR TRADING ACT 1973 and increasingly by EEC legislation. Proposed mergers can be referred to the MONOPOLIES AND MERGERS COMMISSION.

merit award (merit pay). A BONUS paid to an employee for particular merit − such as punctuality, consistently high-quality production etc.

merit pay. *See* MERIT AWARD.

merit rating. An element in a payment system which rewards different individuals according to their performance and value to the company. Factors used in computing a merit rating include punctuality, length of service, aptitude etc.

merit system. A promotion system based on merit rather than on the length of service or other factors.

methods engineer. An engineer specializing in METHOD STUDY and related INDUSTRIAL ENGINEERING techniques.

methods time measurement (MTM). In WORK STUDY, the measurement of standard movements.

method study. The systematic analysis and study of the ways in which work is done and the development of ways of improving performance. It is a major component of WORK STUDY.

metropolitan shift system. A pattern in which workers change shifts twice or more in a week.

MICR. Magnetic ink character reader. *See* MAGNETIC CHARACTER READER.

microcomputer. A small, relatively low-cost stand-alone computer. *See* PERSONAL COMPUTER.

Microelectronics Application Project (MAP). A major UK government initiative launched in 1978 to promote the widespread use of microelectronics in products and processes of manufacturing firms. The scheme has 3 components: (*i*) education and training and general awareness-raising programmes; (*ii*) consultancy support for feasibility studies; and (*iii*) government grants of between 25 and 30 per cent toward the costs of implementing microelectronics projects.

microfiche. A sheet of MICROFILM which carries a number of pages of an original and can be read in a special microfiche reader. It is used in libraries etc to store large amounts of information in a small space.

microfilm. A reduced-size photograph on which documents or books are stored.

microprocessor. The CENTRAL PROCESSING UNIT of a computer on a single chip. Microprocessor systems can be configured to make very small computers and are programmed for a wide range of industrial uses.

microsystems centres. Centres established by the UK DEPARTMENT OF TRADE AND INDUSTRY operated by the National Computing Centre. They offer demonstrations and consultancy support to firms wishing to explore the possibility of using microcomputers.

minimum entitlement. The minimum amount of pay due to an employee under a payment system.

Minimum Lending Rate (MLR). The rate at which the Bank of England lends to CLEARING BANKS and which has a strong influence on INTEREST RATES charged. Introduced in 1972, it replaced the BANK RATE, which dictated interest rates to the clearing banks.

minimum manufacturing quantity (MMQ). The theoretical minimum quantity of products which can be made economically in a batch. The term is used in production planning control. *See* ECONOMIC BATCH QUANTITY.

minimum movements. In MOTION STUDY, the minimum movements needed to carry out a task.

minimum time rate (MTR). The lowest rate of pay per unit of time for an employee.

Ministry of International Trade and Industry (MITI). In Japan, the government ministry often credited with having masterminded the economic success of Japanese industry in world markets.

Ministry of Labour. In the UK, the former name for the DEPARTMENT OF EMPLOYMENT.

MIS. *See* MANAGEMENT INFORMATION SYSTEMS.

misfeance. The carrying out of a legal act in an illegal way.

Mitbestimmung. *See* CO-DETERMINATION.

MITI. *See* MINISTRY OF INTERNATIONAL TRADE AND INDUSTRY.

mixed benefits scheme. A PENSION scheme in which the percentage of benefits includes a lump cash sum and a pension.

mixed cost. *See* SEMI-VARIABLE COST.

mixed economy. A national economy in which a free market operates alongside a PUBLIC SECTOR with the government exerting some measure of control.

MLR. *See* MINIMUM LENDING RATE.

MMQ. *See* MINIMUM MANUFACTURING QUANTITY.

MNC. *See* MULTINATIONAL COMPANY.

mode. In statistics, the most frequently occurring value in a FREQUENCY DISTRIBUTION.

model. Some form of representation of a company or aspect of its business. Models can take a variety of forms (computer simulations, mathematical models, graphical models etc) and their purpose is to explore and experiment to try to predict outcomes in those situations where it would be impossible to make use of the real company which is the subject of the model.

modem (modulator/demodulator). A device used to connect computers via a telephone network to enable communication of data between them.

modulator/demodulator. *See* MODEM.

module training. Training involving units or modules of knowledge which can be learnt piecemeal by the student. Typically, each module involves a combination of experience, formal training and on-the-job training.

monadic product test. *See* DIADIC PRODUCT TEST.

monetarism. A school of thought in economics which suggests that successful management and control of an economy depends principally on controlling the supply of money. It is particularly associated with the CHICAGO SCHOOL OF ECONOMISTS.

monetary union. A form of international cooperation where two or more countries share the same currency and financial infrastructure. *See* EUROPEAN COMMUNITY.

money at call. Money held as a debt or a loan which is repayable on demand.

money broker. An individual or institution dealing in the financial markets in securities, currencies, gold etc.

money purchase pension scheme. A PENSION scheme in which the calculation of the amount payable is based on the years during which an employee has been a member of the scheme and the salary earned during that period. Contributions from the employer and employee are fixed as a proportion of that salary.

money shop. A bank, often located in shopping centres, which is open during shopping hours rather than banking hours. Services offered tend to be consumer-related — for example, hire purchase, credit purchase and cheque cashing — rather than the full range of conventional bank services.

money supply. The total amount of money moving around the economy at any time — as notes, in bank accounts etc. This is hard to identify, and, in practice, is defined by a number of measures — M1 and M3, for example, which give information about money supply measured in different terms.

Monopolies and Mergers Commission. A board set up in the UK to oversee legislation concerning monopolistic and other unfair trading practices (such as the Restrictive Trade Practices Act 1956). The Commission is part of the DEPARTMENT OF TRADE AND INDUSTRY and may be called in when potential MERGERS appear to be leading to a position which would not be in the interests of fair trade.

monopoly. A condition in which a market is dominated or controlled by a single organization. Since this acts in restraint of free trade, there is legislation in most countries to prevent its emergence, such as the antitrust laws in the USA, the Kartellamt in West Germany and the MONOPOLIES AND MERGERS COMMISSION in the UK.

monopsony. A condition in which the purchase of goods or services is dominated by a single organization.

Monte Carlo methods. A range of SIMULATION techniques involving an element of randomness.

moonlighting. Doing more than one job, often without declaring the income from the second and/or others for tax purposes.

morphological analysis. A problem-solving technique which groups together things which have some feature in common. For example, in trying to develop a new product, the possibilities might be examined in systematic fashion in terms of common design features, construction materials etc.

mortgage. A loan made on the security of something — typically a property — where the ownership does not pass to the person taking out the loan until it is repaid but where he may have the use of it, provided he continues to repay the loan in agreed instalments.

mortmain (dead hand). A class of property ownership which is non-transferable — for example, church buildings.

most favoured nation status. In international trade, an agreement between two nations to grant each other preferential and reciprocal treatment in the matter of tariffs and other trade barriers. *See* GENERAL AGREEMENT ON TARIFFS AND TRADE.

motion study. An element in WORK STUDY where movements carried out by a worker are analysed systematically, with the aim of optimizing the performance of the task. The field was pioneered by Frank and Lilian Gilbreth in the USA during the 1920s.

motivation. The set of factors which predispose people to behave in particular ways and, in particular, to exert effort in order to achieve something. A number of theories have been put forward to explain how these factors operate and which of them are more or less significant. Most of these involve the idea of need identification and satisfaction — for example, Abraham Maslow's HIERARCHY OF NEEDS or Frederick HERZBERG'S TWO FACTOR THEORY. Current thinking on motivation divides into content theories (which are essentially concerned with identifying what motivates people) and process theories (which are more concerned about the way in which the mechanism works). Examples of the former can be found in the work of Maslow, Herzberg, David Mc-CLELLAND and Douglas MACGREGOR. Among the latter, attention has been paid to so-called path—goal theories (which explore

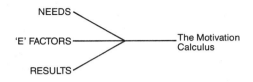

motivation

the paths people take to achieving the goal of meeting their particular needs), of which a good example is the expectancy theory extended by Lyman Porter and Edward Lawler. In this, the assumption is made that people know what they want and direct their behaviour towards achieving it accordingly. Motivation is defined as a function of three factors − the valence (which expresses the preference an individual has for a particular outcome), an expectancy that doing something will lead to that outcome, and a motivational force which results from the expectancy and the valence. As the diagram shows, the individual calculates how far the expenditure of 'E-factors' − energy, effort and enthusiasm − will enable him to meet a need, and will put more 'E' in when the need is stronger.

Such 'motivation calculus' is more complex to grasp than the theories of, say, Maslow, but it is generally accepted as offering a more realistic view of the process of motivation. Summaries of process theories of motivation can be found in V. Vroom and L. Deci, *Management and Motivation* (Harmondsworth: Penguin, 1970), V. Vroom, *Work and Motivation* (New York: John Wiley, 1964) and L. Porter and E. Lawler, *Managerial Skills and Performance* (Homewood, Ill.: Irwin Dorsey, 1968).

motor skills. Basic muscular control skills and manipulative abilities.

mouse. A device developed as part of the attempt by computer manufacturers to design 'user-friendly' computer systems. A mouse is a small box mounted on a roller or ball which is attached to a desktop computer. Instead of using the keyboard, the user moves the mouse around the desk and this moves a pointer around the screen. When the user finds the particular item on

the screen menu which he wants, he pushes a button on the mouse and the program is activated.

Mouton, Jane. One of the orginators of the MANAGERIAL GRID.

moving average. In statistical forecasting, an average which allows for continuous updating of data.

MPA. *See* MASTER OF PUBLIC ADMINISTRATION.

MPS. *See* MASTER PRODUCTION SCHEDULE.

MRP2. *See* MANUFACTURING RESOURCES PLANNING.

MSC. *See* MANPOWER SERVICES COMMISSION.

MSD. *See* MASTER STANDARD DATA.

MS/DOS. A widely-used operating system for personal computers. The name derives from Microsoft Disk Operating System, and is a non-proprietary version of the system originally developed for the IBM PC machine by the Microsoft Company.

MSX. A standard for microcomputers which share common features and which enable considerable compatibility of software and hardware add-ons. It is almost exclusively used by Japanese manufacturers.

MTBF. *See* MEAN TIME BEFORE/BETWEEN FAILURE.

MTM. *See* METHODS TIME MEASUREMENT.

MTR. *See* MINIMUM TIME RATE.

multi-employer bargaining. COLLECTIVE BARGAINING taking place at an industry or sub-sector level involving several employers.

multi-minute measurement. A form of WORK MEASUREMENT where samples are taken at short intervals.

multinational company (MNC) (transnational corporation). A company which operates in a number of different countries and which uses an international strategy based on moving resources and operations around the world to secure local advantages such as labour costs, tax relief or access to local markets. It differs from an international company, which simply sells in different countries.

multiple regression analysis. A statistical technique used to find relationships between variables by finding an equation which fits data points on a graph.

multi-unionism. A situation in which the interests of different groups of workers in an organization are represented by different TRADE UNIONS — as distinct from single factory or industry unions.

multi-user system. A computer system which permits several terminals to access a central computer at the same time.

mutual fund. An investment management company in which securities are bought, held and managed on behalf of shared owners — such as in a unit trust, for example.

mutual insurance. Insurance involving payment into a fund which then pays out to members eligible to make claims.

mutual office. An insurance organization in which there are no shareholders and where all profits are shared out among policyholders.

N

naked debenture. A DEBENTURE which is issued in respect of an unsecured loan.

named vote. A vote in which a record is kept of each personal vote; it is normally used only for very important decisions.

name screening. A MARKET RESEARCH technique designed to check the brand name of a new product or service for connections or interpretations which might be unpopular, embarrassing, ambiguous etc. It is particularly important in international business (e.g. the brand name of an adhesive tape in Australia is the same as that of a leading contraceptive in the UK).

national debt. The total outstanding amount borrowed by a government.

National Economic Development Council (NEDC; 'Neddy'). The council of the NATIONAL ECONOMIC DEVELOPMENT OFFICE (NEDO), chaired by the Chancellor of the Exchequer, formed in 1962. The monthly, private meetings on matters of national economic policy include representatives from employers' organizations, the TRADES UNION CONGRESS (TUC) and the government. Current representation includes six members from the CONFEDERATION OF BRITISH INDUSTRY, six members from the TUC, two representatives of nationalized industries, the Secretary of State for Trade and Industry, the Secretary of State for Employment, the Director-General of NEDO and the Chancellor of the Exchequer.

National Economic Development Office (NEDO). A publicly-funded, independent body in the UK, serving the NATIONAL ECONOMIC DEVELOPMENT COUNCIL and various sectoral economic development committees ('little Neddies') in terms of research, information and integration of activities. *See* ECONOMIC DEVELOPMENT COUNCIL.

National Graphical Association (NGA). In the UK, one of the two main trade unions for printing workers, consisting mainly of machine operators. The other union is the Society of Graphical and Allied Trades.

national income. The REVENUE from resources employed nationally, net of depreciation, measured at a factor cost (i.e. in terms of land, labour, CAPITAL and entrepreneurship). The amount by which the nation's capital assets are deemed to have diminished in value (DEPRECIATION) is deducted from the GROSS NATIONAL PRODUCT to arrive at the national income.

national insurance. An insurance scheme operated by a state, for which contributions are deducted at source from employee and employer. Separate systems exist to cover the self-employed etc. The scheme provides for subsequent illness, accident or other loss of income.

National Insurance Acts. A series of legislative measures pertaining to the UK national insurance scheme.

nationalization. The practice of instituting state ownership of companies. Although normally seen as a socialist policy, it is also used for purposes of saving ailing strategic industries (e.g. British Leyland in the UK) or national interests against foreign ownership in developing countries.

National Research and Development Council (NRDC). A government-funded research body in the UK, responsible to the Secretary of State for Trade and Industry for the funding and stimulation of development of inventions and innovations at pre-commercial stages, and commissioning research into related areas.

National Union of Railwaymen (NUR). One of the two main rail unions in the UK, the other being the Associated Society of Locomotive Engineers and Firemen.

NATO. *See* NORTH ATLANTIC TREATY ORGANIZATION.

NATO Codification System. A 13-digit classification coding system developed by the US military forces based on the American Federal Supply Code. It provides standard reference numbers for all items used by military operations within NATO member countries.

natural wastage. The depletion in the employment size of an organization through death, retirement or resignation (i.e. for reasons other than dismissal or redundancy). In the past, this was often accepted by TRADE UNIONS and used as the basis for a reduction of labour levels. Latterly, however, a move to the principle of jobs in perpetuity − not simply for the present incumbents − has reversed this practice.

NC. *See* NUMERICAL CONTROL.

NDP. *See* NET DOMESTIC PRODUCT.

near money. Funds held in forms which may be easily converted into cash (e.g. DEPOSIT ACCOUNTS).

NEDC. *See* NATIONAL ECONOMIC DEVELOPMENT COUNCIL.

'Neddy'. *See* NATIONAL ECONOMIC DEVELOPMENT COUNCIL.

NEDO. *See* NATIONAL ECONOMIC DEVELOPMENT ORGANIZATION.

need pull. An unsatisfied market or environmental requirement bringing about product or process innovations to meet it. The term is particularly applied to technological solutions for economic or social needs (e.g. lean-burn engines for cars in response to conservational pressures, both social and economic). *See* MARKET PUSH; TECHNOLOGY PUSH.

negative cash flow. The flow of money out of a business, that is, payment for services rendered (including wages of employees) or goods supplied (including raw materials or capital equipment).

negotiable instrument. A financial proof document which entitles the owner to payment by another person (e.g. a cheque or currency note).

negotiation. The formal process of reaching an agreement by discussion. In INDUSTRIAL RELATIONS, negotiation has an important role to play in COLLECTIVE BARGAINING and other forms of bargaining procedures.

net assets. The CAPITAL employed in an enterprise, equal to the total assets minus the CURRENT LIABILITIES. They may also take into account debt capital and long-term loans, in which case the net assets are those of the owner and may be referred to · as OWNER'S EQUITY.

net cash flow. The result of accumulation of positive and negative cash flows over a period.

net domestic product (NDP). The amount by which the capital assets of an economy have been deducted from the GROSS DOMESTIC PRODUCT.

net effective distribution. In MARKET RESEARCH, the number of retail outlets which have a certain product in stock on a certain date.

net income. The NET PROFIT of an organization, including INCOME and payments outside its main activities. It takes into account payment of taxes and interest on loans.

net investment. A GROSS INVESTMENT in equipment and stocks less depreciation. It is a useful measure of actual investment for growth.

net national product (NNP). A NATIONAL INCOME measured without the convention of factor costing.

net operating income (net operating profit). The NET SALES of a firm over a period minus the COST OF SALES and other OPERATING EXPENSES. This income excludes income or expenditure from other activities (e.g. investments).

net operating profit. *See* NET OPERATING INCOME.

net present value (NPV). A method of applying the DISCOUNTED CASH FLOW principle to future income or expenditure by estimating the value of future amounts at the present time, using discounting factors applied to envisaged amounts to allow for INFLATION etc. The net present value of an investment or income is the sum of POSITIVE CASH FLOWS minus the sum of NEGATIVE CASH FLOWS over a period.

net profit (trading profit). The actual financial gain from activities, calculated by deducting all OPERATING EXPENSES from the total sales revenue for a specified activity. It may be calculated with or without allowance for tax and interest payments.

net profit margin. A NET PROFIT expressed as a percentage of sales TURNOVER.

net sales. The total REVENUE from sales after allowing for RETURNS and/or DISCOUNTS.

net statutory income. In the UK, the TAXABLE INCOME of an individual after allowance is made for personal and other reliefs.

network. (1) A schematic diagram used to explain and plan a series of events in a PROJECT or complex activity. The diagram consists of standard symbols denoting work items (activities) with details, such as time required etc, and specific points (events), linking activities. The plan is related to resources required for the operation, the timescale, and the order in which activities must be carried out or events reached. A popular use of networks is CRITICAL PATH ANALYSIS.
(2) A grouping of microcomputers enabling the sharing of memory and data and communication between one machine and others. It provides some of the benefits of MAINFRAME computing while retaining microcomputer flexibility. *See also* LOCAL AREA NETWORK.
(3) Any linked arrangement of resources, outlets, agents etc.

network analysis. The use of a NETWORK to plan a series of activities (a PROJECT), to make best use of RESOURCES and to ensure control may be maintained over progress. It may be used to determine the chain of events

which has the tightest time requirements — the critical path — through the network.

net working capital. (1) The net CURRENT ASSETS of a firm.
(2) The difference between CURRENT ASSETS and CURRENT LIABILITIES at any one time.

net worth. An OWNER'S EQUITY or net total assets.

new game. *See* OFFENSIVE STRATEGY.

new technology agreement (NTA). An agreement between a TRADE UNION and an employer on the introduction of new technology, containing details of implications and impacts on such factors as employment levels, working practices, status differentials etc. For a full explanation see the Trades Union Congress pamphlet, *Employment and Technology* (1979).

NIIP tests. A series of PSYCHOLOGICAL and APTITUDE TESTS devised by the National Institute of Industrial Psychology in the UK.

NGA. *See* NATIONAL GRAPHICAL ASSOCIATION.

NNP. *See* NET NATIONAL PRODUCT.

node diagram. *See* ACTIVITY ON NODE.

nominal share capital. The total value of the nominal shares of a company. *See* AUTHORIZED CAPITAL.

nominal value. *See* FACE VALUE.

nominee holdings (intermediary holdings). SHARES which are held by someone who appears in official registers but which are in fact controlled by someone else who wishes to remain anonymous.

nomogram. A diagramatic calculating/conversion table used in FORECASTING to convert numerical data from one form to another.

non-assignable variables. Observed departures from expected performance which cannot be attributed to known causes. They are used in process control.

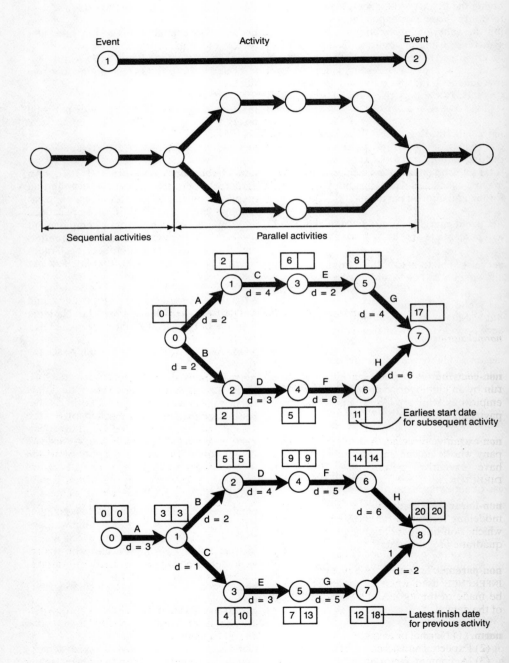

networks (as used in critical path analysis)

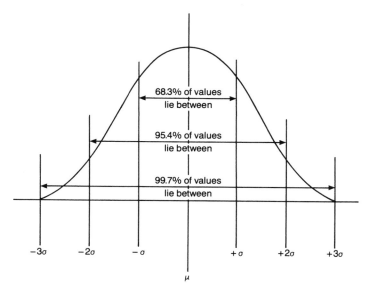

Alternatively: 2.5% of the values lie above $\mu + 1.96\sigma$
2.5% of the values lie below $\mu - 1.96\sigma$

Similarly: 0.2% of the values lie outside $\mu \pm 3.09\sigma$

normal distribution

---

non-contributory pension scheme. A scheme run by an employer to provide PENSIONS for employees who are not required to make payments towards it.

non-executive director. A director of a company who is not an employee and does not have executive power. *See* EXECUTIVE DIRECTOR.

non-linear programming. A mathematical modelling technique for solving problems in which non-linear relationships exist (e.g. quadratic programming).

non-parametric test. A test of STATISTICAL INFERENCE used when no assumption may be made of the PROBABILITY DISTRIBUTION of the data.

norm. (1) Normal or average.
(2) Expected and accepted behaviour.
(3) A context factor in PSYCHOLOGICAL TESTING used to relate data to the type of sample being considered.

normal distribution (Gaussian distribution). A PROBABILITY DISTRIBUTION of randomly occurring events or values, such as the heights of children at a particular age, the weights of components, or the life expectancy of a product. A distibution is 'normal' if 68.3 per cent of the population are within 1 STANDARD DEVIATION from the centre of value, if 95.4 per cent are within 2 standard deviations from the centre value and if 99.7 per cent are within 3 standard deviations.

normal population. A collection of recordings (population) of a random variable which has a NORMAL DISTRIBUTION.

normative forecasting. The process of predicting future NORMS, rather than actual events or values.

North Atlantic Treaty Organization (NATO). A political alliance group formed in 1949 by a defence agreement. The members are Belgium, Canada, Denmark, France, Greece, Iceland, Italy, Luxembourg, the Netherlands, Norway, Portugal, Spain, Turkey, the UK, the USA and West Germany. Political and military headquarters are near Brussels.

notary public. A legal appointment with authority to guarantee the authenticity of signatures and documents.

NPV. *See* NET PRESENT VALUE.

NRDC. *See* NATIONAL RESEARCH AND DEVELOPMENT COUNCIL.

NTA. *See* NEW TECHNOLOGY AGREEMENT.

numerical control (NC). Technology based upon digital/analog numerical information which may be generated, stored, manipulated and retrieved for purposes of controlling the operation of machine tools and other electromechanical equipment. Originating in such early items as music boxes, pianolas and punchcard looms (Jacquard, *c*1800), NC was developed through the 1970s into COMPUTER NUMERICAL CONTROL and DIRECT NUMERICAL CONTROL.

NUR. *See* NATIONAL UNION OF RAILWAYMEN.

nursed account. A supplier who is favoured by a customer in terms of payment of invoices and preference for new business, particularly over other regular suppliers.

nursery units. Small factories on new industrial estates, set up by developers or local authorities, to help new small businesses to find suitable premises in which to begin operations.

O

OAPEC. *See* ORGANIZATION OF ARAB PET-ROLEUM EXPORTING COUNTRIES.

OAS. *See* ORGANIZATION OF AMERICAN STATES.

OB. *See* OBJECTIVE BEHAVIOUR.

objective test. A personality or ability assessment technique designed in such a way that each question has only one correct answer (to rule out subjectivity in an examiner's verdict).

objects clause. The part of the MEMORANDUM OF ASSOCIATION of a company which states the purposes for which the company was set up.

occupational classification. Occupation types are classified by the INTERNATIONAL STANDARD CLASSIFICATION OF OCCUPATIONS (ISCO) and the CLASSIFICATION OF OCCUPATIONS AND DIRECTORY OF TITLES (CODOT). The groupings are similar to the usually quoted SOCIO-ECONOMIC groups: (*i*) professional; (*ii*) employers and managers; (*iii*) scientists, engineers and technologists; (*iv*) clerical workers; (*v*) foremen; (*vi*) skilled manual workers; (*vii*) semi-skilled manual workers; and (*viii*) unskilled manual workers.

occupational mobility. The readiness and practical ability of someone to move from one occupation to another. *See* LABOUR MOBILITY.

occupational profile. *See* PROFILE.

OD. *See* ORGANIZATION DEVELOPMENT.

odd pricing. A selling technique using misleading prices (e.g. £99.99 rather than £100.00).

OECD. *See* ORGANIZATION FOR ECONOMIC CO-OPERATION AND DEVELOPMENT.

offensive strategy. A plan to introduce something new (a product, a process, a service etc) into a competitive situation in order to gain a commercial advantage (e.g. a new or increased market share). It may involve an entirely new idea (new game) or a new way of using an existing idea (OLD GAME).

offer. An indication of desire to sell or buy something.

offer by tender. A means of selling something (especially SECURITIES) to the highest bidder(s).

office automation (electronic office; office of the future). A popular term for the implementation of new technologies (especially INFORMATION TECHNOLOGY) into office functions (e.g. WORD PROCESSING, FAC-SIMILE TRANSMISSION etc).

Office of Consumer Affairs. A US government 'watchdog agency'.

Office of Economic Opportunity. A US government agency responsible for welfare programmes.

Office of Fair Trading (OFT). A UK government office responsible for monitoring consumer affairs and company MERGERS and TAKEOVERS.

Office of Management and Budget. A US government agency responsible for the Federal budget and programmes.

Office of Manpower Economics. An independent UK advisory body concerned with government intelligence on employment issues.

Offices, Shops and Railway Premises Act 1963. UK legislation concerned with conditions of work (e.g. hours of work, environmental conditions etc) in specific places. It is administered by local authorities, and, in certain circumstances, by factory inspectors.

The Act was complemented, but not superseded, by the HEALTH AND SAFETY AT WORK ACT 1974.

official receiver. An individual appointed by a government office (e.g. the Inland Revenue) to supervise the LIQUIDATION of an enterprise.

official reserves. A nation's reserve of foreign currencies, gold, SPECIAL DRAWING RIGHTS and other internationally acceptable credits.

official strike. A STRIKE which has been sanctioned and supported by at least one TRADE UNION.

off-line. In computing, work which is done at a remote WORK STATION while it is not connected to a central processor.

offshore. An operation or investment which is financially regulated in a country or area outside the control of that in which it operates or is employed.

off-the-job-training. Training or retraining for which the individual is absent from the workplace for a period of time (e.g. day release for attendance at a technical college). It is usually combined with ON-THE-JOB TRAINING for best effect.

OFT. *See* OFFICE OF FAIR TRADING.

ogive. A graphical representation of a distribution function.

old game. In STRATEGIC PLANNING, the existing competitive environment and tactics. *See also* OFFENSIVE STRATEGY.

oligopoly. A situation in which a market is controlled or dominated by a few large sellers.

oligopsony. A situation in which a market is controlled or dominated by a few large customers.

O & M. *See* ORGANIZATION AND METHODS.

OMS. *See* OUPTUT PER MANSHIFT.

oncost. (1) An increase in existing cost which would result from a specific course of action.
(2) An INDIRECT COST.

one-point arbitrage. *See* SIMPLE ARBITRAGE.

one-stop shopping. A retailing concept which attempts to group the main types of retail outlet together so that the customer may buy all that is required within one area. *See also* SCRAMBLED MERCHANDISING.

on-line. (1) In computing, when peripherals are directly conneted to the central processor of a computer and are operational.
(2) A computer system in which it is possible to access a central proceesor directly for the purposes of multiple, immediate operations. This is not necessarily the same as interactive or real-time operation.

on-pack giveaway. A marketing device employing gifts given free with a purchase, for example, a free razor with a pack of razor blades. Since the razor is designed to work only with the manufacturer's blades, the object is to encourage further purchases of the blades.

on-the-job training. Training or re-training carried out at the employee's workplace and during the period of work (e.g. operating a new piece of equipment under the supervision of a specialist). This is the opposite of OFF-THE-JOB TRAINING.

OOQ. Optimum order quantity. *See* ECONOMIC ORDER QUANTITY.

OPEC. *See* ORGANIZATION OF PETROLEUM EXPORTING COUNTRIES.

open account. A system of selling by customer's credit. Goods are delivered with an invoice which must be settled within a specified period (e.g. 30 days).

open-door policy. A management policy whereby any individual has unrestricted access to his or her immediate supervisor during working hours.

open-ended payment system. An arrangement under which the pay of an individual is not regulated by a fixed rate or incremental scale, but is decided in an *ad hoc* manner by his or her superior and might be changed at any time without reference to a plan.

open learning. Organized DISTANCE LEARNING, such as that provided by the OPEN UNIVERSITY and the OPEN TECH in the UK.

open loop. (1) In control theory, a system which does not have feedback circuits, driven by error signals, to monitor output and thus modify input.

(2) Any system in which it is assumed that a given instruction will lead to a predicted result and no account is taken of possible error.

open shop. A workplace in which no one union is recognized as representative of all employees and in which membership of a trade union is not compulsory.

open system. A collection of interrelated activities which combine to form a system capable of receiving inputs and producing outputs. Open systems theory is used to analyse management information and operating systems by analogy with natural systems (organisms).

open systems interconnection (OSI). The standard protocol of the International Standards Office for transmitting electronic information between two or more separate computer systems.

Open Tech. A DISTANCE LEARNING technical college founded in the UK in 1982 by the MANPOWER AND SERVICES COMMISSION. The objective of the Open Tech is to provide training and retraining courses for people in or out of work by means of 'packages' of written, recorded (audio and video) and physical form, supported by administrative centres throughout the country (typically technical colleges). The courses are all concerned with modern technologies.

open union. A TRADE UNION in which anyone may become a member.

Open University (OU). A DISTANCE LEARNING institution founded in 1968 in Milton Keynes in the UK. The OU provides distance learning packages in written and recorded

form (including daily BBC television broadcasts) to degree standards (Bachelor and Master) by a credit system. Originally conceived as non-vocational, the OU now has a business school and other practically-orientated departments undertaking research as well as tuition. Students do not need conventional academic qualifications to register, but must be over 21.

operating cycle. The average time taken by a manufacturer between the purchase of materials and receipt of payment by customers (usually expressed as a number of days). The calculation for an operating cycle takes into account COST OF SALES, payment periods (CREDITORS and DEBTORS) and sales and purchases, all on a daily basis.

operating expenses. The total expenditure on operating within a firm, including factory overheads but not costs of finance (interest).

operating leverage. The ratio of FIXED COSTS to total costs.

operating profit. The positive difference between INCOME and operating expenses (i.e. excluding taxation and INTEREST). *See also* TRADING PROFIT.

operating statement. An accounting statement designed to record and explain the use of funds during operations in a specific period.

operating system. (1) The mechanism of interaction and communication within an organization.

(2) In computing, a set of supervisory and utility PROGRAMS which perform routine functions within a computer to connect the user with the machine operating level.

operational research (OR; operations research). A field in MANAGEMENT SCIENCE dealing with the application of mathematical theories to operating system problems and control, especially optimization.

operations management. The management of the central function of a business organization, whether in the manufacturing or service sector. This covers the management of materials, equipment, plant, and people with the objective of matching the activity of the enterprise to its market.

operations research. *See* OPERATIONAL RESEARCH.

operator. (1) An individual who operates a piece of equipment.
(2) In industry, a skilled or semi-skilled worker.

operator performance. The ratio (expressed as a percentage) of the amount of work carried out, expressed in standard hours (CONTROLLED WORK), to the number of actual hours worked. It is a measure of working efficiency in WORK STUDY.

Opitz classification. A PRODUCTION ENGINEERING coding system for classifying TOOLING items and components, using primary and secondary numerical codes.

opportunity cost (shadow price). In economics, the potential value to a firm of the outcome of a course of action which is not taken.

OPT. *See* OPTIMIZED PRODUCTION TECHNIQUES.

optimization. A technique for calculating the best allocation of resources for a given set of objectives and constraints.

optimized production techniques (OPT). A packaged approach to production control based upon selective attention on 'bottlenecks' in material flows and the linking of flow throughout a production system to the output stage, to minimize work in progress and hence costs. For a full explanation see E. Goldratt, *The Goal* (New York: Creative Output, 1985).

optimum order quantity. *See* ECONOMIC ORDER QUANTITY.

option. The right to acquire specific goods or services as a fixed price or on preferential terms at some time in the future, within agreed restraints. Options may be taken up by the original purchaser, may be traded to a third party, or may lapse.

option forward. A CONTRACT which gives the holder the right to buy a commodity or amount of currency at a fixed rate at some time in the future.

option money. A fee paid for the taking of an OPTION.

optoelectronics. Technology combining electronic circuitry and optical circuitry for control, information and communication systems (e.g. the combination of fibre optics and electrical signal cables in telecommunications systems).

OR. *See* OPERATIONAL RESEARCH.

ORACLE. In the UK, the Independent Broadcasting Authority VIDEOTEXT service.

Order in Council. In the UK, Privy Council legislation on behalf of the Crown.

order picking. The selection of goods from stock in a sequence designed to fill customer orders in accordance with a predetermined priority.

order processing. The acceptance, acknowledgment and initiation of response to sales orders (e.g. a typical output of order processing is an internal or works order).

ordinary resolution. A resolution passed at the ANNUAL GENERAL MEETING of a company.

ordinary shares. SECURITIES sold by a company which may be traded within limitations (e.g. if it is a PRIVATE COMPANY etc), and which constitute the EQUITY CAPITAL of that company. These shares usually carry voting rights and take third place, after DEBENTURES and PREFERENCE SHARES, in entitlement to the distributed profits of the company.

organic. An ORGANIZATION which has a task orientation, a flexible definition of jobs, and a readiness to accept change, and in which open communication is encouraged and fresh ideas welcomed. The term was coined by Tom Burns and George Stalker. *See also* MECHANISTIC ORGANIZATION.

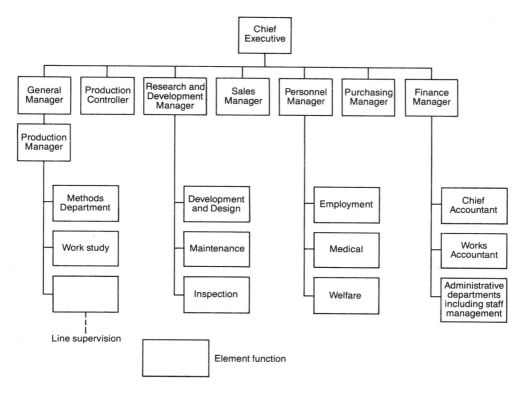

an organization chart

organization. (1) A group of people brought together by common, agreed rules, procedure and management in the use of resources towards defined common goals. It often refers to a company or group of companies.

(2) The practice of setting up and arranging such a group.

organizational behaviour (OB). The manner in which an organization may be said to act as an entity.

organization and methods (O & M). The study of how methods employed and arrangements made in organizing work lead to differing levels of achievement, efficiency and development.

organization chart. A diagramatic representation of an organization, usually in the form of a family tree, showing the functional arrangement of tasks, responsibilities and titles, and often the names of present incumbents. *See* FUNCTIONAL ORGANIZATION, MATRIX ORGANIZATION.

organization development (OD). A technique of managerial adaptation designed to change the arrangement of an organization gradually to improve its efficiency, flexibility, response to change etc. For a full explanation see W. French and O. Bell, *Organization Development* (2nd edn, Reading, Mass.: Addison Wesley, 1982).

Organization for Economic Development (OECD). A group of countries devoted to the improvement of trade and economic development through co-operation, founded in 1961. Members include Austria, Belgium, Canada, Denmark, Finland, France, Greece, Iceland, Ireland, Italy, Japan, Luxembourg, the Netherlands, Norway,

Portugal, Spain, Sweden, Switzerland, Turkey, the UK, the USA and West Germany. The OECD developed from the Organization for European Economic Co-operation, formed after World War II under the Marshall Plan.

Organization of American States (OAS). An international organization formed in 1948 to encourage co-operation and economic development in member states. These include Argentina, Barbados, Bolivia, Brazil, Chile, Colombia, Costa Rica, Dominica, Ecuador, El Salvador, Guatemala, Haiti, Honduras, Jamaica, Mexico, Nicaragua, Panama, Paraguay, Peru, Trinidad and Tobago, the USA, Uruguay and Venezuela. Canada is not a member, but attends as an observer.

Organization of Arab Petroleum Exporting Countries (OAPEC). An international organization, formed in 1968, whose members include Abu Dhabi, Algeria, Bahrain, Dubai, Egypt, Kuwait, Libya, Qatar, Saudi Arabia and Syria.

Organization of Petroleum Exporting Countries (OPEC). An international organization formed in 1960 to develop co-operation between the member countries, and also to provide an international lobby on matters of specific concern to them. Members include Abu Dhabi, Algeria, Indonesia, Iran, Iraq, Kuwait, Libya, Nigeria, Qatar, Saudi Arabia and Venezuela.

organization structure. The arrangement of functional roles within an organization. The structure consists of a basic plan of reporting hierarchies, decision mechanisms, and operating mechanisms, providing the necessary rules, procedures and lines of communication for day-to-day operation and stability. See J. Child, *Organizations: A Guide to Theory and Practice* (2nd edn, London: Harper & Row, 1982).

orientation programme. Induction training for a new task or set of working conditions.

OS/2. An operating system developed by IBM for the 1987 series of personal system computers (PS/2).

OU. *See* OPEN UNIVERSITY.

output. The result of production operation — for example, a product, service, presentation of information etc.

output device. A piece of computer-related equipment designed to provide information produced by the system in usable form (e.g. a printer or plotter).

output per manshift (OMS). A unit of efficiency, mainly used in the coal mining industry, to measure the productivity of an operation. The total output for the shift is divided by the number of men working during that period to obtain the average OMS.

outputs. For VALUE ADDED TAX purposes, the charges made by an enterprise to its customers.

out-source. To obtain materials from or require work to be carried out by another company or individual (the supplier or contractor).

overcapitalize. (1) To provide a company with more capital funding than can be justified by the nature or size of its operation.
(2) To overestimate the value of fixed assets.
(3) To overvalue the nominal capital of a company (this could be illegal, and depends on the circumstances involved).

overhead. *See* INDIRECT COST.

overhead absorption. The spreading of overhead costs across the whole range of a company's operations. *See* ABSORPTION COSTING.

overhead structure. The areas of an organization which do not contribute directly to the production of value (e.g. the supervisory, managerial, commercial, technical, clerical and financial departments).

overtime. Work done outside normal working hours, usually at an agreed special rate of pay.

overtime ban. A RESTRICTIVE PRACTICE technique designed to expose the extent to which a company is reliant upon overtime to complete its operations (and thus how under-resourced it is in terms of labour) and to create operating difficulties which will bring pressure to bear on the company, in support of a specific cause.

overtrading. The position of a company which has insufficient WORKING CAPITAL to support its level of operation, and is thus in danger of becoming insolvent.

own brand. A retailing technique of packaging goods with the retailer's name as the BRAND, often sold at a lower price than proprietary brands.

owner's equity. EQUITY in a company which belongs to the owner (i.e. the party which has a majority (or total) shareholding).

P

Paasche index. A pricing index invented by the German economist Paasche, used to compare the prices of items bought by a specific population during a period time (e.g. one year) with the prices of the same items in a specified base year.

PABLA (problem analysis by logical approach). A system of problem-solving used in improving design processes, using progress cards which must be completed at planned stages.

PABX. The acronym for a private automatic branch (telephone) exchange.

pacer. A fast worker used by management in time-setting activities to arrive at an unfairly low time allowance for a job.

pacing. Allowing time for operations, especially on a moving assembly line. The rate (or pace) of work is controlled by the machinery set by the supervisor.

package. (1) A parcel or an item specially protected for transportation.
(2) A group of facilities constructed around a central theme (e.g. a product or a defined service) in order to boost its sales or efficiency.
(3) Computer SOFTWARE consisting of a set of PROGRAMS written for a common purpose.

packing note. A document, similar to an ADVICE NOTE, enclosed with delivered goods, which lists all items enclosed in the package.

pack test. A marketing technique in which the packaging of a product is tested for consumer acceptability.

pac man defence. A technique in which a company threatened by raiders (e.g. an unwelcome TAKEOVER BID) returns the attack by bidding to reverse the takeover — usually this is a defence tactic, rather than a serious wish to merge.

paid-in capital (contributed capital). Money which a company receives as a result of issuing SHARES, consisting of the total FACE VALUE of the shares and the total PREMIUM paid for them.

paid-up capital. That part of the ISSUED CAPITAL of a company which the subscribers have been required to pay. When issuing SECURITIES the issuer may require only part payment of the issue price. The remainder is the uncalled capital, and may be called up at any time as the financial needs of the company dictate.

pallet. A carrying platform or container of standard size and shape designed for a specific purpose or product, to enable more efficient materials handling (e.g. by robot or machine tool).

palletized. (1) A system of materials handling designed to incorporate the use of PALLETS.
(2) The goods handled by such a system.

panel interview method (audit method). A personnel selection method in which a candidate is interviewed by several people. In this way interested parties are involved in the selection process making it both more efficient and more acceptable (e.g. to line managers).

Panel on Takeovers and Mergers. A UK committee consisting of prominent people in the City of London, charged with the responsibility of maintaining ethical practice in ACQUISITION matters.

paradigm. A set of personal values and norms which constitute a stable situation for an individual, technology or state. A major change (e.g. in technology) is said to cause a paradigm shift — requiring a reassessment of values etc. This is sometimes known as the 'risky shift' syndrome — a basis for resistance to change due to fear of the unknown. For a full explanation see T. Kuhn, *The Structure* *of Scientific Revolutions* (Chicago: University of Chicago Press, 1970).

parallel import. A product which has been imported into a country by someone other than the licensed importer.

parallel interface. A computer connection (e.g. between a computer and a printer) which carries parallel signals. The most common type is known as a CENTRONICS interface.

parallel pricing. An agreement between manufacturers or traders of similar products to increase their prices by similar amounts at the same time.

parameter. In economics, a quantity which remains constant in a given context. The term is commonly used as a synonym for a variable or a factor.

parent company. *See* HOLDING COMPANY.

Pareto analysis. A method of determining the relative importance of certain items within a population in terms of their contribution to the overall effect. It is chiefly used in inventory control to determine the stock items which account for the major proportion of overall stock value, and in sales and marketing to identify those products which provide the majority of sales value. It is often referred to as the 80:20 rule, since it is usually found that 20 per cent of items account for 80 per cent of overall value. *See also* ABC ANALYSIS.

parity. The equality (real or perceived) of fairness in pay of two or more groups of employees.

Parkinson's law. A semi-serious observation, originated by the UK author C. Northcote Parkinson, that 'work expands to fill the time available for its completion'. It is often borne out by experience, especially in related senses (e.g. required space increases to fill available space, and expenditure rises to meet income). There are several variations on the theme, causing the above to be known as 'Parkinson's First Law'. For a full explanation see C.N. Parkinson, *Parkinson's Law or the Pursuit of Progress* (London: John Murray, 1959).

part. A component of a product which is not itself an assembly of other items.

participation. The formal involvement of individuals in decision-making to which they would not previously have been privy.

participative management. A style of management based upon group decision-making and personal involvement. It has been widely studied by such theorists as Robert Blake and Jane Mouton, Rensis Likert and Douglas MacGregor. *See also* THEORY Z.

partnership. A business or professional unit based upon a formal legal agreement between two or more partners. It is not an incorporated company, which means that the individuals remain responsible for actions and decisions, and not the business unit itself.

part programming. A method of preparing numerical control information for manufacturing a product by designing machining or other processes for parts of the product one at a time.

parts list. A record of all parts and components required to assemble into a SUB-ASSEMBLY or product.

part-time. Anything less than full-time. In the UK, a part-time employee is one who is contracted to work less than 30 hours per week.

party plan. A selling technique using domestic parties to which prospective buyers are invited. A good example is 'Tupperware', which was initially only available through 'Tupperware parties'.

par value. (1) The FACE VALUE or nominal value of a share.
(2) The fixed value of a country's currency, as agreed by the INTERNATIONAL MONETARY FUND, in terms of the gold standard.

Pascal. A high-level computer language, named after the French mathematician Blaise Pascal, used for dealing with alphabetic data. It is widely used as a teaching language.

password. A unique, secret individual code used to enable an authorized user to enter a computer system or other protected device.

patent. An official record of specific rights awarded to an individual or group to prevent others from copying a design for goods or manner of procedure (e.g. a manufacturing process) invented by that individual or group for a specified time. In the UK this is 20 years, dependent upon payment of fees, although it is sometimes possible to extend this period after the first 16 years. Patents may be exchanged by firms, or individuals, as part of licensing agreements, particularly between different countries. Protection is normally national, and thus must be obtained in every country in the world to be truly effective. Reciprocal arrangements exist to which most countries subscribe, through the International Convention for the Protection of Industrial Property.

patent pool. An arrangement between groups of companies who agree to initiate licensing agreements automatically upon the issue of a new PATENT to one company for certain types of product or process. Legislation is to be found in the UK Patents Acts 1949, 1977.

paternalism. An attitude of managers to employees based upon the belief that subordinates can make only token contributions to decision-making (i.e. that a manager must take a parental role). Paternalistic management assumes that employees respond to generous conditions both in the workplace and in their personal life.

Paterson method. A JOB EVALUATION technique based on the degree of decision-making required in a job, devised by Thomas T. Paterson. For a full explanation see D. Torrington and J. Chapman, *Personnel Management* (2nd edn, Englewood Cliffs: Prentice-Hall, 1983).

pattern bargaining. A negotiating tactic which brings pressure to bear by referring to agreements made in other firms and/or unions.

PAV. *See* POTENTIAL ACQUISITION VALUATION METHOD.

pay as you earn (PAYE). A payment system whereby an employer deducts income tax at source from an employee's pay and remits it directly to the collector of taxes.

payback. The notion of receiving financial benefit as a result of an investment which justifies the investment.

payback method. An appraisal technique which determines the period of time over which the benefit must accumulate in order to pay back the original investment. *See* DISCOUNTED CASH FLOW.

payback period. The time in which it is expected the benefits resulting from an investment will return the original sum invested.

PAYE. *See* PAY AS YOU EARN.

payment-by-results (PBR). A payment system which links the level of remuneration to quantity of OUTPUT. *See* PIECEWORK; WORK STUDY.

Payment of Wages Act 1960. UK legislation allowing employers to pay employees by cheque where this is requested. In practice, employers prefer to pay in this way and often require the employee to make the request.

pay-off matrix. A technique for comparing the expected outcomes of a set of choices showing the best and worst cases for each option in the light of forseeable events (*see* DECISION RULES). The matrix shows the expected financial outcome from three strategies in the event of reflation of the economy or recession. The decision-maker makes a

		Event	
		Reflation £	Recession £
Strategy	Expand	+750,000	−420,000
	Maintain	+390,000	+150,000
	Cut-back	+210,000	+180,000

a pay-off matrix

strategic choice on the basis of each pay-off and the forecast event.

payola. A colloquial term referring to corrupt influence in business deals involving a paid informant or other form of bribery.

payroll. (1) A list of all employees who must be paid by a company.
(2) The total amount of money required per period to pay a workforce.

pay scheme. A formal arrangement of pay within a company explaining grading levels, SALARY ranges, MERIT RATINGS etc.

PBR. See PAYMENT-BY-RESULTS.

PC. See PERSONAL COMPUTER.

PC/DOS. A disk-operating system used in a PERSONAL COMPUTER.

PDM. See PHYSICAL DISTRIBUTION MANAGEMENT.

peek. In computing, the ability to access specific parts of the memory when using BASIC.

peer group. A group of people perceived by an individual as equals with whom comparisons may be made.

peer goal setting. A problem-solving technique in which a PEER GROUP sets goals to be met jointly.

peg. In currency terms, a synonym for PAR VALUE.

pegboard. A device for testing manual psychomotor skills and dexterity in general by timing various tasks which involve fitting pegs into holes in a board.

penetration pricing. The introduction of a new product to the market at a low price in order to maximize the volume (though not the value) of sales in the early stages.

pension. A payment made to an individual, usually after retirement from employment (but also possibly in respect of injury or loss of a relative etc). Pensions are funded by contributions by an individual and/or employer(s) throughout a working life, and are invested to provide financial strength for a pension fund. Retirement pensions are known as SUPERANNUATION. In the UK, the state provides both a STATE FLAT-RATE PENSION and a STATE-GRADUATED PENSION.

pension fund. A fund set up to receive contributions from employees, to manage the investment of money contributed, and to pay pensions to retired employees.

PEP. See PERSONAL EQUITY PLAN.

PER. See PROFESSIONAL EXECUTIVE RECRUITMENT.

P/E ratio. See PRICE−EARNINGS RATIO.

percentile. A statistical concept with different meanings for 2 types of distribution (n = a number between 1 and 100). For a probability distribution, the nth percentile is the value of the random variable when the distribution function equals $n/100$. The number n is called the percentile rank and the distribution is divided into 100 equal percentiles. For a frequency distribution, the nth percentile is the value of the random variable which is exceeded by $(100-n)$ per cent of the sample items.

per diem. Daily allowance.

perfect market. An economics concept for comparing reality with an imaginary base. In a perfect market, no buyer or seller can bring special pressure to bear to alter prices (e.g. by discounts), and all buyers and sellers are aware of each other; all relevant information is available free of charge.

performance. The notional measure of effort and achievement of an individual or group.

performance appraisal. A technique of measuring or assessing performance with regard to a standard performance (e.g. in physical tasks). The performance of a worker is compared to walking 4 miles per hour, as a notional performance standard of 100.

peripheral. A piece of equipment in a computer system other than the central processing unit (e.g. printer, disk drive etc).

perks. See FRINGE BENEFITS.

perpetual debenture. A DEBENTURE for which there is no fixed time for redemption.

perpetual inventory. A system of STOCK CONTROL involving a periodic physical check on the contents of a store.

perpetual improvement. A Japanese philosophy of never accepting the apparent solution to a problem. The assumption that all solutions are sub-optimal brings about the need for constant improvements.

per pro. *See* PP.

personal computer (PC). A microcomputer designed to be used by one person, rather than a shared facility. It is usually low-priced, with simple hardware (e.g. a processor, a keyboard, a VISUAL DISPLAY UNIT, disk drives and possibly a printer and a MOUSE).

personal equity plan (PEP). A UK government scheme to encourage individuals who do not usually invest through the Stock Exchange to do so by providing tax relief on the income from small amounts of income from shareholdings.

personality promotion. A selling technique using a well-known person who visits specific areas to promote a product.

personal space. A boundary layer which an individual maintains and which may only be penetrated by a sympathetic person. When two people are able to work closely together they may be said to share personal space.

personnel. (1) The people employed in a company.
(2) The function set up to manage the human resources of a company. This covers selection, training, retraining, welfare, pensions, employment, legal matters, social events etc.

PERT (Programme Evaluation and Review Technique). A technique developed in the USA by the US Navy and by the CEGB in the UK (among others) to plan, monitor and control the resources and progress of projects. The term has been broadened to include almost any use of a form technique (e.g. GANTT CHARTS). PERT covers CRITICAL PATH ANALYSIS and various other methods of networking.

Peter principle. The notion that 'in a hierarchy, every employee tends to rise in the organization until reaching his level of incompetence' when promotion stops. For a full explanation see R. Hull, *The Peter Principle: Why Things go Wrong* (London: Pan, 1970).

Peters, Thomas J. and Waterman, Robert H. Management authors who wrote *In Search of Excellence* (New York: Harper & Row, 1983). The principle of the work, which has since been employed by others, was to ask successful US companies about strategic factors which had made them successful, subsequently presenting the overall picture as a set of guidelines for others.

petty cash. A fund administered by a clerical or supervisory person to make small amounts of money available immediately for sundry purposes, accountable on a general basis.

phantom stock plan. A bonus payment system linking the pay of each employee to the increase in a company's SHARE price over a period, using a points rating.

physical distribution management (PDM). The planning, monitoring and control of distribution and delivery of manufactured goods, including the use of transportation, warehousing, agents and retail outlets.

Physiocrats. A group of 18th-century French economists who believed in a simple agricultural economy.

pick. To locate an item in stores and withdraw it for issue.

picking list. A computer-generated list which indicates specific items needed and the order in which they should be picked for maximum efficiency.

pick and place unit. A simple ROBOT-type handling device for moving goods or workpieces.

pictogram. A presentation technique combining the clarity of a diagram with the descriptive quality of a picture.

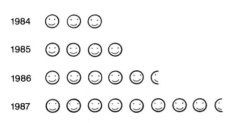

a pictogram

piece rate. An agreed amount of money to be paid to a worker or to a group of workers for production of one unit of OUTPUT. The rate is based upon agreed estimates of time required for the work and targets for overall (weekly) pay levels. It may be linked to a BONUS SCHEME.

piecework. A payment system derived from F.W. TAYLOR's SCIENTIFIC MANAGEMENT theory. Basically, it is a system of linking pay to ouput, using an agreed rate and method. Developed systems incorporate minimum wages and BONUS SCHEMES.

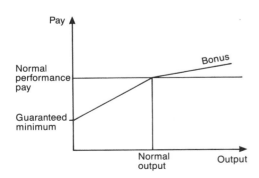

piecework

pie chart. A diagramatic representation of proportions of an overall amount (e.g. shares of a market), illustrated in plan view as slices cut from a round pie.

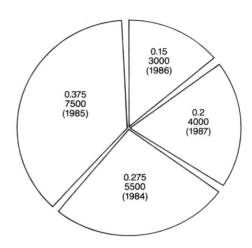

a pie chart

piggy-backing. The selling of another company's goods to complement a product range.

Pittler classification. A coding system for classifying items (e.g. components). It uses a nine-digit numerical code.

place utility. The activity of a company principally concerned with transportation and DISTRIBUTION of goods.

placing. The issuing of SHARES to a buyer or buyers without PUBLIC OFFER. The shares may be for private holding (i.e. not for sale) or for subsequent dealing on a STOCK EXCHANGE.

planning − programming − budgeting system (PPBS). An application of PROGRAMME BUDGETING.

planned maintenance (preventive maintenance). A technique of servicing or replacing equipment in line with a forecast of performance and reliability. The objective is to reduce unexpected downtime by preempting failures and problems.

planned obsolesence. The designing of a product so that it will need replacement within a certain period, to ensure future sales levels are maintained.

planning. (1) The function of preparing a series of events, within the constraints of time and resources, to achieve specific objectives.

(2) In operations management, matching capacity to demand.

planning blight. A drop in property values in an area following an announcement of planning approval for an unpopular building project nearby (e.g. a motorway).

plant. Premises and equipment used in the operation of a company, especially in the manufacturing or PROCESS INDUSTRIES.

plant engineering (plant layout). The function of applying structured management to the acquisition, planning, maintenance and replacement of plant.

plant layout. *See* PLANT ENGINEERING.

plc. *See* PUBLIC LIMITED COMPANY.

PLC. (1) *See* PROGRAMMABLE LOGIC CONTROLLER.

(2) *See* PRODUCT LIFE CYCLE.

PL/1 (Programming Language 1). A high-level, procedure-led computer language compatible with FORTRAN and COBOL.

plug-compatible. Computer equipment which is designed to connect to other items by the use of common standard plugs.

pluralism. A belief in the importance and feasibility of consensus in decision-making, especially in management and industrial relations.

PMTS. *See* PREDETERMINED MOTION—TIME SYSTEM.

point of information. A comment made in a debate which is neither in favour nor against a motion, but seeks to clarify a factual point.

point of manufacture. An identifiable point at which a certain proportion of a product's ADDED VALUE may be said to have accrued.

point of sale. The place where a product is displayed to a customer, and where a TRANSACTION takes place. *See also* ELECTRONIC FUNDS TRANSFER AT POINT OF SALE.

point of sale advertising. The promotional activity or devices employed at a POINT OF SALE.

points ranking (points rating). A JOB EVALUATION system based upon awarding points to specific job functions for responsibility, training, degree of autonomy, dexterity, decision-making etc. Jobs are ranked according to their total points, and graded accordingly for pay-level decisions.

points rating. *See* POINTS RANKING.

poison pill. A colloquial term for anti-TAKE-OVER tactics employed to make a company less attractive.

Poisson distribution. A PROBABILITY DISTRIBUTION in which the VARIANCE equals the average, named after the the French mathematician S.D. Poisson. It is widely used as a model for random events; for example, in the production of polythene sheeting there may be a constant probability of a blemish which makes the film opaque: the number of blemishes per square metre would make a Poisson distribution. It may be used to forecast the likelihood of a rare event happening a specified number of times, when there are many opportunities for it to occur.

policy. A stated position on a specific issue or subject. Company policy is recorded to provide guidelines for decision-making.

pp. Per pro. Beneath a signature on a letter, pp indicates an authorized deputy signing on behalf of the author of the letter.

PR. *See* PUBLIC RELATIONS.

population. (1) In statistical analysis, a group of people or items about which information is obtained, hence 'sample population'.

(2) The group of possible outcomes which may be envisaged for a specific course of action.

Porter, Michael. An influential writer on strategy, from the Harvard Business School. His major writings include *Competitive Strategy: Techniques for Analysing Industries and Competitors* (New York: Collier Macmillan, 1980) and *Competitive Advantage* (New York: Collier Macmillan, 1985).

portfolio. A collection of products, services, investments or SECURITIES upon which a business is based. The various items in a portfolio are interdependent, providing a viable overall business plan even though any one individual item might not be profitable when viewed in isolation.

portfolio management. A strategic method of balancing the various business enterprises of an organization as a PORTFOLIO, rather than as a series of independent activities. A method of portfolio management was developed by the Boston Consulting Group during the 1960s. *See* BOSTON BOX.

POSDCORB. Planning, organization, staffing, directing, co-ordinating, reporting and budgeting. A system of analysis of executive activities, developed by L. Gullick during the 1930s.

position statement. *See* BALANCE SHEET.

positive cashflow. Amounts of money received by a business.

post-entry closed shop. A CLOSED SHOP which accepts new employees on the condition that they join the union immediately upon appointment (i.e. new employees need not already be in the union).

post-industrial society. A concept of an alternative base for societal wealth creation following the adaptation of new technologies for all labour, possibly including the replacement of manufacturing industry by service sector operations as the main provider of wealth. For a full explanation see D. Bell, *The Coming of the Post-industrial Society* (London: Heineman, 1972).

potential acquisition valuation method (PAV). A structured evaluation method for investment appraisal.

power. The ability of an individual or group to bring about specific desired events through influencing the activities of other individuals or groups.

power of attorney. An authorization to act on behalf of another person.

PPBS. *See* PLANNING−PROGRAMMING−BUDGETING SYSTEM.

preceding year basis. A taxation method which bases the tax assessment for the current year on the income declared for the previous year.

predetermined motion−time system (PMTS). An anthropometry technique for estimating the time required for a complex activity (e.g. a sub-assembly task) by breaking it down into basic elements of movement for which accurate times have previously been determined. It is used in basic WORK STUDY.

pre-entry closed shop. A CLOSED SHOP which only agrees to the appointment of new employees who are already members of a specified union.

preference share. A special class of EQUITY in a company which may entitle the holder to payment of a fixed DIVIDEND irrespective of PROFITS and first consideration for repayment of the FACE VALUE of shares if the company is liquidated. Preference shareholders are not normally accorded voting rights at general meetings. The equity held by a company from the sale of preference shares is PAID-IN CAPITAL and cannot be reduced in the same way as other equity.

preferential debt (prior claim). In the case of a bankruptcy or winding-up order, a debt which must be repaid in full before other claims are made upon a company or individual.

preferential shop. A workplace in which membership of a specific union may be a prerequisite for new employees for certain types of work.

preferred ordinary share. A participating PREFERENCE SHARE (i.e. the shareholder may have voting rights).

preferred stock. The US equivalent of PREFERENCE SHARE capital.

preliminary expenses. Costs incurred in setting up a company which may be claimed against the first year's accounts even though they were dated before the start of trading.

premium. (1) An extra amount paid for something in order to secure its acquisition – usually as a result of the level of demand exceeding that of supply for the item.
(2) With respect to SHARES, the difference between the FACE VALUE and the price paid for a share.
(3) A payment made by a client to an insurance company for specific cover for a certain period.
(4) A prize.

premium bonus scheme. A PAYMENT-BY-RESULTS scheme in which a BONUS is paid over and above the standard rate, linked to time savings related to STANDARD TIME.

pre-production. An activity in a manufacturing company covering preparation for a new product, including design proving, production facility preparation etc.

present value. The worth of a future stream of returns or costs in terms of their value now. The purchasing power of an amount of money decreases over time as prices rise, thus an expected future income compares with a smaller amount of money available immediately. Standard tables are available for the DISCOUNT factor, and these must be applied to a future sum, dependent upon the number of years before the income would occur.

president. An individual who presides over a meeting or a company. The term is used particularly in the USA to denote the chief executive of a company.

Prestel. A viewdata system in the UK developed and run by British Telecom.

prestige pricing. A technique for attracting buyers for an item by increasing the price to imply special quality. It is used where potential buyers might shun a low-priced product despite its actual high quality or specification.

preventive maintenance. *See* PLANNED MAINTENANCE.

price–earnings ratio (P/E ratio). The ratio of a company's SHARE price to its EARNINGS PER SHARE figure for the current year.

price elasticity. The degree to which sales of a product are affected by its price (e.g. a drop in sales as a result of an increase in price).

price-fixing. An agreement by two or more competitors on the prices each will charge for specific products or services.

price-leader. A company which increases its prices first, usually followed by its competitors.

price lining. The pricing of several similar products at the same level even though their production costs may vary.

price mechanism. The means by which prices are regulated – either by market forces (e.g. the relationship between supply and demand), or by some legislative measure designed to bring about desired economic events (e.g. tariffs).

price plateau. The level at which a price is considered fair by the customer, as perceived by the supplier. It may be thought unwise to increase a price beyond such an established plateau, since the PRICE ELASTICITY may be such that sales would drop.

price ring. An agreement between manufacturers to increase prices together, rather than to compete, and thus drive up the price of their common products. This practice is illegal in most parts of the world.

price sensitivity. The degree to which the sales of an item are affected by an increase or decrease in selling price. *See* PRICE ELASTICITY.

pricing methods. Techniques used to determine the best price at which to market a product.

pricing policy. A decision on price levels set for products. This incorporates information on costs (of production, administration etc) and market factors (competition, PRICE SENSITIVITY etc).

primary labour market. Workers with narrow SKILLS, perhaps applicable to one type of work only.

primary legislation. The treaties which constituted the TREATY OF ROME. All other legislation passed by the EUROPEAN COMMUNITY is secondary legislation.

primary market. A market in which those who sell goods are the manufacturers or producers of those goods.

primary product. Goods which are the product or result of PRIMARY SECTOR operations.

primary sector. The organizations and activities of agriculture, mining and quarrying, fishing, and forestry (i.e. those in which the end product is not substantially altered by processing).

primary standard data (PSD). WORK MEASUREMENT TECHNIQUES employing a synthesis of activity times from predetermined element times.

prime cost. *See* DIRECT COST.

principal. (1) An amount of money invested.
(2) An individual who is represented by an agent or other deputy.

prior claim. *See* PREFERENTIAL DEBT.

private Act of Parliament. (1) The result of a successful private bill.
(2) An act that applies only to one individual or corporation.

private company. In the UK, a company whose shareholders are restricted in sale of EQUITY. SHARES of a private company are not bought and sold on the open market.

private placing. The issue of SHARES or SECURITIES for private sale (i.e. not on a STOCK EXCHANGE).

private sector. That part of commerce and industry consisting of business organizations not owned by a government.

privatization. The FLOTATION of a previously state-owned organization as a PUBLIC LIMITED COMPANY, often with some remaining government interest, perhaps of a special nature. It is seen as a political move rather than a purely economic one. *See* NATIONALIZATION.

proactive. A management style which takes the initiative to make things happen. *See* REACTIVE.

proactive inhibition. The tendency to adhere to known methods rather than learn new techniques, as a result of conditioning over a long period of time.

probability. The likelihood of an event occurring, usually expressed as a decimal number between zero and one. Probability theory is the branch of mathematics concerned with the concepts of prediction on a numerical assessment basis. This is applied to business management in the fields of forecasting and decision-making. Where there are two or more possible events, out of which one is certain to occur (e.g. either it will rain or will not), the arithmetic sum of their probabilities is one. *See* BAYES THEOREM.

probability distribution. The pattern of PROBABILITIES for a specific POPULATION using probability theory, mathematically expressed as a function. The function may refer to the items in the population (e.g. the number of women in the armed services over a period of time), or some random variable (e.g. the height of women in the army), in which case it is termed a frequency function. Probability distributions may compare with well-known phenomena which have been expressed as functions (e.g. NORMAL DISTRIBUTION, BINOMIAL DISTRIBUTION, POISSON DISTRIBUTION etc), and are used for testing the significance of a result by comparing it to an expected norm. This is known as STATISTICAL INFERENCE.

problem analysis by logical approach. *See* PABLA.

problem-solving technique. A method of approaching problem-solving along established lines (e.g. the KEPNER–TREGOE method of problem-solving by eliminating the temptation to 'jump to conclusions').

problem-oriented language. A high-level computer language designed to enable a computer user to solve problems simply by describing the factors involved.

procedure flow chart. *See* DATA FLOW CHART.

procedure-oriented language. A high-level computer language designed for specifying the procedures which should be encompassed by a computer's operating system (e.g. FORTRAN).

process. A series of events which takes place to alter the nature of material or information, for subsequent use. Manufacturing processes range from FLOW PRODUCTION (e.g. the production of oil) to batch processing (e.g. the machining of metal parts). *See also* BATCH MODE.

process audit. A technique in SOCIAL AUDITING developed at the Harvard Business School.

process chart. A diagrammatic representation of a process.

process control. A quality control approach based upon close, constant monitoring of a process to determine quickly when it is not performing to specification. Corrective action to avert serious or prolonged departure from the specification is taken immediately, and thus the process may be relied upon to produce little or no defective work.

process industry. An industry converting bulk materials.

process manufacture. (1) A manufacturing activity which involves continuous flow.
(2) Any manufacturing process through which a 'flow' or path of work may be discerned.

process intervention. The introduction of new ideas (e.g. new technology into an established process) for the purpose of improvement in efficiency etc.

process planning. The function of preparing facilities and resources for a necessary process, usually on a long-term basis.

processor. An electronic device which receives information, processes it and provides an output in the form of information or control signals. *See* MICROPROCESSOR.

procurement. *See* PURCHASING.

produce. (1) Primary food products.
(2) The act of manufacture.

producer market. An industrial market, that is, one in which the customers are industrial companies rather than individuals.

product analysis pricing. A marketing/pricing technique which determines the price at which to sell an item, based upon cost, market considerations (e.g. PRICE ELASTICITY), and perceived value to the customer.

product development. The activity involved in converting a design concept into a physical reality and matching it to its market requirement, in practical terms.

product differentiation. The designing of interdependent products to have related but clearly differing specifications, in order to appeal to specific sections of the target markets. For example, the standard model of a saloon car, the deluxe, the estate car version and the sports model are all differentiated products within a range.

product diversification. A strategic move aimed at reducing dependence upon one or a few types of product, perhaps to avoid commercial decline with changing technology or buyer requirements, or as the basis of expansion by broadening the manufacturing or sales operations.

production. (1) The function of manufacture.
(2) *See* OUTPUT.

production control. The function of balancing ouput with demand, with reference to the sales information and capacity factors. *See also* MATERIALS REQUIREMENTS PLANNING.

production engineering. The application of engineering principles and techniques to the design, planning and provision of facilities and resources required in a production process.

production flow analysis. A technique for cost reduction through improving the logic of a work path through a production process. *See* STRING DIAGRAM.

production line. A linear workplace designed to enable sequential operations to be interrelated in the course of manufacture.

production-oriented company. A company which bases its strategy on proven strengths in specific production processes and techniques.

productivity. The measure of production achievement or efficiency comparing the quantity of output with the use of necessary RESOURCES. Several methods exist, some based solely upon labour ratios (e.g. output per employee, value added per direct worker etc). The basic efficiency ratio of output to input is usually employed in some way.

product layout. A technique of arranging production facilities to suit the manufacture of specific products, or group of products. *See* GROUP TECHNOLOGY.

product life cycle (PLC). The concept of four discrete stages in a product's 'life'. The first is development, before the launch; the second is growth of sales following the launch; the third is maturity, once the product has become established and sales have reached their maximum rate; the fourth is decline, when the rate of sales begins to reduce and the product approaches withdrawal from the market. The dynamics and market factors of each stage are extensively studied in MARKETING; LIFE CYCLE COSTING also employs the concept.

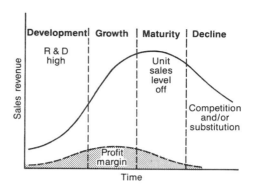

a product life cycle

product life cycle costing. A financial project appraisal technique which seeks to assess the validity of an investment on the basis of varying return over the life of the product which will be sold as a result of it. For example, during the development and early post-launch stages, the cost of the product (or service) to the company will by high and the revenue low. As sales increase, so the revenue increases and the investment begins to 'pay back'. During the maturity and decline stages of the PRODUCT LIFE CYCLE, no further costs of development should be encountered, so that the revenue from sales of the product consolidates the investment in a planned manner.

product line. A group of similar or related products marketed by a company.

product management. A method of apportioning managerial responsibility on the basis of products or product groups. The product manager has overall responsibility for all aspects of the product, from design and development, through production, to sales and marketing.

product mix. All the products produced or marketed by a company.

product-oriented company. A company which is driven by consideration of product details and technology rather than existing market factors.

profession. (1) An occupation controlled by an established group of practitioners who may be entitled to restricted entry (e.g. legal, medical, architectural etc).

(2) An occupation which requires a high degree of intellect and prior study.

Professional Executive Recruitment (PER). A division of the DEPARTMENT OF EMPLOYMENT concerned with locating unemployed professional people and identifying occupational opportunities for them. PER charges fees to employers, but not to individuals.

proficiency. A measure of individual ability to perform a specific task.

profile. A collection of PARAMETERS on a certain subject (e.g. personal details, expressed graphically in combination). It takes the shape of a graphical representation drawn from such details being listed along one axis with the value for each factor being plotted perpendicularly.

profiling systems. A JOB EVALUATION technique which uses profiles of specific factors in jobs (e.g. responsibility, degree of experience needed etc) to compare one with another for purposes of RANKING.

profit. The difference between REVENUE and expenditure over a certain period within specific conditions (e.g. before or after tax etc). This is basically the same as EARNINGS or margin, or, in some cases, income. Profit may be 'gross' — the difference between TURNOVER and the COST OF SALES (including all OPERATING EXPENSES), or 'net' — taking into account interest items etc. *See* NET PROFIT.

profitability. The measure of PROFIT in the light of the amount of expense required to generate it.

profitability index. A DISCOUNTED gross COST-BENEFIT ratio.

profit and loss account (income statement; revenue account). A statement of income over a specific period (usually a FINANCIAL YEAR), showing a summary of the revenue and expenditure of an enterprise. It is one of the the major performance measurement documents, the others being the BALANCE SHEET and the FUNDING STATEMENT.

profit centre. A department within a firm with designated targets for use of resources and contributions — in effect, a small company within a larger firm. The profit centre approach to cost accounting has become popular (following the COST CENTRE APPROACH) because it brings the commercial aspects of the business directly to the place of operation, and provides an incentive for improvement, based upon sharing responsibility.

profit margin. The PROFIT per unit of OUTPUT expressed as a percentage of price.

profit sharing. An incentive scheme for employees, based upon a periodic bonus payment linked to the degree of PROFIT made by the company.

profits tax. The forerunner of CORPORATION TAX in the UK.

profit—volume chart. A diagram which shows the level of profit to be expected from various volumes of production. It is similar to a BREAK-EVEN CHART.

pro-forma. An invoice sent to a client for settlement prior to the delivery of goods.

program. A computer command sequence written in formal language to direct the computer to carry out certain activities. When several programs are combined for complex multi-functioning, it is referred to as a suite or package.

programmable logic controller (PLC). A computer PROCESSOR designed to receive complex data on the status of specific production PROCESS facilities, providing OUTPUT in the form of information reports, control signals and error warnings (e.g. the central management HOST COMPUTER in DIRECT NUMERICAL CONTROL systems).

Programmable Read Only Memory. *See* PROM.

programme budgeting. The setting of financial targets for expenditure and achievement within a company on the basis of individual programmes or projects, rather than by departments or divisions.

Programme Evaluation and Review Technique. *See* PERT.

programmed instruction. *See* PROGRAMMED LEARNING.

programmed learning (programmed instruction). A computer-based technique for self-teaching methods. It was originally devised for the so-called 'teaching machines', which were non-interactive and therefore not successful. Programmed learning has been given a new lease on life with the advent of ON-LINE, USER-FRIENDLY computers.

Programming Language 1. *See* PL/1.

progress billing. *See* PROGRESS PAYMENTS.

progress chasing. An expediting function, particularly used by manufacturing companies, set up to sort out the many small problems which impede the progress of production work. Progress is sometimes said to contain 'head people' − responsible for thinking out the problems and making plans, and 'feet people' − who are required to move throughout the plant to accomplish the problem-solving tasks in a practical sense.

progressive customer. A consumer who is prepared to pay higher prices for goods or services of a higher specification or QUALITY.

progressive part method. A training technique in which the operator learns a task one part at a time, mastering each part on its own and then in conjunction with the subsequent part, before going onto the next.

progressive tax. An INCOME TAX for which the rate increases with the level of income. For example, in the UK in 1986, income (after allowances) up to £17,000 per annum was taxed at 29 per cent, and at 40 per cent above this level, and so on upwards. Levels may be determined by using SLAB SCALE or SLICE SCALE methods.

progress payments (progress billing; stage payments). Payments on account made by a client to a supplier to assist with the financing of a long project (e.g. the purchase of materials etc). Long-established as a necessary arrangement in building and heavy plant construction, the sharp increases in inflation and borrowing rates during the 1970s made progress payments a usual feature of any contract for capital equipment, often including a percentage of the contract price with an order, to enable work to commence.

project. A specific, discrete operation with defined start and finish points which requires special management to ensure completion on time and within a BUDGET. A project may be the design, development and introduction of a new product, implementation of new plant, or simply an INVESTMENT.

project assassin. An individual inside or outside a company who perceives a threat to the status quo which is currently to his advantage in a project.

project champion. An individual whose personal drive, vision and achievement may be identified as fundamentally important to the success of a project. Projects involving new technologies are often said to founder because of the lack of a project champion. For a full explanation see J. Langrish et al, *Wealth from Knowledge* (London: Macmillan, 1972).

project management (project planning). A special type of management activity chiefly concerned with the planning, execution and consolidation of a project of any type within the constraints set by the company and its environment. Project management has recently emerged as a crucially important technique for controlling costs and timescale in projects, in some cases preventing financial failure which might otherwise be experienced. In particular, the value of quantitative planning and control techniques has been realized. For a full explanation see D. Lock, *Project Management* (3rd edn, London: Wildwood House, 1986).

project network techniques. The application of NETWORK ANALYSIS for controlling a PROJECT.

project planning. *See* PROJECT MANAGEMENT.

project purchasing. The purchasing of items for a specific PROJECT in line with a project BUDGET, rather than within the terms of a specific department. This type of purchasing often calls for expedients, not normally used in purchasing, to ensure that timescales are maintained.

PROLOG. A high-level computer language used in ARITIFICIAL INTELLIGENCE applications.

PROM (Programmable Read Only Memory). A memory chip used in computer or MICROPROCESSOR control devices to perform a special function determined by the programming used.

promissory note. A document which records an agreement between two parties for one to pay the other a specific sum by a specific date. It is held by the party who is to be paid.

promotion. The elevation of an individual to a position of greater authority, responsibility or importance within a company.

promotional campaign. An activity to support the sale of a product or service by improving customer awareness.

promotional mix. The various techniques and methods which a company uses in combination to promote its business, particularly below the line. *See* ABOVE THE LINE.

proprietary insurance office. An insurance company which has shareholders. *See also* MUTUAL OFFICE.

prospectus. A public notice, published in advance, of the public sale of SECURITIES in a PUBLIC LIMITED COMPANY. The prospectus projects the company as a good investment, including details of performance to date, current worth and future plans.

prospectus issue. The issue of SECURITIES, based upon a PROSPECTUS, for public purchase. The prospectus is a legal requirement before shares are issued in this way.

protectionism. The support for a national industry or company provided by a government by preventing the import of competitive goods (or penalizing such import by heavy tariffs or other means). This is an extreme policy, usually limited to developing countries eager to boost their economy.

Protestant work ethic. The notion that 'to work is good', based upon the teaching that God works and therefore man should too. The philosophy was propagated by factory, mill and mine owners, closely involved in the Protestant church, in the UK during the 18th and 19th centuries, in order to discourage dissent or industrial unrest. The work ethic still has a great influence today.

protocol. (1) An agreed formal manner of conducting a meeting or other engagement.
(2) In computer communications, a sequence of commands based upon logical priorities.

provident benefit. A fund set up to receive contributions and provide financial support for its subscribers in times of need (e.g. prolonged absence from work due to illness). It is a technique especially favoured by TRADE UNIONS.

PSD. *See* PRIMARY STANDARD DATA.

psychodrama. A technique of creative BRAINSTORMING, based upon the unconventional idea of assuming the personality of inanimate objects (e.g a product, for purposes of improving its design).

psychological inventory. A psychological assessment technique based upon recording what an individual claims to think or feel.

psychological pricing (charm price). The use of prices which appear frequently and thus seem acceptable or normal to customers. '

psychological testing. Tests that are used widely in PERSONNEL selection. These include APTITUDE TESTS, personality tests and intelligence tests.

psychomotor skills. Skills which require co-ordination between thought and physical action.

public corporation. A CORPORATION founded by statute or decree to perform some public service (e.g. the British Broadcasting Corporation).

public limited company (plc). A limited company in the UK whose SHARES are bought and sold in public and quoted on the STOCK EXCHANGE. Such a company must use the letters plc after its name.

public relations (PR). The activity within a company responsible for dealing with the press, local residents, complaints etc. It is either part of the personnel management function (e.g. for statements on employment issues), or that of marketing (for generally improving the public image of the company). Major issues are dealt with as part of the duties of senior management, or handled on a long-term basis by public relations consultants.

public offer. A sale of SECURITIES in a company which is made public.

public sector. Those industries, organizations or companies which are owned by the state.

public utility. A community service (such as a mass transit railway), or supply (such as water), provided and maintained by a public or private organization.

pull-down menu. The visual representation of available options in a software package on a computer screen. A pointer on the screen can be moved (usually with a MOUSE) to select an option, which will then appear on the screen. This system has become popular with WORD PROCESSING and DESKTOP PUBLISHING systems. It was pioneered by Apple on the Macintosh computer. *See also* WIMP.

punched card. A data storage device used in early computer systems. It was replaced in the late 1970s by disk and tape storage.

punt. Any venture which is deemed to have only a limited chance of success.

purchase order. An official commitment of company funds to the purchase of goods or services. It may employ a BLANKET ORDER format, supported by MATERIAL CONTROL schedules, for VENDOR SCHEDULING of production items.

purchasing (procurement). A MATERIALS MANAGEMENT function responsible for buying all items required by a company. Purchasing denotes a strategic, planned approach to the procurement of materials and services, rather than the tactical nature of 'buying'.

purchasing agent. (1) An individual outside the company who purchases materials or services for them.
(2) A senior member of the purchasing organization in a group of companies or a multinational company, who has strategic responsibility for supplies.

Purdue tests. A series of PSYCHOLOGICAL TESTS developed in the USA.

pure strategy. In GAME THEORY, a simple choice move, rather than a series of interdependent sequential moves.

put option. An option to buy for which the holder (the prospective purchaser) must pay a fee, whether or not the transaction eventually takes place.

pyramid of ratios. A pyramid-shaped diagram containing interrelated FINANCIAL RATIOS appertaining to one company. The pyramid structure comes about as the result of one ratio feeds into the ratio down the pyramid and so on.

pyramid selling. A system of selling by agents. Each agent is originally a customer, who then buys the rights to sell the items on offer, subsequently selling similar rights to other customers and so on. Each customer thus becomes first an agent and then a managing agent, not selling the product but co-ordinating the selling activities of others.

Q

QA. *See* QUALITY ASSURANCE.

QC. *See* QUALITY CONTROL.

quadratic programming. A nonlinear programming OPTIMIZATION technique using quadratic equations when the factor which is to be optimized appears as a square.

quality. (1) A notional excellence giving rise to satisfaction in the user or customer.

(2) The degree to which a product or service fulfils its function or conforms to specification. The traditional idea of higher quality resulting in higher OPERATING EXPENSES has now largely been replaced by the realization that improved quality may reduce costs (by reducing SCRAP, REWORK, WARRANTY costs etc).

quality assurance (QA). A strategic function within a company aimed at ensuring long-term achievement of appropriate quality levels and targets, specifications, test and inspection procedures etc. It is responsible for defining and recommending quality policies.

quality circles (quality control circles). A Japanese technique, part of COMPANY-WIDE QUALITY CONTROL, developed by US and Japanese industrial engineers in the 1960s. The circles consist of groups of operatives who collectively employ formal and informal PROBLEM-SOLVING TECHNIQUES to find potential solutions to quality shortfalls and other subjects of relevance to the company and its employees. It is now used widely throughout the world in both manufacturing and service environments. Specific techniques and arrangements vary. Some circles meet during working hours, others after work, others employ a mixture of the two. It is generally agreed that membership must be totally voluntary − examples of failures usually indicate the shortcoming of coercion on the part of the company. They are often known by different names : for example, Corrective Action Teams (CATS);

Customer in Focus teams (CIF); and Big Brother/Sister movements (in Japan). For a full explanation see D. Hutchins, *Quality Circles Handbook* (London: Pitman, 1985).

quality control (QC). The operational function within a company responsible for carrying out quality policies through inspection and formal procedures.

quality control chart. A diagrammatic representation of conformance to specifications in a particular product or PROCESS. Various designs of control chart exist, usually comparing specific measurements or attributes with established norms or TOLERANCES, to show up any variations which may result in poor quality.

quality control circles. *See* QUALITY CIRCLES.

quality market. A market in which the quality of the product or service is considered to be more important to the customer than the price.

QUAGO (quasi-autonomous governmental organization). In the UK, a body set up by the government to report on or monitor some defined subject.

QUANGO (quasi-autonomous non-governmental organization). In the UK, a body set up by the government, and practically controlled by it, to report on or monitor a specific subject. For a full explanation see A. Barker (ed.), *QUANGOs in Britain: Government and the Networks of Public Policy-Making* (London: Macmillan, 1982).

quasi-autonomous governmental organization. *See* QUAGO.

quasi-autonomous non-governmental organization. *See* QUANGO.

quasi-professional organization. An organization formed by a group of people with a shared occupation which is not strictly a PROFESSION, but which has a similar nature (e.g. management consultants).

quartile. Quarters of the coverage of a DISTRIBUTION. For a FREQUENCY DISTRIBUTION this means the values of the RANDOM VARIABLE which are exceeded by the rest of the items; that is, the first quartile is that value which is exceded by 75 per cent of the items, the second, that value which is exceeded by 50 per cent of the items (also called the MEDIAN), and the third, that value which is exceded by 25 per cent of the items. In a PROBABILITY DISTRIBUTION, the first, second and third quartiles are the values of the RANDOM VARIABLE for which the distribution function is ¼, ½, and ¾ respectively. Quartiles are used to categorize items approximately: if an item is in the top quartile of a probability distribution it means that the function is more than 75 per cent.

questionnaire. A method of recording survey data in a formal written manner, for the purposes of subsequent comparison and DATA PROCESSING. Usually it is a form, filled in personally by a respondent, for a set of questions designed to discover required information. The object of a questionnaire is to ensure good validity and reliability in the information collected.

queuing theory. A branch of OPERATIONAL RESEARCH mathematics which seeks to analyse and understand the nature of queues as they occur in natural or actual circumstances.

quick ratio. *See* ACID TEST RATIO.

quorum. The number of members of an executive body (e.g. a group of shareholders or members of a committee) who must be present at a meeting for the decisions of that meeting to be binding upon the body. A meeting is thus described as quorate (or inquorate, if the number of authorized members attending is less than the quorum).

quota restriction. The limit agreed between two or more parties on an item of trade.

quotation (quote). (1) A formal indication of ability and willingness to provide a service or to supply goods. A quotation always records details of prices, payments, specification, delivery or timescale, and limits to responsilbility.
(2) The share price for a company listed on a STOCK EXCHANGE.

quote. *See* QUOTATION.

R

rabble hypothesis. A MOTIVATION theory which holds that each individual in a group will behave in accordance with self interest, so that the group becomes a rabble. It is the opposite of much sociological thinking which attributes behaviour to influences from other group members' interests.

Race Relations Acts 1968, 1976. UK legislation designed to remove the effects of racial prejudice in employment.

Race Relations Board. A UK organization, set up by the 1968 Race Relations Act to monitor progress and take legal action against transgressors where appropriate.

rack jobbing. A retailing technique whereby a WHOLESALER provides a rack full of goods for sale at an outlet, charging subsequently for items sold, by refilling the rack. It is especially popular for controlling POINT OF SALE operations.

R & D. *See* RESEARCH AND DEVELOPMENT.

raid. In a TAKEOVER bid, a planned buying rush on a company's shares in order to obtain a large holding before the company can prepare a defence.

rake-off. Improper income resulting from the arrangement of a deal.

RAM. *See* RANDOM ACCESS MEMORY.

random access memory (RAM; random access storage). That part of a computer system's memory which is made available to the user for short-term storage of data and mounting programs for use. The size of the RAM is measured in KILOBYTES, often referred to simply as 'K'. The larger the RAM a computer has, the more powerful programs it can operate (including storage of necessary input and output data).

random access storage. *See* RANDOM ACCESS MEMORY.

random sample. A SAMPLE of a specific size taken from a POPULATION which has been chosen so that any sample of items has the same PROBABILITY of being taken. This is important in STATISTICAL INFERENCE because it means that the sample upon which observations are based may be accepted as fair and unbiased.

random variable. A variable which takes on values according to its PROBABILITY DISTRIBUTION. For example, a normally distributed random variable will take on values in a certain range with the probability given as integral under the NORMAL DISTRIBUTION curve lying between the limits of that range.

random walk. A forecasting technique which deals with successive probabilities attached to events which may be seen as steps in a walk, joined by changes of direction, at random intervals and in random directions at each turn. If the walk exists within a fixed area, then, given sufficient time, all points in that area will be visited at least once. The technique is used in MARKETING to provide a random SAMPLE in a survey.

range. The difference between the largest and smallest values of an observed factor in the items in a SAMPLE.

ranking. The placing in order of importance. If several aims exist, they may be ranked in order of priority. Ranking coefficients may be employed to add weight to some factors within the order to allow for special circumstances or considerations.

rate buster. In the USA, an operator paid by PIECEWORK who works faster than the standard in order to earn more money. The rate for the job might be altered as a result, and thus the rate buster is frequently unpopular with TRADE UNIONS.

rate fixing (rate setting). A fixed rate for a job (especially in PIECEWORK) by discussion, possibly without formal measurement techniques.

rate of return. The degree to which the benefit from an investment compensates for the outlay. This usually consists of the ratio of the annual return (the amount of income attributable to the investment) to the amount of the original investment, expressed as a percentage. Long-term investments may make use of DISCOUNTED CASH FLOW TECHNIQUES to allow for inflation etc.

rate setting. See RATE FIXING.

rating. The process of measuring factors. In insurance, this is applied to the level of risk of a requested underwriting, and in television it is applied to the size of the audience.

rationalization. (1) The reconsideration of a company's resources and their use, with a view to improving the competitive position of the company.
(2) A reduction in the scope of operations in line with reduced company performance in the market.

rational management. A management style based on optimizing input/ouput ratios by the application of quantitative techniques. It is the opposite of PARTICIPATIVE MANAGEMENT.

ratios. FINANCIAL RATIOS referring to a specific company, used for assessment of performance, stability, potential etc. Normally simple ratios are used, comparing one factor as a proportion of the other (e.g. NET PROFIT as a percentage of TURNOVER).

Raven's progressive matrices. An intelligence test which uses non-verbal communication as the basis for assessment.

raw data. Information collected in a survey or experiment, before it has been processed for use in determining results.

raw materials. That part of INVENTORY which consists of items bought for use in a company's operation. This may consist of bulk materials, components, sub-assemblies and complete products. The categorization depends on the nature of the operation. The term is normally used in manufacturing operations, but service organizations also have identifiable raw materials (e.g. food supplies in a restaurant).

reactive. A management style based on taking executive action only when called upon to do so by a subordinate. See PRO-ACTIVE.

reactive maintenance. The policy of servicing or repairing items of plant only when a fault or breakdown occurs. This policy is more effective for some items than MAINTENANCE.

read only memory (ROM). A random access data storage device in a computer which cannot be overwritten (as opposed to RANDOM ACCESS MEMORY which normally can be overwritten). See also DRAM; EPROM.

real income. Disposable income. It is used as a national economic indicator, allowing for inflation etc.

real time. In computing, operations in conversational mode when the processor is dealing with information as it receives it, rather than being provided with data which is then processed in BATCH MODE. This enables records to be kept up to date, and changes in circumstances to be taken into account instantly.

receivable. A DEBT, or an amount of money, which may be expected to be paid to a company at some future stage.

recession. A period when an economy ceases to grow in terms of output, trade etc, or registers a decline. In a recession, investment is less attractive and companies tend to consolidate rather than to expand. Employment levels may fall as RATIONALIZATION takes place.

reciprocal trading. An agreement between two companies or countries which governs trade between them in various items. For example, one country may agree to buy another's motor vehicles, if in return it can sell them agricultural produce. This form of trading is particularly important for developing economies.

recommended retail price (RRP). The price for an item which a manufacturer suggests a retailer might charge.

redeem. (1) To settle an account.
(2) To pay off a loan or to buy back a SECURITY.

redeemable preference share. A PREFERENCE SHARE specifically designed to be bought back at some future stage.

redeployment. To find alternative employment for someone or something.

red—green—blue monitor. *See* RGB MONITOR.

red-ringing. The practice of ringing an employee's name in red ink on a printed list when the employee has reached the top of a payment range. An employee who is red-ringed may not be included in a general annual increase for merit, but only for basic rate increases.

reducing balance method. A DEPRECIATION method which considers the remaining value of items each year and applies a depreciation factor to that sum.

redundancy. The state of being surplus to requirement and legally provable. Redundancy may come about through company circumstances (loss of business etc) or personal situation (loss of skills etc). If proven, it may be a legal basis for dismissal.

reference group. (1) A group used for comparison and contract purposes in an experiment.
(2) A group of colleagues which an individual compares with on a personal basis in developing a PARADIGM.

reflation. The stimulation of an economy by support measures instigated by a government (e.g. investment incentives).

regional development. A policy of providing selective financial and moral support to specific geographical regions which are deemed to be in need of help. Policies on regional development are political and are liable to frequent changes.

regional management centre. A department of a business school or faculty of management and/or business which pays particular attention to a particular geographic region.

registered company. A limited or unlimited company, usually with shareholders, which has been incorporated under the COMPANIES ACTS, having complied with all required regulations.

registered office. The address which a REGISTERED COMPANY records upon incoporation. It is also the legal address for correspondence to that company.

registered trade mark. A legally-defined TRADEMARK owned by a recorded individual or group in the Register of Trademarks.

Registrar of Companies. In the UK, the government officer responsible for ensuring that new companies register and also that the requisite information on companies is available to the public.

regression analysis. A statistical technique used primarily in FORECASTING. The principle is to find the pattern of correlation between a 'dependent' variable (a factor which is being forecast) and one (simple) or more (multiple) independent variables which affect it.

regressive tax. INCOME TAX which has lower percentage rates at higher levels of income — thus favouring the better-paid.

reinsurance. The practice of 'backing-up' an insurance agreement by finding a reinsurer to indemnify the insurer on specific parts of the claim.

related company. A company in which another holds a substantial stake (over 15 per cent), thus holding influence while not being a majority shareholder.

relation analysis. An organizational analysis technique, developed by Peter DRUCKER, used to assess relationships between managers within a company. He also developed two other such techniques: ACTIVITIES ANALYSIS and DECISION ANALYSIS.

relaxation allowance (compensating rest). An allowance made to basic time in WORK MEASUREMENT to allow for the incidental use of time over prolonged periods, depending on the nature of the job.

relevance analysis. A technique for assessing the relevance or importance of individual or grouped RESEARCH AND DEVELOPEMENT projects to an overall programme plan.

reliability. (1) The degree to which an item continues to perform to a specification over an expected period of time.
(2) The degree to which the information gathered in a survey might be regenerated in an identical form if a similar survey was carried out at another time.

remuneration. Money paid to an individual as a result of an occupation.

reorder cycle. The period between replenishment orders in STOCK CONTROL.

reorder point (ROP). The stock level of an item at which a replenishment order should be made to avoid running out of stock during the time taken for a new delivery to be made.

reorder quantity. The standard quantity of an item to be ordered whenever the RE-ORDER POINT is reached or the REORDER CYCLE is complete, depending on the system being used.

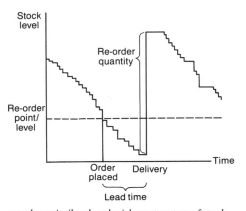

reorder point/level replenishment system of stock control (one item)

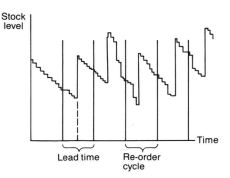

reorder cycle replenishment system of stock control

repeat business. Further work for an existing customer; possibly proof of satisfaction with prior performance.

repeat demand. Consumer demand for items which are purchased regularly (e.g. toothpaste).

replacement analysis. An OPERATIONAL RE-SEARCH technique designed to predict life cycles of pieces of plant to provide efficient policies of updating and renovating facilities.

replacement demand. A demand for durable items or capital plant which are only purchased as replacements for worn-out items (e.g. an electric toaster). The reason for replacement may not be functional obsolescence; technological developments or fashion may make the item 'out of date'.

replacement theory. A technique in DIS-COUNTED CASH FLOW which aims to predict the best time to replace items on financial terms (allowing for inflation, second-hand prices, changing maintenance costs etc).

replenishment system. A STOCK CONTROL system based on estimated usage rate and delivery lead time for each item. The principle is to avoid running out of stock of an item by ordering a replenishment delivery at a predetermined point, in order to use up a safety stock amount during the time it takes for the delivery of the items. The replenishment point may be a stock level or a point in time, depending on the policy. In either case (and more complicated systems have developed, combining the two), the system requires safety stock and relies upon standard delivery lead times and usage rates — both factors are liable to vary. *See* REORDER CYCLE; REORDER POINT; REORDER QUANTITY.

reporting by responsibility. The provision of information to individuals on the basis of the 'need to know', rather than providing everyone with all available data.

representational right. The right of a TRADE UNION to represent the interests of a member, short of negotiating terms of employment or pay.

resale price maintenance. The practice, made illegal in the UK in 1964, whereby the manufacturer of an item dictates at what price it should be sold by the retailer.

research and development (R & D). The function within a company, responsible for discovering new ideas, or new applications of old ideas, which might be to the commercial advantage of the company at some point in the future. A company's strategy will limit the scope of R & D to those areas which are deemed feasible within overall plans, but allowances should always be made in such planning for unforeseen factors which could alter strategy.
  The degree to which R & D is linked to current operations depends on the type of company and its strategy. For example, 'blue sky' R & D may be without clear relevance to today's products or services but deemed important for future operations. The complexity and costs of new technologies may require the company to collaborate with others to carry out R & D.

research associations. Organizations set up to encourage research projects, often between industrial and academic partners. All types of research are now covered in this way, often by benevolent foundations, started by a major investment and funded by the interest income. Trade and industry sector organizations often set up research establishments (e.g. the British Food Manufacturing Industry Research Association at Leatherhead in the UK).

research councils. QUANGOs set up to co-ordinate academic and industrial–academic research into specific areas (e.g. the Science and Engineering Research Council in the UK).

reserve currency. A currency that is kept in a country's official reserves (e.g. US dollars).

reserve price. *See* UPSET PRICE.

reserves. Retained PROFITS which are not allocated to a specific future purpose (e.g. tax).

resource. Something which is available to a company or individual to achieve its purpose. Resources are usually categorized into finance, property, premises, plant/equipment, personnel, and materials.

resource smoothing. The planning or scheduling use of resources to remove periods of very high or very low utilization.

responsibility accounting. A system which sets up specific centres within a company to take responsibility for financial transactions. *See* PROFIT CENTRES.

restrictive endorsement. Endorsement or approval which specifically stops the individual who receives the endorsement from using it to endorse other people or items.

restrictive practice. A policy of organized labour to control the way in which work is organized, particularly with respect to new technologies, in order to preserve consideration for the interests of the workforce.

retail audit. A market research survey based upon retail outlets.

retail banking. The personal business of a bank (e.g. current accounts).

retailing. The practice of buying consumer goods from WHOLESALERS or manufacturers for sale to the public through shops.

retail multiple. A retailer who has many outlets, often using the same trading name and style, covering a wide geographic area.

Retail Price Index (RPI). A UK index designed to show the purchasing power of currency with regard to a basket of consumer item prices.

retained earnings. The sum of money left of a company's PROFITS after payment of TAX, INTEREST and DIVIDENDS.

retention. The witholding, by agreement, of money due to a contractor at the completion of a contract, until it is clear that the work has been satisfactorily carried out.

retirement benefit. A sum paid to an employee upon retirement in addition to a PENSION.

retrogressive consumer. A customer who wishes to pay less for a product and will accept a lower specification in return.

return. (1) A financial benefit resulting from some specific financial activity.
(2) A statement of financial activity for official purposes (e.g. a tax return).

return on assets managed (ROAM). The financial benefit (TURNOVER less cost of goods) derived by a business as a result of using specific ASSETS. The ROAM is a key indicator of performance.

return on capital employed (ROCE). The financial benefit derived by a business expressed as a percentage of the CAPITAL EMPLOYED in obtaining it.

return on investment (ROI). The return achieved expressed as a percentage of a specific investment.

returns. Goods which have been sold but sent back by the customer for some reason (e.g. poor quality).

revaluation. (1) A government decision to raise the value of its currency against international standards, in accordance with new factors in its economy.
(2) A new assessment of the value of a company's ASSETS for purposes of updating the figures on a BALANCE SHEET etc.

revenue. Money received by a business as a result of its trading activity.

revenue account. *See* PROFIT AND LOSS ACCOUNT.

reverse takeover. A MERGER between two companies in which the smaller company gains effective control of the larger.

revolving loan (continuous credit). An overdraft or similar CREDIT facility with a fixed credit limit (e.g. a credit card).

rework. Corrective action to make goods saleable despite initial rejection in the production stage.

RGB monitor (red−green−blue monitor). A colour VISUAL DISPLAY UNIT for use with computers, with a higher picture/character definition than a normal television set.

right of recourse. The right to recover a bad debt.

rights issue. An issue of new SECURITIES for purchase by existing shareholders (or holders of other securities) only. Each shareholder is offered new securities and may accept or decline the offer. Alternatively, he may sell the rights, or sell the securities 'cum rights'.

ring. A group of people who collaborate for commercial purposes (e.g. to bid in an auction) for mutual but separate benefit.

ring-fenced. Items in a set of accounts which are not to be integrated into the main figures for some special reason.

risk. (1) Something covered by an insurance policy.
(2) Probability of failure.

risk analysis. An OPERATIONAL RESEARCH technique employed in decision-making to estimate the probabilities of forecasts being wrong at various points in the future, and the implications of such errors. *See also* GAME THEORY; UTILITY THEORY.

risk capital. Finance made available for a venture in a risky area of business. Risk capital is usually made available for ventures which, if successful, should produce a high financial yield.

risk manager. A specialist insurance underwriter who deals in risk estimation and long-term policy.

risky shift. The perception of an individual who is asked to accept a new PARADIGM as a result of changing circumstances (e.g. a new technology), and who is naturally cautious of embracing the unknown.

ROAM. *See* RETURN ON ASSETS MANAGED.

robot. A programmable, computer-controlled mechanical handling device, used in various manufacturing environments. It may be equipped with vision, touch sensitivity, voice recognition and machine intelligence.

robotics. The study of the development and application of ROBOTS.

ROCE. *See* RETURN ON CAPITAL EMPLOYED.

Rogers, Everett. *See* ADOPTION THEORY.

ROI. *See* RETURN ON INVESTMENT.

role. An individual activity or behaviour pattern.

role ambiguity. Frustration felt by an individual who is unclear as to the role required for his position.

role conflict. Frustration experienced by an individual who is required to take two roles which have conflicting objectives.

role play. A training technique in which trainees assume defined roles in specific situations for learning purposes.

rolling plan. A strategy statement covering a standard future period (e.g. five years ahead), which is updated annually to allow for changing circumstances. *See* STRATEGIC PLAN.

ROM. *See* READ ONLY MEMORY.

ROP. *See* REORDER POINT.

Rowan incentive payment system. A method of calculating a premium BONUS in terms of time saved on a particular operation.

royalties. Fees paid to an author in respect of sales of a published work.

RPI. *See* RETAIL PRICE INDEX.

RRP. *See* RECOMMENDED RETAIL PRICE.

RS232. A computer connection; a standard serial interface for connecting PERIPHERALS such as printers etc.

Rucker plan. An incentive scheme similar to the SCANLON PLAN.

running costs. Expenses incurred in the daily operation of a business or project.

running yield. The income derived from an investment expressed as a percentage of the amount invested, on an annual basis.

S

SA. (1) *See* SOCIEDAD ANÓNIMA.
(2) *See* SOCIÉTÉ ANONYME.

safety officer. An individual within a company who monitors adherence to codes of practice and laws relating to safety at work. The HEALTH AND SAFETY AT WORK ACT 1974 also requires the safety officer to report on accidents etc, and to make employees aware of their obligations and rights with respect to themselves and others.

safety representative. An honorary position instituted by the HEALTH AND SAFETY AT WORK ACT 1974. The safety representative is an employee (often a trade union official) with specific responsibilities and powers under the Act, to ensure that SAFE WORKING CONDITIONS and practices are maintained.

safety stock. *See* BUFFER STOCK.

safe working conditions. Under the HEALTH AND SAFETY AT WORK ACT 1974, the FACTORIES ACT 1961 and the OFFICES, SHOPS AND RAILWAY PREMISES ACT 1963, an employer must provide conditions of work which all parties (employer, employee and authority) agree to be safe. Once these conditions are provided, the employee shares responsibility for correct use of facilities, and thus safe working.

salary. A fixed regular payment to an employee, expressed as an annual amount of money.

salary band. *See* SALARY GRADE.

salary bracket. *See* SALARY GRADE.

salary classes. SALARY GRADES used specifically in calculations for pensions etc.

salary club. A communications network between employers, usually in geographical proximity, and often in the same type of business, through which salary levels etc may be discussed informally. In this way each company benefits from comparing their own position with that of neighbouring firms.

salary grade. A specified position within an ORGANIZATION which is defined by the salary paid to the person who occupies it. Salary grading is a common method of defining the hierarchy of an organization, by relating individual functions in terms of salaries paid.

salary progression curve. A graphical projection of salary increasing with length of service or age, used to determine an appropriate salary level for an individual employee.

salary sacrifice. The practice of reducing an employee's salary level, paying the amount of reduction in another form (e.g. into an ENDOWMENT account or other investment).

salary structure. The manner in which an ORGANIZATION fixes levels of remuneration (salaries) to various grades of employees, including interlinking of grades and scales of increments.

sale and leaseback. An arrangement whereby a company or individual sells something to another party and then LEASES it from them. This is usually done with property for tax reasons (e.g. the lease rental may be claimed as tax-deductible expenses, whereas owning the building would not provide such a desirable situation).

sale or return. An arrangement whereby a supplier agrees to accept items returned from the customer who is unable to retail them (e.g. unsold newspapers are returned by newsagents to WHOLESALERS). The supplier will award some credit for the returns, often 100 per cent of the price paid for the items.

sales. The provision of goods or services for which a company or individual receives income.

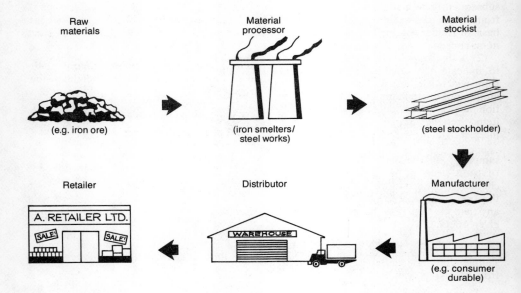

Raw materials (e.g. iron ore) → Material processor (iron smelters/steel works) → Material stockist (steel stockholder)

Retailer (A. RETAILER LTD.) ← Distributor (WAREHOUSE) ← Manufacturer (e.g. consumer durable)

a sales chain

sales audit. A quantitative analysis of sales on the basis of relevant parameters – by product, by region, by month etc.

sales chain. The passage of a product between manufacturer and consumer – traditionally comprising agents, DISTRIBUTORS, WHOLESALERS, and retailers.

sales coverage. The degree to which a sales force can cover the potential client base in a specified area.

sales depth test. A detailed analysis of a sales administration procedure.

sales ledger. The formal accounts record of goods or services which have been sold by a company. For a business operating on credit, this is sometimes called ACCOUNTS RECEIVABLE.

sales mix. The desired or actual mixture of products which are currently being sold.

sales operation planning and control. A MANAGEMENT INFORMATION SYSTEM based upon sales performance.

sales order processing (SOP). The acceptance procedure for customers' orders for goods or services. The orders will vary in their format and must be processed to be fed into the company's system for action. This is a critical part of the supply chain and one which has been substantially improved by new computer software systems in many cases. The time for an order to pass through the process is sometimes called the response time of the company.

sales planning. A strategic approach to organizing a sales effort. A comprehensive plan showing product or services details and volumes of sales planned for each enables the performance of a sales department to be more closely monitored.

sales promotion. An advertisement or public awareness campaign for a particular service or product designed to increase sales levels.

sales revenue. *See* TURNOVER.

sample. (1) A small number of items chosen at random from a population which are subjected to some analysis. Observations may subsequently be made about the population from which the sample was drawn on the basis of results obtained from inspecting the items chosen.

(2) A small portion of something provided to indicate the qualities of the substance from which it is taken. This may be an example of a component, provided for inspection purposes, or a special presentation of an item, free of charge, intended to create interest from prospective customers.

sampling distribution. The PROBABILITY DISTRIBUTION of a RANDOM VARIABLE characteristic or statistic of a sample showing the occurrence pattern for that statistic in any sample that may be chosen from the given population.

sampling error. The degree to which a sample does not represent the population from which it is drawn.

sampling frame. A catchment of the population for a survey from which a sample may be chosen.

sampling order. An initial order for a small quantity of an item, made by a customer for exploratory purposes.

sandwich course. A course of full-time higher education which includes periods of experience in industry or other practical, relevant employment as part of the learning process. It is found mainly in polytechnics (e.g. business studies) and some universities.

sapiential authority. The notion that authority is respected in some individuals on the basis of their innate wisdom and experience.

SAPPHO (Scientific Activity Pattern Predictor from Heuristic Origins). A UK research project carried out in 1971–2 by the Science Policy Research Unit of the University of Sussex, into the factors which enable manufacturing companies to make the best use of new process technologies. See C. Freeman, *The Economics of Industrial Innovation* (2nd edn, London: Francis Pinter, 1972).

satellite. A supplier company which is strategically dependent upon one major client and locates close to the manufacturing plant.

satisficing. The reaching of a compromise, usually sub-optimal.

satisfiers. *See* HERZBERG'S TWO FACTOR THEORY.

SBU. *See* STRATEGIC BUSINESS UNIT.

scab. *See* BLACKLEG.

scalar principle. An organizational theory that authority should exist in single personal links only (e.g. each member of a company receives instructions only from one immediate superior, who has in turn only that one subordinate).

scalogram. A data analysis technique, invented by Louis Gouttman, which uses visual representation to clarify a complex position.

Scanlon plan. An incentive scheme invented by the US trade unionist, Joseph Scanlon. The principle is to reward production workers by paying them a BONUS made up from financial savings resulting from improvements in performance. The nature and extents of improvements and cost savings are decided by a committee, comprising management and labour representatives.

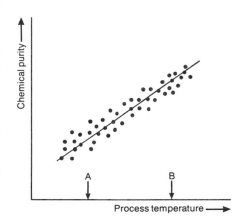

scattergram: temperature v purity

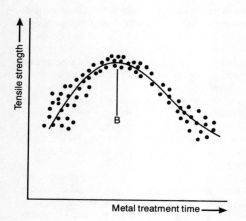

scattergram: metal treatment time v tensile strength (example of scattergram)

scattergram. A graph on which the points are not connected by lines in the usual manner. The main purpose is to show how the points form groupings.

scenario generation. *See* SCENARIO-WRITING APPROACH.

scenario-writing approach (scenario generation). A FORECASTING technique in which a series of expert predictions are combined and extended to form the basis of a broad series of events which might follow a specific set of events. *See also* BRAINSTORMING; DELPHI TECHNIQUE; NORMATIVE FORECASTING.

schedule. (1) A plan of events with respect to time.

(2) A list of supportive or explanatory details attached to a document.

(3) A taxation class in the UK (e.g. Schedule D covers self-employment).

science park. A high-technology industrial development area situated close to a centre of learning. The idea is to encourage progressive companies (particularly manufacturing) to locate in premises which are close together − thus generating high-technology-based employment for a region, and to make use of potential collaborators within a university or polytechnic, in order both to reduce the costs of RESEARCH AND DEVELOPMENT and to improve the practical learning experience of the research staff and students.

scientific management. A theory relating to worker motivation and work measurement, based largely upon the work of the US engineer Frederick W. TAYLOR. The principal tenet is that managers should define the one best way of doing any particular job, using scientific methods, and that the selected and trained operators should then follow instructions without deviation. In this way, the operator becomes an extension of the mechanical task and may be measured as such, while the manager's task is to derive the greatest benefit for both company and employees from the overall operation.

The motivational theory derived from this is that an operator would work harder if offered greater extrinsic incentives (e.g. more money). This gave rise to the idea of PIECEWORK and hence formed the basis of payments systems used during the 20th century.

scrap. (1) Material which becomes unusable excess as a result of a production process.

(2) Faulty items resulting from poor work, which may or may not be recoverable by rectification.

scrambled merchandising. The use of unconventional PRODUCT MIXES in RETAILING to increase overall sales levels (e.g. supermarkets selling clothing).

screening. A process of selection (of people, ideas product names etc) designed to prevent future problems by recognizing potential weaknesses and strengths.

scrip. The abbreviation of subscription receipt, and a general term for any SECURITY.

scrip dividend. A payment of a DIVIDEND in further securities in lieu of cash.

scrip issue. An issue of shares, free of charge, to existing shareholders.

seal. The unique sign of a person, company, institution etc, formed by pressing a metal form into warm wax, often at the bottom of a signed document. Although less frequently used in present-day business, the legal character of a seal is still of great importance in many transactions.

SEAQ. *See* STOCK EXCHANGE AUTOMATED QUOTATIONS SYSTEM.

seasonal. The description of some factor which varies in relation to the time of year at which it is observed.

seasonal index. The index used to provide seasonal adjustments. *See* TIME SERIES FORECASTING.

seasonality. The variation in some factor which may be observed to follow a similar pattern each year (e.g. the sale of lawn-mowers might be expected to rise in spring and decline in autumn).

seasonally-adjusted. Figures which have been calculated from actual results and some SEASONAL INDEX, to arrive at levels which might be expected if there were no SEASON-ALITY effect.

secondary banking sector. Banks, other than the main national CLEARING BANKS, which offer a range of facilities (e.g. cash withdrawal cards, credit cards, cheque books etc).

secondary market. A market in which items are produced by one party but sold by another. The item may be a product, service or security.

secondary penetration. The adoption of a product by its TARGET MARKET at the second attempt.

secondary picketing. The picketing of a workplace by union members who are not employees of the company being picketed. In the UK, the practice is limited by law in terms of numbers of pickets and their rights.

secondary sector. The sector of industry in which goods are produced from RAW MATERIALS (i.e. manufacturing).

secondary worker. An individual who works part-time, often in an informal arrangement, as a result of their situation (e.g. a retired person).

secondment. A form of benevolent support whereby a company or organization provides one or more of its employees, free of charge, for a specified period of time, to carry out duties in another company or organization (e.g. a voluntary youth training scheme or a charity). The secondment amounts to financial support (the individual's salary) and technical help (his skills).

Secretary of State. A senior member of government with responsibility for a whole department.

secured creditor. A CREDITOR who has some arrangement to cover a debt, partially or wholly, by a MORTGAGE or charge on the property of the DEBTOR.

Securities and Exchange Commission. In the USA, the national office responsible for maintaining proper practice in all dealings in SECURITIES.

Securities and Investments Board (SIB). The body set up in the UK under the Financial Services Act 1986 to supervise investor protection and investment businesses generally, including SECURITIES trading. The SIB oversees the day-to-day regulation of the markets which is conducted by the SELF REGULATORY ORGANIZATIONS. The SIB is ultimately responsible to the Secretary of State for Trade and Industry.

security. (1) SHARES, DEBENTURES, BONDS and STOCKS. One party (the issuer) gives the security to another (the bearer), to record the receipt of money and the rights of the bearer to some agreed benefit (e.g. voting in a company ANNUAL GENERAL MEETING). Securities may become the subject of trading (e.g. shares on a STOCK EXCHANGE).
(2) A deposit left by someone as guarantee that something will be done, or not done, on penalty of losing the security in case of default.
(3) Provision made to guard against loss or damage as a result of intrusion, robbery etc.

security export controls. National restrictions on the types of goods which may be exported – usually applied to items of defence technology which are seen to be of strategic importance to a country. Limitations may also be placed for political reasons (e.g. limitations on the sale of arms to a country whose regime is considered unacceptable). Control is usually exercised through the use of licences.

security of tenure. The right of an individual to remain in a current position of employment or residence.

SEFIS (Small Engineering Firms Investment Scheme). A two-phase UK government incentive programme designed to encourage investment in strategically important technologies (e.g. microelectronics) in manufacturing. Set up in 1980, the scheme provides grants to small engineering firms to assist with capital expenditure.

self-actualization. The motivational concept of achieving personal creative goals or realizing one's potential.

self-administered fund. A PENSION fund run by an employer designed to provide the required future sums of money from long-term, fairly simple investments made at the present time (e.g. annuities), rather than more complex investment in SECURITIES. The fund is intended to require a minimum of management and to provide only what will be required for employees' pensions. See also DEPOSIT ADMINISTRATION FUND.

self-assessment question. A question included in a DISTANCE LEARNING test, designed to check the comprehension of the reader by referring to points covered in the preceding pages.

self-employment. The state of conducting a business activity on one's own behalf as a SOLE TRADER.

self-fulfilling prophecy. A statement of forecast which is likely, as a result of being made, to bring about the events which it predicts.

self-liquidating premium. A special extra feature which is offered to boost sales, but which is actually covered in cost terms by the price charged for an item.

self-optimizing control. See ADAPTIVE CONTROL.

Self Regulatory Organizations (SROs). The self regulators, responsible to the SECURITIES AND INVESTMENTS BOARD, which cover the different components of the financial services industry (i.e. The Securities Association; The Association of Futures Brokers and Dealers; The Financial Intermediaries, Managers and Brokers Regulatory Association; The Investment Management Regulatory Organization; and The Life Assurance and Unit Trust Regulatory Organization).

sellers' market. A situation in which demand exceeds supply, so that a PREMIUM may be charged for an item and will be willingly paid by buyers to secure a purchase.

selling costs (selling expenses). Amounts paid by a company in the process of MARKETING and selling its goods.

selling expenses. See SELLING COSTS.

selling price. The price at which a company's goods are offered to the market.

sell short. To agree to sell items which are not currently possessed but which, it is expected, will be acquired before the required delivery date.

semi-fixed cost. See SEMI-VARIABLE COST.

semi-manufactures. Items which consist of RAW MATERIALS, partly processed towards being end products and which are subsequently supplied to manufacturers for completion.

seminar. A discussion session led by a specialist in the subject to be covered, usually on the basis of some previously circulated written material.

semi-skilled work. Work which is related between UNSKILLED WORK and SKILLED WORK, usually on the basis of a requirement for dexterity but not decision-making or judgment.

semi-variable cost (mixed cost; semi-fixed cost). An operating cost which will increase with a rise in output, but not in strict proportion. For example, labour cost is variable in proportion to production output, but the cost of supervision will only increase with a substantial increase in output (as a further supervisor is required for extra operators). The cost of supervision is thus semi-variable. The diagram shows an example of semi-variable cost. As the amount of produce stored in warehouses increases, the cost of holding it (insurance, capital, extra staff etc) increases proportionately. At certain points it is necessary to open a new warehouse, hence incurring extra fixed costs. *See also* BREAK-EVEN CHART.

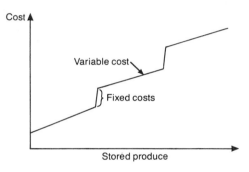

semi-variable cost

sensitivity analysis. A method of analysing how an estimated outcome might vary as the result of variations in the factors upon which it is based. *See also* RISK ANALYSIS.

sensitivity training. A behavioural training technique using LABORATORY TRAINING.

sensors. Devices in control systems used to monitor specific factors by receiving signals.

separable programming. A mathematical programming technique employing multi-factor, neo-linear approximation for non-linear constraints.

sequence arrow. A part of a NETWORK diagram showing the sequence of events within a network.

serial bond. One of a number of connected BONDS which mature individually over time.

serial correlation. a simple TIME SERIES FORECASTING technique.

serial interface. A computer connection device through which data is transmitted and received in serial mode (i.e. one BIT of data at a time). *See* RS232.

serial storage. A BATCH MODE computer storage device which works on the first in, first out principle.

service. (1) An operation which provides activities to order (e.g. cleaning contractors, insurance agents, hotel accommodation etc).
(2) The maintenance and/or repair operation on a piece of equipment.

service level. The degree to which the requirements of customers are entirely met (e.g. it might be decided that 95 per cent of customer orders are to be delivered in full and on time). This would be a service-level policy decision, taking into account the cost of providing such service, and the loss of potential business as a result of dissatisfaction etc. The diagram shows that above a certain level of service the cost of improving (towards 100 per cent service) becomes exponential, whereas the revenue increases only in proportion to the level of service. A trade-off is thus made at this point − an acceptable level of service.

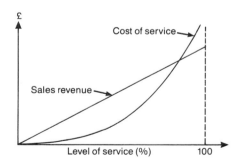

service level

service sector. The tertiary sector of business − that in which no product is produced, nor material converted. Service sector industries include transport, communications, education, leisure, insurance, consultancy, finance, and health.

set. A collection of items or ideas which is clearly described by one definition.

set off. To reduce the amount of DEBT by lending money back to the CREDITOR.

setting (setting-up). The preparation of a piece of equipment for the next operation.

setting-up. *See* SETTING.

setting-up cost. The cost of setting up equipment, especially in BATCH MODE. It is an important factor in decisions concerning batch size and ECONOMIES OF SCALE.

settlement day. *See* ACCOUNT DAY.

set up. To prepare a piece of equipment for an operation.

seven-point plan. A personal assessment questionnaire developed by the UK occupational psychologist Alec Rodger.

severance pay. An amount of money paid to an employee who is to be dismissed for reasons other than his own fault.

Sex Discrimination Act 1975. UK legislation designed to eliminate discrimination on the basis of gender in selection for employment. *See also* EQUAL OPPORTUNITIES COMMISSION and EQUAL PAY ACT 1970.

SFI. *See* SUPPORT FOR INNOVATION.

shadow price. *See* OPPORTUNITY COST.

share. The part ownership of a company in the form of certain rights to which a SHAREHOLDER is entitled. These may include voting in company meetings, selling shares (within certain restrictions in some cases), a share in the residual value of the company if it is wound up, and other special privileges (e.g. reduced prices for the company's services or products). Shares are issued by a company to raise CAPITAL. Thereafter, the shareholders are said to own EQUITY in the company. The shares of a PUBLIC LIMITED

COMPANY are bought and sold on a STOCK EXCHANGE through stockbrokers. Ownership of the shares of a private limited company is controlled by the company and may not be sold without its approval.

share capital. The PAID-IN CAPITAL or EQUITY and PREFERENCE SHARE CAPITAL of a company. This is normally expressed as the FACE VALUE of the shares issued (i.e. excluding the PREMIUM paid for them, either the potential amount or fully paid-up).

share certificate. A certificate issued by a company to a shareholder recording the number of shares held and the FACE VALUE of each.

shareholder. An individual or organization which has bought or acquired a SECURITY in a company.

share incentive scheme. A scheme introduced in 1973 in the UK by the Finance Act, which enables full-time employees to buy shares in a company on a long-term savings basis at a reduced price.

share index. An ECONOMIC INDICATOR calculated for a basket of shares on a stock exchange. The prices of the shares are monitored on a continuous basis and the computed index is published as a measure of buoyancy in the market. In the UK, the FINANCIAL TIMES − STOCK EXCHANGE 100 SHARE INDEX is the best-known, although many others exist. In the USA, the DOW JONES INDEX is the most commonly quoted.

share-of-production plan. A plant-wide incentive scheme, similar to the SCANLON PLAN, based upon linking employees' rewards to overall achievement in a production facility.

share option. An agreement which gives an individual the right to buy shares in a company at some future point at an agreed price. Options may sometimes be bought and sold, often at a PREMIUM.

share premium. The difference between the FACE VALUE of a share and the price paid for it. The premium on the shares is a measure of confidence shown in the company.

share warrant (bearer share). A certificate, similar to a SHARE CERTIFICATE, which states that the bearer is the legal owner of a number of shares in a company. No record of the bearer's name is kept by the company, however, and the warrant may be sold without the company's knowledge. The bearer must register with the company and exchange the warrant for a certificate to obtain voting rights and other privileges.

shark repellant. A colloquial term for tactics employed by the board of a company to deter TAKEOVER BIDS, usually by increasing the complexity of the company's rules.

shell company. A limited company set up for a specific purpose at a later date and which has, for the present, no trading activity and no ASSETS.

shift. (1) A period or portion of the day during which a section of the workforce is in operation. Normal shift refers to the normal working day somewhere between eight am and five pm. Double shift usually means one shift from early morning to mid-afternoon and another from then until late evening. The maximum is usually 3 shifts, covering 24 hours between them. A shift need not fill eight hours, however, and special arrangements are often made to suit the particular requirements of the business.
(2) A group of employees.
(3) With respect to tax payments, to make a special arrangement to raise the necessary cash, thus avoiding paying from previous income (e.g. increasing prices to improve revenue to pay overdue tax).

shift premium. An extra payment made to an employee in return for working a shift other than normal hours, especially 'unsocial hours'. The amount is usually linked in some way to the normal rate of pay, in a similar manner to OVERTIME calculations.

shipping and forwarding agent. A company offering a service in freight transportation. In addition to arranging transport and storage, the agent may offer to deal with authorities (customs etc), breaking bulk shipments down into individual requirements, insurance and so on.

shop. (1) RETAILING business premises.
(2) A location of manufacturing or other operations.

shopfloor. (1) The area of operation in a shop, particularly in production.
(2) A production workforce.

shopfloor data collection. The process of recording information from shopfloor activities and equipment for purposes of feedback into PRODUCTION CONTROL systems, either computerized or otherwise. This is increasingly being carried out automatically by process plant control systems, but the term applies equally well to manual systems of collecting readings and measurements.

shopping goods. CONSUMER DURABLE and similar goods for which the purchasing procedure involves careful consideration on the part of the buyer.

shop steward. A representative of a TRADE UNION at shopfloor level, with some time allowed by the company for union activity during the working day. He is elected by colleagues to serve a fixed term of duty.

shortage. The absence of component parts from an otherwise finished product, resulting from a lack of supply or quality problems.

shortage costs. Costs associated with a shortage. These range from some simple rectification costs (e.g. post-completion fitting of parts) to substantial penalties (e.g. stopping a moving mass production line), which may, in the case of automobile assembly be measured in millions of £ sterling per hour.

short account. An account of SHORT SALES over a period of time either at an individual or national level.

short gilts. GOVERNMENT SECURITIES redeemable in less than five years.

short-interval scheduling (SIS). A method of WORK MEASUREMENT and control based on dividing routine work into small groups of tasks which can be covered by an operator in a short interval (often one hour), during which time performance ratings can be made and feedback data obtained.

short sales. Selling something which is not actually owned by the seller, but which will be his by the time the sale goes through. The term is applied to COMMODITIES, SECURITIES and futures.

short-time working. The practice of employees agreeing or being required to reduce the working week, and thus the weekly wage, to relieve difficulties for the company in a recession.

shrinkage. Stock losses resulting from damage, deterioration or theft.

shrinkwrap. A process of protection coating for goods, consisting of a plastic film, sprayed in semi-molten form, which forms a strong, waterproof wrapping. It is also used in thicker forms to secure items to pallets for stability in transportation.

shutdown. A period of closure of plant (or a section thereof), usually for common holiday arrangements, to minimize disruption to output. The shutdown period may be linked to that of a major customer (who would thus not require deliveries during the period) and is used for maintenance work which would otherwise impede production.

SIB. See SECURITIES AND INVESTMENTS BOARD.

SIC. See STANDARD INDUSTRIAL CLASSIFICATION.

sickness benefit. Money paid to an employee by a company during periods of absence from work due to illness. It is usually a feature of STAFF STATUS.

sight bill. See BILL OF EXCHANGE.

simo chart (simultaneous motion–cycle chart). A graphic representation of analysing human movement in physical operations to provide scientific techniques of WORK MEASUREMENT, invented by Frank Gilbreth.

Simon, Herbert A. A US economist, winner of the Nobel Prize for Economics in 1978 for his pioneering research into the decision-making process in economic organizations. See J.G. March and H.A. Simon, *Organizations* (London: Wiley, 1958).

simple arbitrage (one-point arbitrage). ARBITRAGE which involves only one pair of transactions (i.e. a single purchase and a single subsequent sale).

simple debenture. A naked or unsecured DEBENTURE.

simple discount. A calculation resulting from the multiplication of the amount to be discounted by the discount rate and the number of years. Thus

$$discount = original\ sum \times discount\ rate\ pa \times number\ of\ years$$

simple regression analysis. REGRESSION ANALYSIS using only one independent variable.

simplex method. A LINEAR PROGRAMMING technique for solving operational problems with several variable factors and constraints in order to arrive at an optimal solution.

simulation. A technique for replicating a system of activities or functions in another more convenient form for purposes of design, development, experiment, training etc. For example, a computer simulation of the world economy has been constructed which allows the user to test the effects of suggested events ('what if' questions). Similarly, a training simulator for aircraft pilots provides the behaviour responses of the actual aircraft under various situations, using only computer-controlled systems and computer-generated visual displays.

simultaneous motion–cycle chart. See SIMO CHART.

single entry. An accounting technique where only one record is kept of a transaction, as opposed to a DOUBLE ENTRY in which both the issuer and receiver accounts are updated.

single industry union. A TRADE UNION whose membership is drawn entirely from one industry (e.g. the National Union of Railwaymen in the UK).

single premium costing. A PENSION scheme which is designed to link pension cover to premium on an annual basis – as opposed to averaging the total amount which will eventually be required over the years of paying premiums.

single status. The Japanese concept of all employees having the same status in non-functional roles. For example, all employees from the most menial to the most senior executive wear the same company uniform (which must therefore be practical enough to withstand factory conditions, but smart enough to be worn in commercial offices), use the same canteen etc.

single task role. A role which requires the individual to carry out only one task in the course of duty.

sinking fund. Money invested in order to pay off a debt by earning interest.

SIS. *See* SHORT-INTERVAL SCHEDULING.

sit-in. A protest by employees agains a company decision (usually connected to redundancies, plant closures etc) which involves them in occupying the company's premises and refusing to leave, thus bringing the matter to public attention, and disrupting the process of administering the company business.

situation profile. A technique for designing a company's payment system, based upon features of the company's operation and nature (its profile). For a full explanation see A. Bowey and T. Lupton, *Job and Pay Comparisons: How to Identify Similar Jobs in Different Companies and Compare their Rates of Pay* (London: Gower: 1973).

SI units (Système Internationale). An internationally-agreed, monitored and controlled system of units of measurement.

size effect. A notional increase in the complexity of INDUSTRIAL RELATIONS problems linked to the increase in size of organizations.

skewness. The degree to which the results of a statistical analysis, based upon sampling, shows a bias or imbalance.

skill. (1) The ability to perform a certain task.
(2) A common working attribute of a group of employees (hence skill group).

skilled operator. An individual who has specific skills, assessed in relation to specific types of work. A skilled operator may have a great deal of ability in a small range of tasks, or in a broad range of skills.

skilled work. A task which requires a SKILLED OPERATOR.

skills analysis. A technique for analysing specific tasks to develop training programmes using KINAESTHETICS. *See also* LEARNING CURVE.

skimming. The practice of setting a high price to maximize revenue on a non-PRICE SENSITIVE product.

slab scale. An income tax scale which applies higher rates to whole income, rather than to a band (which is called a SLICE SCALE). For example, if the rate of income tax is 30 per cent on incomes less than £15,000 per annum and 35 per cent above this level, then for an income of £16,000 per annum, using a slab scale method, the whole amount would be taxable at 35 per cent. A slice scale would apply 35 per cent only to the top £1000 (i.e. the amount above the £15,000 level). *See also* PROGRESSIVE TAX.

slack. The available time within a PROJECT programme which may be employed during the project to cover for slippage in performance against the schedule. A series of events within the programme which contains no slack is a critical path. *See* CRITICAL PATH ANALYSIS.

sleeper. (1) A dummy address in a postal survey which is not a respondent but merely a check to ensure that deliveries are being received.
(2) A large non-progressive company (i.e. a sleeping giant).

slice scale. An income tax method which applies higher rates only to incremental bands, not to the whole income. *See* SLAB SCALE. *See also* PROGRESSIVE TAX.

sliding parity. A technique for minimizing the effect of differing values of currencies. Short of direct linking of currencies, sliding parity allows differences to be taken up over a period of time.

sliding scale. The notional or actual means of measurement which can be adjusted to fit the circumstances.

slip chart. A graphical method of representing the slippage in a project (i.e. the degree to which the project is late, measured during its progress). The chart plots planned times for the sequence of events on a vertical axis against actual times, on a horizontal axis. A line at 45 degrees is thus the perfect position. A steeper gradient means the project is being completed in less time than planned, and vice versa.

slippage. The falling behind in a programme or project.

Sloan, Alfred P. A US entrepreneur who took control of General Motors during the early part of the 20th century, turning it into the world's largest vehicle manufacturer, chiefly by a strategy of the acquisition of other motor companies. His work on developing mass production techniques was as important as that of Henry Ford and Fredrick TAYLOR (*see* SCIENTIFIC MANAGEMENT). Sloan founded a management school at the Massachusetts Institute of Technology.

slogan. A catchphrase used in sales promotion.

slump. An economic depression, especially in the manufacturing industry.

slumpflation. A hybrid term combining a slump and inflation.

slush fund. Money held to pay informal gratuities in order to maintain important but unofficial relationships in business.

sm. *See* STANDARD MINUTE.

Small Engineering Firms Investment Scheme. *See* SEFIS.

smokestack industries. Manufacturing industries which suffered decline during the 1970s and 1980s, typified by an image of factories with smoky chimneys.

smoothing. A technique for interpreting graphical data by lessening the effects of atypical data on an overall result (smoothing a bumpy line). Mathematical methods are employed, particularly exponential smoothing.

snake. The group of currencies in the EUROPEAN MONETARY SYSTEM which, by common agreement, rise and fall in value with respect to international standards (e.g. the US dollar) while remaining constant in relation to one another.

Snellen chart. A chart for testing eyesight and other vision factors.

social audit. The process of evaluating the impact of a company's plans upon the environment in which they will take effect, with particular regard for the people who will be involved.

social costs. The costs of a project which are incurred as a result of the company's duty to neighbours and the general public (e.g. restoration of natural beauty after laying a pipeline through open countryside).

social investment. Investment in public facilities (e.g. schools, shops, hospitals etc), often as part of a large scheme. This may be to provide facilities specifically for employees (but under public administration) or for truly open access.

social security. A state-administered scheme to provide financial support for individuals unable to support themselves (e.g. as a result of unemployment).

sociedad anónima (SA). In Spain, a company with limited liability.

società per azioni (SpA). In Italy, a joint stock company.

société anonyme (SA). In France, a company with limited liability.

société simple. *See* EINFACHE GESELL-SCHAFT.

Society for Worldwide Interbank Financial Statements. *See* SWIFT.

socio-economic factors. Factors which are the result of social and economic factors (e.g. civil unrest caused by unemployment).

socio-economic status. A sociological classification of individuals with regard to factors such as type of occupation, income, family history, likes and dislikes etc.

socio-technical system. An organization of people and technological equipment, designed for specific purposes, analysed principally in terms of the ways in which the people and the equipment have effects upon one another.

soft currency. A currency which is not considered to be totally stable, perhaps reflecting a country's political position.

soft loan. Financial aid to developing countries. A soft loan is very long-term and often repayable in the borrower's own currency.

soft sales promotion. A PROMOTIONAL ACTIVITY which is designed not to offend potential customers, using subtle approaches.

software. (1) Computer programs designed to perform specific functions.
(2) Written support material for any computer system.

software piracy. The act of copying proprietary software for use in a computer, without paying for the service. Since software is stored on disks or tapes, it is relatively easy to duplicate, despite attempts to protect it by scrambling devices etc. Piracy is a breach of copyright.

sole licence. A PATENT licence which prevents the holder from licensing others to use the patent.

sole trader. Someone carrying out business on an individual basis (i.e. without a partner and without forming a company), for example a person who is self-employed.

solid modelling. A technique in COMPUTER-AIDED-DESIGN for constructing an apparently three-dimensional picture of an item on a computer screen. The solid model may then be used in experimental combinations with other items, subjected to simulated stress, temperatures and vibration etc.

solus position. The placing of an advertisement in the news or editorial section of a publication – away from other advertisements.

solvency. The state of being able to settle one's debts.

SOP. *See* SALES ORDER PROCESSING.

sore-thumbing. A technique, especially used in JOB EVALUATION, of identifying people or items from a group who do not appear to fit in with the general pattern. Once identified, the sore-thumb cases may require special treatment.

source code. The original code in which a computer program was specified by the analyst or programmer.

source program. A computer program written for user-level communication. The source program must be compiled into MACHINE CODE in order for the computer to run it.

SpA. *See* SOCIETÀ PER AZIONI.

span of control. The number of people who report to a manager within an organization. Experiments have shown that there is a practical maximum span of control, related to the type of work being carried out, and that this is linked to the number of levels of hierarchy within the organization.

spatial reasoning. The ability of an operator to carry out tasks which involve judgments of distance and relative position.

SPC. *See* STATISTICAL PROCESS CONTROL.

special deposits. In the UK, money which CLEARING BANKS must deposit with the Bank of England. It is notionally used as a control on lending.

special development area. A defined geographical region in the UK where the government wants to encourage industrial and/or commerical development by offering financial incentives to investors. Conditions and incentives change periodically to reflect shifts of policy.

special drawing right (SDR). The international standard unit of account of the INTERNATIONAL MONETARY FUND, expressed as the dollar equivalent of a BASKET OF CURRENCIES.

specialty goods. CONSUMER DURABLE goods which appeal to a minority group whose choice is determined by careful consideration of technical factors (e.g expensive cameras).

speculate. To invest in something with a view to making profit by a subsequent resale, without making actual use of the item purchased. *See* ARBITRAGE.

speech processing. The ability of a computer to understand, respond to and generate the spoken word. *See* FIFTH GENERATION COMPUTER.

speed test. A test of manual dexterity in assembly operations. It is used both for assessment of individual operators and for setting performance norms.

spin-off. A peripheral benefit which is received as a chance result of some other, intentional activity.

split inventory system. *See* ABC ANALYSIS and PARETO ANALYSIS.

split-level investment trust. An INVESTMENT TRUST which has two types of shares. One type entitles the SHAREHOLDER to a share of profits; the other type entitles the shareholder to a share of the assets when the trust is liquidated. Both may be traded.

split shift. A SHIFT which has been divided into two teams and/or two time periods.

sponduliks. Physical units of money, coins etc.

spot. Immediately available. The spot price of an item or COMMODITY is that which must be paid to gain immediate possession.

spot market. A trading market upon which items or commodities are bought and sold for immediate transfer.

spot rate. The exchange rate for currency bought or sold for immediate transfer.

spreadsheet. An accountancy technique for displaying cost items across a broad page, in columns, such that calculations may be done by line, column or item, and analysis carried out of the figures contained. Many computer software packages have been designed specifically to generate and manipulate spreadsheets and the term is often used to refer to such a package (e.g. *Lotus 123*), rather than to the original accountancy concept.

	South	North	East	West	Total
January	4.73	2.61	2.62	4.33	14.29
February	5.19	3.00	3.91	5.64	17.74
March	6.20	3.11	3.96	5.61	18.88
April	8.72	4.22	5.00	5.90	23.84
May	10.64	7.41	7.00	6.90	31.95
June	10.64	7.00	7.11	7.00	31.75
July	10.00	4.78	6.21	6.99	27.98
August	9.40	3.61	5.00	4.97	22.98
September	7.43	3.62	4.10	3.97	19.12
October	5.50	2.90	3.00	3.00	14.40
November	5.10	3.00	2.90	2.90	13.80
December	4.99	2.97	3.20	3.20	13.91
Total	88.54	48.23	53.46	60.41	250.64
Sales: figures in £000s					

an example of a spreadsheet for sales income

SPSS (Statistical Package for Social Science). A computer SOFTWARE package for analysis of statistical survey data.

SQA, *See* SUPPLIER QUALITY ASSURANCE.

SQC. *See* STATISTICAL QUALITY CONTROL.

SROs. *See* SELF REGULATORY ORGANIZA-TIONS.

stability/neurosis syndrome. A scale on which personality is tested in psychological testing.

staff association. A formally recognized organization of employees within a specific company or sector, which acts in some ways like a TRADE UNION, but is usually less politically motivated. Such associations are common in the financial sector (banks, insurance etc).

staff functions. Positions within an organization which are seen as support to an operation rather than part of it (i.e. not line functions).

staff status. A basis of employment traditionally associated with weekly or monthly payment, rather than an hourly wage, often augmented by special benefits (e.g. company cars).

stag. An individual who buys shares in a public offer in order to resell them at a profit after a short period.

stage payments. *See* PROGRESS PAYMENTS.

stagflation. An economic situation in which output is static despite rising prices which might otherwise encourage producers to increase supply.

stamp duty. A duty which must be paid for some documents (e.g. title deeds to property) to record a transaction formally, with an official stamp.

standard cost (direct cost). An estimated cost for an operation, based on measurements of labour requirement, material usage and overhead apportionment, which is used in conjunction with others for purposes of cost control and forecasting. For example, valuation of work in progress depends upon accounting for value added to each point in the process, and thus needs standard costs

for items observed at each stage. Standard costs may also be used to stabilize prices over a forward period by estimating a level of costs which might be reached half-way through the period and thus fixing a standard cost for the whole period.

standard deviation. In statistics, the extent to which a distribution is dispersed about its mean. For a probability distribution, this is also called the population standard deviation and is equal to the square root of the variance, usually denoted by σ. For a frequency distribution, the letter 's' is used, and it is called the sample standard deviation.

standard error. The standard deviation of a sampling distribution.

standard hour. A measure of work, not time. In WORK STUDY a standard hour is the amount of work which may be completed by an operator, working at standard performance, for one hour, allowing for all reasonable interferences.

Standard Industrial Classification (SIC). A codified classification system used to describe different types of industries in official statistical reports. The SIC is derived from the International SIC, administered by the the Central Statistical Office and published by HMSO.

standard minute (sm). A measure of work equivalent to one-sixtieth part of a STANDARD HOUR.

standard performance. A notional rate of operational performance used for measurement of work. Defined by a British standard, the standard performance is used as a reference point, equivalent to the effort required to maintain a walking speed of four miles per hour.

standard rating. The WORK STUDY practice of estimating the rate at which a specific operation is being carried out, with reference to STANDARD PERFORMANCE. A rating out of 100 (but never expressed as a percentage) is estimated for each operation, and the time taken for the operation, as measured by the work study engineer, is multiplied by the reciprocal of the rating to arrive at the basic minutes for the job.

standards. (1) Agreed values, practices, conventions etc for carrying out technical or business activities. Standards are usually maintained by a national or international organization (e.g. the British Standards Institute, the International Standards Organization etc).

(2) Within a company, established norms upon which estimates for output, costing etc are based.

(3) In manufacturing, standard times for operations, established by WORK STUDY methods.

standard time. The amount of work contained in an operation as defined by WORK STUDY. The standard time is calculated from the observed time, amended by standard rating to arrive at the basic time, which is then augmented by allowances for interruptions etc. It is used as the basis of cost accounting (for DIRECT LABOUR costing), and often in PAYMENT-BY-RESULTS systems (e.g. PIECEWORK). Such a payment system is referred to as a 'standard time payment system'.

standing committee. A committee which is set up to monitor some special subject over a period of time and which reports back periodically to its superior committee (or other authority) on the subject.

standing orders. The established ground rules for the operating practice of an organization.

start-up. A new business venture.

start-up costs. Costs incurred in starting up a new business venture, which may be claimed as expenses against subsequent income.

stated value. The lowest amount acceptable in payment of a no-par share.

state flat-rate pension. In the UK, the normal basic pension which is payable to all persons over retirement age and no longer employed who have previously paid NATIONAL INSURANCE contributions. Those who have been employed are also entitled to a STATE-GRADUATED PENSION, or a similar provision made through their employer's scheme.

state-graduated pension. In the UK, a pension payable to all individuals who have paid NATIONAL INSURANCE contributions as employed people, in addition to the STATE FLAT-RATE PENSION, unless they have opted out of the state scheme and chosen instead to pay into an employer's scheme.

statistics. Numerical information processed from results of observations, used to characterize the subjects of such observations.

statistical inference. The use of PROBABILITY theory to make assumptions and assertions about observed PROBABILITY DISTRIBUTIONS, employing sampling techniques.

Statistical Package for Social Science. *See* SPSS.

statistical process control (SPC). The discipline of recording observed measurements of process parameters and taking corrective action immediately to maintain the process (and thus the output) within predetermined limits. STATISTICAL INFERENCE is used to determine the acceptable limits within which such observed parameters should lie, to varying levels of significance. For a full explanation see J.S. Oakland, *Statistical Process Control − A Practical Guide* (London: Heinemann, 1986).

statistical quality control (SQC). The use of STATISTICAL INFERENCE to determine TOLERANCE levels for inspection of process output, upon which an accept or reject decision may be based. A practical application of SQC is the practice of inspecting a sample of a few items from a batch of many and accepting or rejecting the batch on the basis of the outcome of such an inspection.

status. (1) The degree of respect in which an individual is held by others within a group or organization. A person's status may reflect his perceived individual value or importance, or that of a particular rank or office (e.g. a chief executive officer may have a high status as a result of his position, but may be held in relatively lower personal esteem by his peers).

(2) The status of a document (e.g. when tabled at a meeting) is important when the people receiving it decide how to respond.

An official consultative report may demand some formal response, whereas a draft paper for information only may require only cursory reading or discussion.

statutory audit. An AUDIT of a company's accounts which is carried out to satisfy legal requirements.

statutory company. A company formed by a private Act of Parliament (i.e. a statute) which thus becomes a corporation, intended for public service.

statutory corporation. A corporation established by a public Act of Parliament, sometimes a nationalized industry.

statutory instrument. A set of orders and legislation made by a government official (e.g. a Minister or Crown in Council).

statutory meeting. The general meeting of members of a public company, held in the first three months of the company's existence to disseminate information on the company.

statutory minimum wage. The minimum wage which may be paid by an employer, as stipulated by the law of the land.

stepped cost. An operating cost which is fixed for a certain range of output and then rises in a step (rather than a gradient) at some level. For example, the cost of supervision is not linked to the level of output until a certain level at which it is necessary to employ an extra supervisor. At this point the cost of supervision increases to reflect the extra wages cost of the new supervisor. *See also* SEMI-VARIABLE COST.

stewardship accounting. Proper accounting procedures which satisfy legal and commercial needs but are less rigorous and detailed than the professional practices of management or financial accounting. It is usually applied to small businesses who do not need the more sophisticated techniques.

sticker. An individual who is content to remain in his current position rather than seek promotion.

Stilling tests. Tests for colour blindness in which images are presented in a confused manner in order to test the viewer's ability to distinguish between different colours.

stochastic. Random. A stochastic approach to something is usually the reverse of a deterministic approach, and is based on the assumption that the situation in question will be affected by sundry random factors and cannot therefore be treated simply as an ideal arrangement of inputs and outputs.

stochastic decision tree. A DECISION TREE in which the outcomes of sets of decisions are seen as continuous RANDOM VARIABLES and are expressed as PROBABIBLITY DISTRIBUTIONS. The method employs risk analysis techniques to arrive at optimum courses of action.

stochastic game. A method in GAME THOERY in which outcomes are assumed to be random.

stochastic PERT. A version of PERT which includes random factors which may affect progress through a project. The forecast and actual effects of such factors are regularly reconsidered in the course of project control.

stock. (1) INVENTORY − RAW MATERIALS, work in progress and FINISHED GOODS contained in a production process.
(2) In a non-manufacturing company, goods held for sale or use in service. Stocks appear on the BALANCE SHEET of a company as an asset but are not considered liquid.
(3) CAPITAL STOCK, or the SHARES of capital stock held in a corporation.
(4) An entitlement to payment of a regular DIVIDEND from a public company or corporation, bought and sold by holders much the same way as shares, with a FACE VALUE which may be increased by a PREMIUM on a STOCK EXCHANGE.

stockbroker. An individual who arranges the sale of STOCKS and SHARES, or other SECURITIES, without owning them during the transaction.

stock certificate. Written proof of the ownership of stock in a company, retained by the stockholder, showing the nominal value of the stocks owned.

stock control (inventory control; inventory management). The control of materials used and stored in a company, with the objective of providing exactly what is required, where and when it is required, employing a minimum of residual stock, and thus incurring the least possible cost. Stock may be controlled by monitoring and replenishing individual items on a timed basis or physical check routine, or by employing a computerized planning system, such as MATERIALS REQUIREMENTS PLANNING, to reduce the need for holding BUFFER STOCK. *See* REORDER CYCLE; REORDER POINT; REORDER QUANTITY.

stock cover. The time period for which current stocks will last, assuming that a usage rate is predictable.

stock exchange. A nationally recognized, formally organized place of dealing in SECURITIES. Because of the importance of sales in securities, transactions may only take place between authorized people (JOBBERS and STOCKBROKERS) acting on behalf of others. This business is restricted to stock exchanges, or stock markets, which exist in major cities throughout the world. Membership of exchanges is carefully controlled. Since computerization of systems, some deregulation of transactions has been inevitable (*see* BIG BANG), broadening the scope of dealing and lessening to some extent the importance of the stock exchange as a physical place of business. The control of such dealing remains, however, a priority for the national interest, and the stock exchange is still the only official channel.

Stock Exchange Automated Quotations System (SEAQ). In the UK, a system which provides electronic price displays for SECURITIES. SEAQ requires all MARKET MAKERS to quote buying and selling prices along with the number of shares in which they are prepared to deal at that price. These quotes are displayed on screens in brokers' offices. Dealing takes place by telephone and is subject to negotiation between the broker and the market maker.

stockholder. (1) An individual who owns STOCK issued by a company.

(2) A company which holds stocks of goods or materials to sell for use by other companies.

stockholding cost. The cost of holding stock, consisting of actual costs (warehouse rent, lighting, insurance, damage, wages etc) and notional costs (lost interest on capital tied up in stocks held). If stocks have been bought on credit, then the period of payment may be used to cover their length of storage, thus diminishing the notional costs. However, stockholding costs are a substantial matter, often estimated as over 20 per cent of stock value per annum.

stocking agent. A STOCKHOLDER who may procure and hold specific items or goods for use by particular customers.

stock-in-trade. Goods held by a company for purposes of sale.

stockist. A STOCKHOLDER who is nominated by a manufacturer to be the sole source of their products in a certain geographical area.

stock jobber. A JOBBER on the STOCK EXCHANGE.

stock losses. Losses incurred as a result of the price of material in stock falling on the market. The current value of stocks may thus be less than the price originally paid for them – a straightforward loss. *See also* STOCK PROFITS.

stockout. The situation when stock of an item has been used up and not yet replenished.

stock profits. Realizable financial gains due to the increase in value of material stocks bought at a lower price and potentially sellable at a higher price. *See also* STOCK LOSSES.

stock purchasing. The purchasing of materials to be held in stock, rather than used immediately.

stocktaking. A periodic physical audit of all materials currently held by a company for the purpose of correcting records for stock control and financial calculations.

stock turnover (inventory turnover; turnover of stock). The number of times the value of material stocks is used and replaced per year. It is calculated by dividing the annual cost of materials bought by the average value of stocks held at any time during the year and expressed as a 'times' (e.g. 12 times per year), or in weeks' or months' worth of usable stock (e.g 1 month's stock). The higher the figure, the better. Traditionally, a stock turnover of between 10 or 15 was good for a manufacturing company; however, new techniques (such as JUST-IN-TIME PRODUCTION) have increased this target to double or 3 times this. In non-manufacturing, the picture is different: some types of RETAILING may have much higher or lower figures due to very different types of stock (e.g. green-grocery produce compared to consumer durables).

store. (1) An area of a company's premises which is used to store materials.
(2) Part of a computer system used to record and retain data.

storyboard. A presentation technique used in product development, advertising, project management etc, which employs the clarity of explicit visual symbols to get across the desired message.

straightline depreciation. A depreciation technique which reduces the notional value of an asset by a fixed equal amount each year.

strategic business unit (SBU). The management concept of dividing up a company into finite business units, each responsible for progress and profitability. It was developed in the USA by the General Electric Co.

strategic plan. A long-term plan which describes in detail the way in which it is intended a company should develop, but not necessarily the fine details of how this will be achieved. The strategic plan was traditionally drawn up to cover a five-year period, but this has now become too long a timescale due to the increasing rate of technological and economic change. A more common

technique today is a 'rolling plan', which is updated periodically to reflect new opportunities and threats identified by a company and ways in which it is intended to deal with them. The strategic plan not only describes the current position of a firm and that which it is intended to occupy after a defined time period, but also major actions which will be undertaken in the process of moving from one to the other.

stratification. The division of a POPULATION in a survey according to some desired factor (e.g. age, size etc).

strike. An interruption in work following disagreement, normally between employer and employee, on some matter relevant to the contract or conditions of employment.

strike pay (dispute benefit). Financial support paid to union members involved in a strike (and thus not receiving normal pay). Strike pay is funded by the trade union(s) concerned.

string diagram. A diagram drawn on a plan of a factory to show the path of materials or products through the process. This technique is intended to show up any anomolous distance travelled by such items which might be reduced by logical reorganization, thus revealing a potential cost reduction and improvement in responsiveness (a reduction in lead time). *See* diagram p. 196.

structural determinants. Identifiable environmental influences upon the behaviour of individuals.

Stuctural—Functionalist School. A US school of thought in the social sciences (particularly psychology) which believes that groups of people have shared values and wish for stability through organization.

structural unemployment. Unemployment which is accepted by a government as part of the economic balance of the country.

structured interview. *See* DIRECTIVE INTERVIEW.

structured programming. The technique of building a computer program from basic

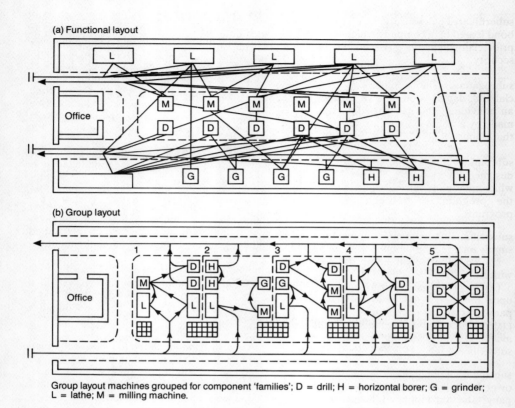

(a) Functional layout

(b) Group layout

Group layout machines grouped for component 'families'; D = drill; H = horizontal borer; G = grinder; L = lathe; M = milling machine.

an application of a string diagram to show a simplification of production process flow

routines, following an overall structure. This is intended to provide a more efficient, faster program, in a simpler fashion.

student-centred learning. A teaching technique which places the onus upon the student to 'find out' the information and knowledge required to complete a project, rather than attend a course of lectures.

Student's t-distribution. *See* T-DISTRIBUTION.

sub-assembly. An assembly of components which is itself a component part of a larger assembly in a product.

subcontract. An agreement between two parties for the supply of goods, manufactured by one (the subcontractor) for the other (the contractor, or customer) usually to the latter's specification. Subcontracting may also cover process work to be done by the subcontractor on materials supplied by the customer.

subliminal advertising. The technique of inserting an advertising or propaganda image very briefly into a film, in such a way that the human mind receives the message but the viewer does not remember seeing the image. The practice has been banned by most authorities as immoral.

suboptimize. To reach a compromise plan of action, usually as a combination of activities, which is less than ideal for the task in hand.

subordinate. An individual who is of lesser rank or importance in an organization.

subordinated debenture. A DEBENTURE bond issued by a company which already has prior claim debentures issued on the same security.

subrogation. The practice of an insurer claiming damages on its own behalf against an individual who has caused a claim to be made by a policy-holder, after settlement of that claim.

subroutine. Part of a computer program designed to complete a specific function which may be required several times during the program, or subsequently in other programs.

subscribe. (1) To pay for some service or supply on a regular basis.
(2) To endorse something by identifying with it.
(3) To pledge payment for securities (e.g. upon the FLOTATION of a new public company). If more shares in a new PUBLIC LIMITED COMPANY are requested than are available, the issue is said to be over-subscribed.

subsidiary. A company whose shares are owned wholly or mostly by another company. The controlling company may be called the HOLDING COMPANY (usually when several subsidiary companies are owned in a group) or the parent company. If the parent company owns all the shares, the subsidiary is defined as wholly-owned.

substantive agreement. An agreement reached between management and trade union representatives as a result of COLLECTIVE BARGAINING, which concerns some substantial reform of working practices, payment systems etc.

substitution effect. The impact on sales for a company caused when its products are unavailable to customers who therefore switch to competitors' products. Some products are particularly vulnerable to this, and are said to have substitutionality. Others, such as specialist medical equipment, may not be easily replaced by competitors' goods and therefore have low substitutionality.

subsystem. A series of functions within a SYSTEM, grouped for a specific purpose.

succession plan. A personnel management technique of recording details of present incumbents in all managerial (or other) positions and the names of potential replacements for them.

succession planning. See MANAGEMENT SUCCESSION.

successive approximations. A method of estimating something by beginning with a rough approximation and gradually improving the result by repeating the calculations with more precise input data. It is used in several areas of quantitative decision-making (e.g. FORECASTING).

suggestion scheme. A scheme which encourages all employees in a firm to suggest ways in which any part of the operation might be improved to reduce costs, increase quality, remove anomalies etc. Financial rewards are usually made for suggestions which are implemented and provide subsequent benefits. See also QUALITY CIRCLES.

suite of programs. A collection of computer programs designed to operate together in an integrated fashion for a specific purpose (e.g. a manufacturing control suite might contain programs to deal with STOCK CONTROL, PURCHASING, PRODUCTION CONTROL, cost accounting, WAGES, design interface, machine tool control interface, SHOPFLOOR DATA COLLETION etc).

sum of the year's digits. A technique used in DEPRECIATION based on the useful life of an asset, using the formula

$$s = 1 + 2 + 3 + 4 + 5 + \ldots + L = \tfrac{1}{2}(L + 1)$$

where L is the estimated useful life of the asset. The second formula shows the depreciation in the nth year as

original cost of asset $\times (L - n)/s$.

sunk cost. The cost incurred in acquiring a fixed asset (e.g. a piece of equipment) which, it is deemed, cannot be reclaimed after the event.

sunlighting. Continuing in full-time employment after official retirement.

sunrise industry. An industry which is in a growth period early in its life cycle, usually due to a technological development. The classic example is microelectronics products, based upon the invention of silicon chip technology. Sunrise industries are usually seen in contrast to others which they replace, again on the basis of technological development.

sunset industry. An industry which is in decline, in the latter stages of its life cycle, usually due to technological developments which have rendered its products uneconomic or redundant (e.g. mechanical cash registers).

superannuation. The provision of a pension after retirement on the basis of contributions made during years of employment, either by the individual or on his behalf. *See also* STATE FLAT-RATE PENSION; STATE-GRADUATED PENSION.

supernumerary. An individual who is extra to the numbers required for a group task, either as a result of poor labour planning (i.e. overmanning) or as a training project.

superstore. A large retailing outlet designed to provide ONE-STOP SHOPPING. Originally the province of food chains, superstores are now operated by all manner of retailers, often in large shopping complexes.

supervisor. An individual employed to co-ordinate the activities of others, often at a designated salary scale position within a company. The variety of roles played by supervisors within various companies means that there is no clear STATUS attached to the title (as there is, for example, to a managing director of anything but the smallest of firms).

supervisory board. The upper level of a two-tier board, consisting of management and trade union representatives.

supervisory program. A program which forms part of the operating system in a computer, with responsibility for locating other programs in an executive fashion.

supplementary benefit. In the UK, non-contributory pensions and benefits administered by the Department of Health and Social Security.

supplier (vendor). An individual or company which supplies goods to a customer.

supplier quality assurance (SQA). A QUALITY ASSURANCE technique developed in the 1970s in Japan, the USA and Europe. It is based on the principle that goods used by a manufacturer contribute to the overall quality of the end product and thus the supplier of such goods must be seen as part of the process. Quality assurance engineers from the customer company visit the supplier to ensure that the latter has (and is using) systems and procedures which comply with a formal manual of requirements, and may thus be accepted as an approved supplier of parts and materials. *See also* STATISTICAL PROCESS CONTROL; TOTAL QUALITY CONTROL.

supply. The process of providing appropriate goods in response to and in strict accordance with customer demand.

Supply of Goods Act 1973. UK legislation which is designed to prevent the use of disclaimer clauses in contracts for supply of goods which would avoid the responsibilities covered by common law.

support buying. The support of a nation's currency by organized buying of that currency by a government agency in order to prevent the price from dropping too sharply.

Support for Innovation (SFI). A UK government programme of incentive grants to industry to encourage the use of new technologies in product and process innovation. Introduced in 1980, the scheme has been subsequently extended to cover other specialized support programmes (e.g. ROBOTICS). *See* DEPARTMENT OF TRADE AND INDUSTRY.

supportive leadership. A management style based upon enabling subordinates to suggest ideas and to achieve objectives.

surcharge. An extra charge added to the quoted price of goods or services as a result of external circumstances not under the control of the contractor (e.g. during the oil crises of the 1970s many holiday companies made surcharges on top of the quoted and pre-paid prices of package holidays, to allow for increased transport charges made to them by airlines, for increased fuel costs).

surety. A guarantee provided by a third party in support of an application for a loan.

surface bargaining. A negotiation in which there is a hidden agenda, which renders the subject of the bargaining of secondary importance.

surface chart. A graph on which the area under the curve is shaded or coloured in, to give more of an impression of magnitude than would be provided by a single line.

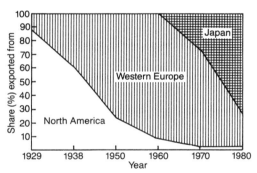

an example of a surface chart

surface mounting. The technique of fitting discrete components and integrated circuits onto printed circuit boards without the need for leads to pass through drilled holes in the laminate. Surface mounting enables the design of more compact board circuitry and simpler assembly operation, both resulting in potential cost reductions and improved product quality.

surrender value. The value of a BOND which will be reimbursed to the holder when it is returned.

suspense account. A special account which is used to hold receipts and payments which are incomplete and require clarification.

swap. An agreement by two parties to link a spot sale and a forward purchase, particularly of currency.

sweetheart contract. A contract placed by a company with a supplier in preference to other potential sources, partly because of their special relationship.

SWIFT (Society for Worldwide Interbank Financial Telecommunications). A computerized international banking transactions system.

swing shift. A group of employees working in a flexible manner, without set hours to a SHIFT, in order to cover for fluctuations in workload requirements.

switch selling. A selling technique in which the salesperson encourages the customer to buy a more expensive model than that originally requested.

SWOT. A strategic analysis technique, based upon consideration of a company's internal factors (strengths and weaknesses), and environmental factors (opportunities and threats).

syllogism. Chaining logic in decision-making. If a implies b, and b implies c, then a must imply c.

symbolic models. Methods employed in SIMULATION to represent physical entities.

symmetrical movements. In ergonomics, human movements which require the left and right hand to carry out the same actions in mirror image to one another.

sympathy strike. A STRIKE called by one group of employees to bring pressure to bear upon the employers of another group, by way of the first group's employers.

symposium. A meeting arranged to discuss and debate specific subjects of interest to selected participants.

syndicalism. An international early 20th-century movement which promoted workers' ownership of industry and the use of industrial action to achieve such ends.

syndicate. A group of independent companies or individuals which co-operate towards some common goal for mutual benefit.

synergy. Complementary activities in two or more parties which might lead to a strong capability if collaboration, to mutual benefit, could be arranged on aspects of common work.

synectics. A problem-solving technique based on group discussion, developed by W.S. Gordon. It is similar to BRAINSTORMING but is intended to generate a refined, specific idea rather than several broader proposals. For a full explanation see T. Rickards, *Problem-Solving through Creative Analysis* (London: Gower, 1974).

synthetic data. Data which has been built up from estimated elemental data, particularly in a PREDETERMINED MOTION—TIME SYSTEM.

synthetics. (1) the technique of combining factors to achieve an overall result.

(2) In WORK MEASUREMENT, the STANDARD TIME for a complex operation synthesized from elemental times which have been estimated rather than actually measured, enabling the job to be costed without the need for a work study exercise.

(3) In materials technology, materials that are formed artificially from the combination of other constituent materials not naturally found in such a combination.

system. A group or series of independent functions which are designed to combine towards one or more common objectives and which may be treated as one entity.

systems analysis. The analysis of a physical system (e.g. of communication flows within a company), often for the purposes of simulating it on a computer and subsequently developing a SOFTWARE package to operate the system in place of the manual activity.

systems engineering. The function of sales/ marketing/design co-operation in a computer manufacturer or similar company to combine hardware and software products into systems which potential customers require.

systems of production. Production facilities that are grouped together in accordance with some specific approach to production (e.g. mass production, flexible manufacturing systems etc).

systems selling. A selling method that adheres to procedures, techniques and philosophy laid down by the originator of the system. It is often claimed to be applicable to any product or service.

T

tachistoscope. A device used in planning advertising techniques such as SUBLIMINAL ADVERTISING. An image is displayed for a brief controlled time and the viewer's response is used to judge the best exposure to be used in practice.

tactical. Relating to a mode of operation employed in pursuit of strategic goals.

tactics. Modes of operation employed in pursuit of a strategic goal.

takeover bid. An attempt by one company to gain control of another by purchase of a majority shareholding. The bidder usually writes to the shareholders of the company in question, with an offer (in cash or shares or both) to purchase shares. The offer, which each individual shareholder is free to accept or decline, may be endorsed or rejected by the board of the target company, but it is up to the shareholders to decide the outcome of the bid.

TALISMAN. An automated system of quoting and listing on the UK STOCK EXCHANGE, implemented in 1979.

tallyman. The traditional practice of delivering goods regularly without receiving payment, keeping a tally in a book, and requiring payment, on the basis of the tally periodically. An example of this method is a milkman in the UK who delivers milk each day, in varying amounts as requested, and who requires payment each week. The system is also the basis of some ideas in JUST-IN-TIME delivery systems, where the principle is to do away with as much paperwork as possible and base the supplier/customer relationship on trust – the supplier's tally.

talon. A counterfoil on a SHARE WARRANT (or similar document) which is retained by the bearer when all the coupons have been used. The talon may be exchanged for more coupons.

tangible assets. Physical properties of a company, used in the course of its business, which might be sold or transferred (e.g. vehicles, equipment etc).

tap. A method of selling SECURITIES employed by an individual who holds a large quantity of them.

tapered increase. A gradual increase in a variable, as opposed to a sudden change.

tape streamer. A computer data storage device which is used to record back-up (security) copies of information processed and stored on disk. The tape storage mechanism is inherently safer and less vulnerable than disk storage, but slower in access. The streamer is designed to pass tape very quickly, recording the data at high speed. Thus a great deal of data can be 'dumped' onto tape quickly (often at the end of a day's business).

tap stock. UK GOVERNMENT BONDS issued through the Government Broker. The market in GILT-EDGED STOCKS is influenced by controlling the supply of such securities, through the 'tap'.

tare. The proportion of the weight of packaged goods which is deemed to represent the weight of the packaging.

target marketing. The practice of identifying specific MARKET SEGMENTS for which products or services will be designed and subsequently aimed.

target population. A group of people to which the output of a company is directed, usually with specific set sales achievement figures. *See also* MARKET SEGMENTATION.

target price. (1) A piece price estimated by purchase analysis departments as a guide for buyers to keep to.
(2) In the EUROPEAN COMMUNITY, the basic Common Agricultural Policy price for

each commodity as fixed annually by the Council of Ministers. Community policies or price support for farmers are related to these target prices.

tariff. (1) A price list.
(2) An import duty, or a list of such duties.

tariff barrier. A measure taken by a country to limit imports of specific items, sometimes from specific countries, by imposition of an import tariff, making the item more expensive to buy within the country of import and thereby reducing sales potential.

task. A specified activity to be carried out by an individual, in accordance with set rules and procedures, to achieve some defined result.

task analysis. The analysis of a task into elements for the purposes of improving methods and identifying skill and/or training requirements for an operator.

task-based appraisal. Appraisal by a superior on the basis of performance measured against set tasks.

task-based participation. Worker participation on the basis of work design consultation, employing TASK ANALYSIS.

task force. A group of individuals brought together to achieve some specific task. A task force may be kept together on a regular basis or be disbanded after successful completion of the task.

tax. A charge levied by a national or local government on companies and individuals in respect of specific items (e.g. income, purchases etc).

taxable income. Income after allowances are made for tax-deductible items (e.g. personal mortgage interest payments), upon which income tax will be charged by the INLAND REVENUE in the UK or the INTERNAL REVENUE SERVICE in the USA.

tax avoidance. A legal practice of using prescribed allowances and accounting procedures related to taxable items to avoid paying tax.

tax credit system. In the UK, an income tax/social security system to provide cash rebates to those earning less than the level at which they would pay tax. It is administered through the PAY-AS-YOU-EARN system.

tax evasion. An illegal practice of non-disclosure of taxable items (e.g. income), beyond allowed procedures, in order to evade tax which is legally payable.

tax haven. A country whose taxation laws are lenient (i.e. a low rate of income tax) and to which individuals emigrate to avoid paying tax in their country of origin. This only applies to people whose income is substantial and for whom the self-imposed exile from their home country is worth the financial gain.

tax holiday. A temporary deferment of tax due, allowed by a tax office for a specific reason — possibly part of a government-sponsored incentive scheme to support industry.

tax schedule. A set of rules and procedures designed for a specific employment pattern, under which individuals are assessed for taxation (e.g. Schedule D in the UK covers self-employed people). See INCOME TAX.

tax return. A declaration made by every employed individual of the income and expenditure relating to his employment during a certain period.

tax year. The 12-month period chosen by a company, at the end of which results will be published, and a tax assessment made.

Taylor, Frederick Winslow. A US industrial engineer who pioneered the principles of SCIENTIFIC MANAGEMENT, applying them to his industrial activity. His doctrine of defining the one best way of carrying out any production task and paying operators in direct proportion to their output level has survived to the present day as PAYMENT-BY-RESULTS, PIECEWORK, and WORK STUDY. Much discredited for his simplistic view of MOTIVATION, Taylor is still studied today and many of his principles, adapted to modern social conditions, are practised. See F.W. Taylor, *Scientific Management* (New York: Harper & Row, 1947).

Taylorism. A synonym for SCIENTIFIC MAN-AGEMENT, or the linking of remuneration to ouptut through a PAYMENT-BY-RESULTS scheme.

t-distribution (Student's t-distribution). A probability distribution of sample statistics which is very similar to the NORMAL DISTRIBUTION (as the sample size increases, so does this similarity). It is commonly used to test whether or not a sample is a reasonable representation of a POPULATION with a characteristic that is 'normally' distributed (e.g. to test whether a change in the production method of electric light bulbs has improved the life expectancy of the bulbs). It was developed by the UK statistician, W.S. Gosset, writing under the nom-de-plume of 'Student'.

teaching machines. An abortive attempt to mechanize teaching and/or learning processes, launched in the 1960s. The display of items to be learned, questions to be answered etc, was non-interactive and the experiment failed. Subsequent work on computerized, interactive systems benefited from the experience, however, and advances in the field of INTELLIGENT KNOWLEDGE-BASED SYSTEMS have shown that there are potential areas of use for such technology in teaching.

Teamsters Union. See INTERNATIONAL BROTHERHOOD OF TEAMSTERS, CHAUFFEURS, WAREHOUSEMEN AND HELPERS OF AMERICA.

technological change. Changes in environments, practices, attitudes etc which are brought about by developments in available technologies for product and process design. During the last two decades the development of microelectronics technology has had a profound influence on social, economic, and political issues, giving rise to many changes of a fundamental nature in everyday life throughout the world.

technological forecasting. Forecasting based upon predicted trends in technological development, the implications of which are consolidated into possible scenarios (e.g. if remote shopping via interactive television is possible by 1990, the patterns of building

new retail outlets will be altered to allow for lesser numbers of pedestrian shoppers). See DELPHI TECHNIQUE; NORMATIVE FORECASTING; SCENARIO-WRITING APPROACH.

technological unemployment. Unemployment brought about by new technologies, reducing the requirement for human input. The advent of many new technologies during a worldwide recession, and following a prolonged period of industrial labour unrest, clouds the issue of the degree to which technology can be said to result in job losses, but it is clear, in specific cases, that capital equipment can be employed to carry out a task previously done by people, in some instances more efficiently.

technology. A developed means of achieving general or specific ends through the use of materials, equipment, processes and protocols made available by scientific study.

technology agreement. See NEW TECHNOLOGY AGREEMENT.

technology push. The concept of changes taking place in society, companies, individuals etc as a direct result of pressure generated by a particular technology which is available and whose use presents potential commercial benefits.

technology transfer. The application in one industrial area of a technological process successfully installed in another. In this way, good ideas are spread across sectoral boundaries, and the exploitation of a particular technology is improved (e.g. the extrusion process, well-established in the plastics industry, has been transferred to the food industry, initially for the manufacture of biscuits).

teleconferencing. Holding a multi-way conversation between several different geographical locations, using telephone lines and/or satellite channels. Early equipment used modified telephones; these have now been developed into high-quality devices. Video conferencing is now a practical reality, enabling several people in different countries to meet 'face to face'. When combined with FACSIMILE TRANSMISSION of documents, the effect can be as communicative as an actual meeting.

telegraphic transfer. An instruction sent from one bank to another to credit or debit funds from an account. The term is still used, even though such instructions are now usually sent by telex. *See also* ELECTRONIC FUNDS TRANSFER.

telefax. A FACSMILE TRANSMISSION device employing a photographic recording process (a send terminal), modems and a telephone link, and a photographic reproduction process (a receive terminal). Written text, diagrams etc on the paper fed into the send terminal are received almost instantaneously at the other terminal.

Teletext Output of Price Information by Computer. *See* TOPIC.

teletype. The transfer of typed text by an electronic device, from a keyboard to a remote printer.

teleworking. The concept of individuals working on shared communication lines without leaving their homes (i.e. not needing a shared office). The development of WIDE AREA NETWORKS, TELECONFERENCING and FACSIMILE TRANSMISSION during the first half of the 1980s meant that the concept became a reality. The social aspects of working alone, however, have yet to be weighed.

telex. The transfer of text from one teletype terminal to another via a telephone link.

tel quel rate. The exchange rate at which a financial instrument may be bought in one country, using the currency of another country.

tender. A formal offer by one party to carry out work for another party, in accordance with specific conditions. In the USA, a tender offer is a TAKEOVER BID in which a company offers to buy all the shares in another company.

term assurance. A LIFE INSURANCE policy which pays out only upon the death of the policyholder during the term of the policy, as opposed to an ENDOWMENT policy which pays at a certain date even when the policyholder is still alive.

terminal. A computer input/output device consisting of a keyboard, a VISUAL DISPLAY UNIT and other specialized equipment (a MOUSE, tablet, LIGHT PEN etc). A terminal may be a 'slave' – able only to receive information and respond, or 'intelligent' – able to process data itself, OFF-LINE from the CENTRAL PROCESSING UNIT.

terminal market. *See* FORWARD MARKET.

terminal qualification. A qualification gained at the end of a course of study.

terminal value. The result of investing a specified amount for a certain number of years, at a known rate of interest. *See* COMPOUND INTEREST.

term loan (time loan). A loan which is to be paid back by a certain date, either in a lump sum or scheduled repayments.

terms and conditions of employment. A formally-agreed arrangement between an employer and an employee regarding the manner of working and all aspects of the CONTRACT between the two parties.

term shares. SHARES which the holder is not allowed to sell until after a specified agreed period.

terms of business. A formal statement of the conditions which a company applies to any commercial contractual agreement.

terms of reference. A formally-agreed description of objectives, aims, activities, resources and timing related to a particular project or piece of work.

terms of trade. A comparative measure of increases in export prices and increases in import prices, expressed as a fraction (the price index for exports divided by the price index for imports) on a national basis. If this is less than one, then import prices are rising more quickly than export prices – which is not good for the economy. The reverse is also true.

terotechnology. An all-embracing term concerned with capital investment and implementation of practical technology (e.g.

manufacturing plant). All aspects of the investment are taken into account, from financial to maintenance. The idea is to consider the project as a whole — balancing one factor against another (e.g. an apparently sound investment from a financial viewpoint might be a long-term problem in terms of maintenance costs).

territorial rights. The perceived rights over a certain geographical space or functional activity. If an individual feels that his territorial rights have been abused (e.g. by someone else intervening in his work), frustration will give rise to conflict. *See also* ROLE CONFLICT.

TGWU. *See* TRANSPORT AND GENERAL WORKERS' UNION.

T-group. *See* LABORATORY TRAINING.

Theory X and Theory Y. Management styles, characterized by Douglas MAC-GREGOR, which divide approaches to employees into two types. Theory X bases management behaviour on the assumption that people work as little as possible and are basically self-centred, and that the manager has a supervisory role. Theory Y assumes that people are keen to be innovative and that the manager has an enabling rule.

Theory Z. A management strategy developed by William Ouchi. It has three basic principles: a collective work ethic (everyone in a group works for the overall benefit of the group), loyalty to fellow workers, and trust between individuals. In an organization this can provide the basis for improved communication, teamwork and the recognition of a common goal. Decisions are made collectively and group sacrifice is expected in times of trouble (e.g. everyone taking a cut in pay if a company is losing money). For a full explanation see W. Ouchi, *Theory Z: How American Business can meet the Japanese Challenge* (Reading, Mass.: Addison Wesley, 1981).

therblig. An element of bodily movement, used in ERGONOMIC analysis of physical activity in WORK STUDY. Frank Gilbreth recorded 17 such elements and invented the term by reversing his own name. A therblig

chart is used to record a series of elements involved in a complex activity, such as working a machine tool.

thermal copy. A low-quality hard copy of a computer (or other) printout.

30 Share Index. *See* FINANCIAL TIMES INDUSTRIAL ORDINARY SHARE INDEX.

threat matrix. A part of SWOT analysis. The threats to a company are placed in a square matrix, one axis showing how serious the threat is, the other showing how likely it is to occur. Serious threats which are very likely to occur are dealt with first.

three-bin system. A stock control method, similar the to TWO-BIN SYSTEM, employing a third bin as extra safety stock.

3i. *See* INVESTORS IN INDUSTRY.

threshold agreement. An agreement between two parties that a price or wage will be increased by a set amount when some relevant factor reaches a certain threshold value (e.g. when the RETAIL PRICE INDEX passes a certain level, an automatic increase in wages will be awarded).

threshold limit value (TLV). A measured level of some environmental factor (e.g. noise) which must not be exceeded. For example, in some industrial premises, the level of ambient noise is not permitted to exceed 80 dBa on a constant basis, although short-duration increases may be allowed. Thus 80 dBa is the TLV for this noise regulation.

threshold price. (1) The price for an item above which its selling characteristics may be expected to alter.
(2) In the EUROPEAN COMMUNITY, the minimum import price, set by the Common Agricultural Policy, at which supplies of cereals, milk and milk products, and sugar, from non-Community countries may be delivered to Community ports. The threshold price differs from the TARGET PRICE insofar that transport costs are added from the port to the inland destination. If import prices are below the threshold price, the difference is made up by agricultural levies.

throughput. Production output expressed in quantitative terms.

through-the-wall banking. *See* AUTOMATED TELLING MACHINERY.

tight rate. A PIECEWORK rate which is set so that an operator has difficulty in making a reasonable wage.

time and motion study. A WORK STUDY exercise designed to quantify the labour aspects of a task for purposes of accounting and method improvement.

time bill. *See* BILL OF EXCHANGE.

time card. A personal record of attendance of a specific period (usually a week). It may be signed by a person in a supervisory position, or 'punched' in a clock designed to record the time of arrival and departure (in which case it is called a 'clock card').

time clock. A clock mechanism designed to print information on cards inserted into it for the purposes of recording times of attendance at a place of work (hence 'clocking-in and out' and 'punching the clock').

time deposit. A deposit account in a bank, building society etc from which money may be withdrawn only after notice of a specified period is given (e.g. seven days). Higher interest may be paid on this type of account than on those without the notice requirement.

time loan. *See* TERM LOAN.

time preference. The degree to which something could be invested and used at some point in the future, rather than used now, and the financial benefit which would be gained by so doing. The time preference is either to use it now or to invest it.

time series forecasting. A forecasting method providing predictions for future values of some variable based upon studying past values over set periods of time (e.g. forecasting the annual heating bill for the next year by examining the heating bills for the past three years and allowing for known or assumed unit price increases).

time sharing. Two or more parties making use of one computer (or other piece of expensive capital equipment), thereby sharing the cost of such an item.

time sheet. A written record of activities over a period of time, particularly for a specific operation.

time span of discretion. A period for which an individual is permitted to be responsible for an operation before a review is made by superiors.

time study. *See* WORK STUDY.

tip. *See* GRATUITY.

TIR. *See* TRANSPORT INTERNATIONAL ROUTIER.

TLV. *See* THRESHOLD LIMIT VALUE.

TNC (transnational corporation). *See* MULTINATIONAL COMPANY.

tolerance. A defined degree to which a dimension may depart from its nominal value.

tommy shop. In the UK during the 19th century, a shop, owned by the employer, in which employees could buy household provisions and other normal requirements with coupons provided by the employer in lieu of wages. This presented grave problems for employees who frequently obtained poor value and often ran into their employers' debt. The practice was abolished by the TRUCK ACTS.

tooling. Wholly- or partly-specialized equipment used in conjunction with capital plant in a production process. For example, a power press is a machine tool but the dies used within it to produce a particular pressed part are referred to as tooling.

top down. A method of disseminating ideas (e.g. for change), which starts at the highest levels of an organization and employs an iterative process of persuasion downwards through the hierarchy. The opposite of 'bottom up'.

top hat pension scheme. A company PENSION scheme designed to provide extra benefits to senior managers on retirement. It is used as an attractive part of a job 'package' in recruitment.

TOPIC (Teletext Output of Price Information by Computer). The London Stock Exchange viewdata price distribution service.

top out. To finish (e.g. a special project).

tort. An action which causes injury or harm to someone else for which they may claim damages in court. This may not include breach of contract or criminal acts.

total cost approach to distribution. A method of calculating distribution costs which attempts to include all costs, not just the obvious items (e.g. waiting time from drivers, costs of handling returnable containers etc).

total quality control (TQC). The philosophy of all-embracing quality consciousness initiated by the US industrial engineers W. Edward Deming and Joseph Duran in Japan in the post-war era. TQC is based upon meticulous attention to detail in operation, rigid adherence to self-discipline in providing quality at each stage, and an enthusiasm for quality improvements created by a genuine identification with this goal by all members of an organization. It has been applied to both manufacturing and service operations. For a full explanation see P. Crosby, *Quality is Free* (New York: Free Press, 1982). *See* COMPANY-WIDE QUALITY CONTROL; JUST-IN-TIME PRODUCTION; SUPPLIER QUALITY ASSURANCE.

touch screen. A computer VISUAL DISPLAY UNIT which allows the user to give commands to the OPERATING SYSTEM by touching the screen at specific places, instead of by typing on the keyboard.

touch trigger problems. Minor industrial relations problems which are seen to lead to much larger disputes.

Towne, Henry. An early writer on SCIENTIFIC MANAGEMENT who encouraged Frederick TAYLOR in his work. Towne's paper,

The Engineer as an Economist (American Society of Mechanical Engineers, 1886) called for research into the area and is generally agreed to have inspired the early work in this discipline.

TQC. *See* TOTAL QUALITY CONTROL.

track system. A PAY SCHEME for staff or management employees within which rules are set which will strictly control each individual's salary increases with respect to time. The 'track' is the path, drawn on a graph, which each salary level will follow.

trade. (1) A specific occupation which requires definable skills and abilities, particularly of a manual nature.
(2) A business activity consisting of buying and selling goods without altering them.
(3) Bartering – exchanging goods for goods.

trade association. An organization designed to serve the common needs and interests of companies sharing an industrial or commercial sector, funded by members (e.g. the Society of Motor Manufacturers and Traders in the UK).

trade cycle. A notional behaviour pattern of national and international economic activity, characterized by alternating peaks and troughs in levels of employment, growth, income etc. *See* BUSINESS CYCLE.

Trade Descriptions Act 1968. A UK statute covering the manner in which a product or service may be described to the market, in order to prevent ambiguity which might disadvantage the consumer.

trade discount. A discount given by a seller to a buyer in recognition of their bona fide activity in a common trade (e.g. a builders' merchant sells materials to builders at a trade discount).

trade dispute. (1) A disagreement between employer and employees centring on working practices.
(2) A disagreement between two or more countries, debating the equitability of the balance of trade between them, sometimes escalating into a 'trade war'.

Trade Disputes Acts 1960, 1965. In the UK, the laws which made peaceful picketing legal, enabling trade unions to strike without fear of prosecution.

Trade Disputes and Trade Union Acts 1927, 1946. In the UK, legislation which dealt with: (*i*) whether or not union dues paid by a member should include a political levy only if the member contracted in (the latter law decreed that a political levy should be included in the dues unless the member contracted out); and (*ii*) the degree to which a SYMPATHY STRIKE could be taken.

trade drive. A concerted effort on the part of one country to export goods to a particular TARGET POPULATION.

trade fair. An exhibition mounted to promote specific trade activity by providing facilities for sellers to advertise and demonstrate their services or products in one location where potential buyers can easily visit them all. Trade fairs may be organized by trade associations, for their specific sectors, or at a national level, for one country to promote itself in an international environment.

trade investment. The purchase by one company of shares in another for the purposes of gaining control.

trademark. A motif or emblem which is owned by an individual or company, used to identify a product or BRAND, which may not be used by another company or individual without the express permission of the owner. *See also* LOGO.

trade name. A name used by an individual or company in the course of operation. This may be expressed as 'Company X' trading as 'Trade Name'.

trade-off. A compromise based upon balancing advantages and disadvantages of various options and choosing a position which avoids the worst levels of the combined effects.

trade press. Journals and newspapers covering news and features concerning a particular trade.

Trades Union Congress (TUC). A UK organization, founded in 1868 to promote trade union development and strength by providing a forum for discussion and policymaking, and by representing trade union views in consultative bodies such as the NATIONAL ECONOMIC DEVELOPMENT ORGANIZATION.

trade union. An organization of employees formed to represent common viewpoints and interests, and to protect individuals from malpractice in employment, through lobbying from a position of strength. Some unions are formed to represent members from one industry (e.g. the National Union of Mineworkers); others cover several industries but one or two specific trades (e.g. the Amalgamated Union of Engineers); others still cover broad areas of employment (e.g. the Transport and General Workers' Union). Some unions have strong political ties including substantial financial support for political parties (e.g. to the Labour Party in the UK).

Trade Union and Labour Relations Act 1974. In the UK, legislation which repealed the INDUSTRIAL RELATIONS ACT 1971, abolished the National Industrial Relations Court and increased immunity for trade unions involved in strikes.

trading account. A statement of gross profit for a period, showing only revenue and expenses, with a minimum of detail.

trading down. The reduction of service to customers and prices in the hope of increasing sales volume, and thus TURNOVER.

trading post system. The practice of trading SECURITIES at a fixed place inside a STOCK EXCHANGE.

trading profit. *See* NET PROFIT.

trading stamps. A promotional technique popular in the 1960s and 1970s based on retailing discounts in the form of cash or free goods, in return for stamps given to the customer at the point of sale and handed back in set quantities to the retailer or a trading stamps company at a later date.

trading up. The introduction of new products or services which intentionally involve a company for the first time, in a more exclusive sector of the market. This may result in lower sales volume (because of a higher price) but increase TURNOVER and PROFIT.

traditional society stage. The first stage in a developing economy, including the establishment of basic infrastructure, agriculture and simple industry.

training board. An organization set up to promote and develop specific training activities within an industrial sector (e.g. the Engineering Industry Training Board in the UK).

training function. The functional area within a company which is responsible for developing the skills of new and existing employees in line with identified requirements for the future of the company.

training levy. A charge made by an industrial training board on companies in the sector which it covers. In return for this money the board provides a service in advising and developing training programmes, information on skills etc.

training manual. A set of instructions designed to enable someone to complete a programme of training in accordance with the intended methods, timescale etc.

transaction. (1) An activity which takes place in the course of business.
(2) A computer operation.

transaction cost. The cost associated with carrying out a transaction (e.g. STAMP DUTY).

transducer. A device in an electromechanical system which enables a signal, generated in one form, to be relayed in another form (e.g. a sonic echo may be converted into an electrical impulse signal and relayed through a circuit).

transfer. (1) A change of ownership or responsibility for an item from one party to another. This is sometimes purely for accounting reasons (e.g. the transfer of stocks from one account to another).
(2) An alteration of physical position.

transfer line. Production equipment designed to carry out several operations in a particular sequence, moving the workpiece from one station to the next automatically. A transfer line may be dedicated or flexible.

transfer pricing. An accounting procedure which covers the transfer of goods between two companies in the same group in accordance with the company's financial policy (i.e. without profit). The cost to the receiving company is referred to as the transfer price.

translating routine. *See* COMPILER.

transnational corporation (TNC). *See* MULTINATIONAL COMPANY.

Transport and General Workers' Union (TGWU). In the UK, the main trade union representing unskilled and general workers.

transportation problem. An algorithmic method in LINEAR PROGRAMMING which attempts to optimize a combination of resources and requirements through a succession of matrix diagrams. It has now been largely superseded in practice by the use of computers.

Transport International Routier (TIR). A European system of transport regulations for heavy goods vehicles. As well as acting as a regulatory body (on factors such as loading, drivers' hours etc), TIR also provides customs clearance carnets which can be used to clear trucks through international borders en route from origin to destination.

travel to work area. The catchment area for employees at a company's site. It is used in location choice, by calculating the time and distance involved in reaching a location from various aspects (e.g. local towns etc).

Treasury. (1) The central government financial authority with responsibility for controlling income and expenditure at a national and international level.
(2) The financial operation of a company or organization.

Treasury bill. A promissory note sold by tender by the Treasury entitling the buyer to payment from the government's loan fund.

Treaty of Rome. The original agreement covering the formation of the European Economic Community, signed at Rome on 25 March 1957. *See* EUROPEAN COMMUNITY.

trend. An identifiable tendency in some variable which may be taken as an indicator of future behaviour.

trend extrapolation. Projecting the trend in a variable forward in time on a chart, making assumptions about the future based upon known performance.

triadic product test. A marketing research technique in which the consumer is presented with three unmarked products, of which two are the same. The consumer is asked to pick the product which is different. STATISTICAL INFERENCE from the data thus generated (over a large number of tests with the same product) can be used to establish whether a significant difference is being perceived.

trial balance. An accounting practice to provide a simple check on the integrity of recorded figures in DOUBLE ENTRY book keeping. All credit balances and all debit balances are totalled and should be equal.

tribunal. A formal hearing of a case in the presence of a person of authority.

trigger price mechanism. A price level which is used to bring some special action into play (e.g. when an import price falls below a certain level, government action may begin to curb levels of importation).

Trist, Eric. A UK writer on industrial sociology, particularly concerned with small group working practices in the coal mining industry. For a full explanation see E. Trist and K. Bamforth, 'Some Social and Psychological Consequences of the Longwall Method of Coal Getting', *Human Relations* 4, 1951; see also D. Pugh, D. Hickson and C. Hinings, *Writers on Organizations* (3rd edn, Harmondsworth: Penguin, 1983).

Truck Acts 1831, 1896, 1940. UK legislation which required employers to pay employees in legal tender, with some particular condition (e.g. the rights of hourly-paid employees to be paid in cash, not credit transfer). One early effect of the Truck Acts was to abolish the practice of payment by vouchers which could only be used at a company's TOMMY SHOP. *See also* WAGES ACT 1986.

trust. (1) A formal agreement under which a trustee takes responsibility for some property or amount of capital and uses it (e.g. by investment) for the benefit of someone else, on behalf of the original owner.
    (2) In the USA, a monopoly which arises as a result of two or more companies in a similar field merging by all stock being entrusted to one new board of trustees. Antitrust legislation was designed to prevent such collaboration leading to actual monopolies.

trust company. An organization which acts as a trustee, often investing money on behalf of clients. *See* INVESTMENT TRUST; UNIT TRUST.

trustee. An individual or organization empowered to make use of resources on behalf of someone else.

t-score. The ratio of a deviation from the MEAN, or other PARAMETER, in a DISTRIBUTION to the STANDARD ERROR. The resultant 'score' is compared with the critical value of the T-DISTRIBUTION.

t-test. A test using the T-DISTRIBUTION to test whether a correlation coefficient is significantly different from zero.

TUC. *See* TRADES UNION CONGRESS.

turnkey contract. A project in which the contractor has responsibility for completing all aspects, leaving the customer with a system which requires him simply to 'turn the key'.

turnover. (1) Sales revenue. The revenue from sales received by a company or individual in the course of business over a set period of time.

(2) A cycle of replenishment (e.g. of inventory or staff). For example, if half the people in a company leave and are replaced each year, the company may be said to have a 50 percent per annum turnover of staff.

turnover value. The total money value of transactions (i.e. the SHARE price multiplied by the number of shares bought or sold).

tutorial system. A method of teaching employing formal lectures supported by follow-up sessions between the lecturer and small groups of students, to allow for questions, related exercises etc.

twilight shift. A SHIFT which is arranged for working in the early evening (i.e. between the day and night shifts, possibly with some overlap).

two-bin system (last bag system). A simple STOCK CONTROL method used for low-value items in production. When one bin becomes empty, another binload is ordered and should arrive before the second bin has been used up. The empty bin itself is the signal to reorder, and the order quantity is fixed at one bin full.

two factor theory. *See* HERZBERG'S TWO FACTOR THEORY.

two-handed process chart. An ERGONOMICS device used in WORK STUDY to analyse the motion of both hands during an operation.

two-tier board. The practice in some European countries (e.g. West Germany − where the idea originated) of having an upper and lower tier in the management structure. Workforce representatives form part of the upper tier − the SUPERVISORY BOARD, while the lower tier is the management board, responsible for the day-to-day running of the company.

two-tier monetary system. A system used to protect currency or balance of payments by using two different systems of EXCHANGE CONTROL.

U

UCCA. *See* UNIVERSITIES CENTRAL CLEARING ADMINISTRATION.

UDCs. *See* URBAN DEVELOPMENT CORPORATIONS.

ultra vires. A UK law, repealed in 1973, concerned with debts of companies in extraordinary circumstances and activities outside their articles of association.

unabsorbed cost. An overhead cost which has not been recovered due to a shortfall in productive OUTPUT (i.e. insufficient sales will be made to cover the costs which had been apportioned over a planned but unachieved volume).

unattended time. Time for which a piece of equipment is not in use nor being serviced.

uncalled capital. The difference between the paid-up capital and issued capital of a company if the latter is the larger of the two (i.e. money owing to the company for the sale of shares which have not yet been paid for).

uncontrolled work. Parts of an operating process which cannot or have not been measured by WORK STUDY techniques and which must thus be estimated for purposes of calculation.

UNCTAD. *See* UNITED NATIONS CONFERENCE ON TRADE AND DEVELOPMENT.

underinsure. To insure an item for less than its realistic value.

undermanning. Assigning less labour resources to an operation than it is deemed to require.

underrecovery. The incurring of UNABSORBED COSTS.

underwrite. (1) To provide insurance for something.
(2) To guarantee the purchase of SHARES in a FLOTATION in the event that they are not all sold on the market.

undiscounted gross benefit cost ratio. The COST BENEFIT RATIO for an investment which includes no allowance for DEPRECIATION, nor for the PRESENT VALUE of future money.

undiscounted net benefit cost ratio. The COST BENEFIT RATIO of an investment which takes into account the DEPRECIATION costs of an investment over time (as a reduction in the cash inflows), but does not include a consideration of the PRESENT VALUE of future money.

undistributed profits. *See* RETAINED EARNINGS.

unearned income. Income received as a result of money invested, as opposed to remuneration for work carried out. The two are the same for income tax purposes.

unemployed. An indivdual without formal, paid employment. *See* STRUCTURAL UNEMPLOYMENT; TECHNOLOGICAL UNEMPLOYMENT.

unemployment benefit ('the dole'). Money paid by the government to unemployed people who are unable to find paid work.

UNESCO. *See* UNITED NATIONS EDUCATIONAL, SCIENTIFIC AND CULTURAL ORGANIZATION.

unexpired cost. The cost of an ASSET which may be used to generate income in the future.

unfair dismissal. A dismissal which is judged to be unfair by a TRIBUNAL. The case is usually brought against an employer by the individual concerned, supported by a TRADE UNION. The employer must prove to the tribunal that the dismissal was fair.

unfunded debt. A DEBT which must be repaid at some future point. *See also* TERM LOAN.

UNICE. *See* UNION DES INDUSTRIES DE LA COMMUNAUTÉ EUROPÉENNE.

UNIDO. *See* UNITED NATIONS INTERNATIONAL DEVELOPMENT ORGANIZATION.

unilateral arbitration. A situation in which one side in an industrial dispute decides unilaterally to go to an arbitration body to seek a solution to the problem.

Union des Industries de la Communauté Européenne (UNICE). An association of the confederations of industry in the EEC member states, formed in 1958 and still active in industrial policy-making in the EUROPEAN COMMUNITY.

union shop. A POST ENTRY CLOSED SHOP.

unique selling point (unique selling proposition). In marketing, something which must be stressed in selling an item or service, since it is not offered by competitors and thus gives the company a unique advantage.

unique selling proposition. *See* UNIQUE SELLING POINT.

unissued capital. The difference between the AUTHORIZED CAPITAL and the ISSUED CAPITAL of a company (i.e. the FACE VALUE of shares which the company has chosen not to offer for sale yet).

unit. A SECURITY sold by a UNIT TRUST company, entitling the holder to a share in the income which that company generates as a result of its dealing in securities. It may be redeemed at any time for its original or 'bid' price.

unitary system. An INDUSTRIAL RELATIONS system designed on the basis of one central policy which does not allow alternative interpretations. Typically, a company run on the unitary 'model' is seen as 'one big happy family' in which disagreement on any issue is considered a failure in management to resolve all differences.

unit cost. The cost of one unit of a product. For discrete products this would be 'each' or 'per 100' etc. For dimensional products, it might be 'per metre' or 'per litre' etc. Unit cost is the best focus for cost reduction, since it is the basis for the selling price, and represents the combination of all other factors.

United Nations Conference on Trade and Development (UNCTAD). An organization, established by the United Nations in 1964, to promote international trade, and especially to accelerate economic development. It is the main forum for discussion between developed and developing nations on trade etc. The Conference meets at least once every four years. It is co-ordinated by the UK Trade and Development Board.

United Nations Educational, Scientific and Cultural Organization (UNESCO). A UN agency, established in 1946, based in Paris, responsible for promoting international harmony and respect for law and human rights.

United Nations Industrial Development Organization (UNIDO). A UN agency, established in 1966, responsible for promoting industrialization in the developing countries. It was declared independent of the UN General Assembly in 1985 – the first UN agency to be given its own treaty status.

United Stock Exchange. The result of the combination of all UK and Irish stock exchanges in 1973, carried out to remove anomalies in prices and administrative duplication.

unit of account. A monetary unit used for measuring or comparing values, amounts etc. Within countries this is usually the unit of currency. Between countries, international standards or specially invented units are used (e.g. the European Currency Unit).

unit price. The price of a unit of some item (e.g. £100 per kilogram).

unit production. The manufacturing of products one at a time.

unit trust. An organization set up to manage investment on behalf of many individuals, using the strength, power and securitiy of a large body to provide benefits to small investors. The management company of the unit trust sells redeemable units and invests the money in various ways, to optimize the return. A unit trust also has a trustee, often a bank, and an agreed set of payment procedures and charges.

universal bank. *See* BANQUE D'AFFAIRES.

universe. In the context of statistical surveys, the large group about which observations and predictions may be made on the basis of the experimental sample taken.

Universities Central Clearing Administration (UCCA). The central UK office for universities through which all applications are made and administered.

UNIX. A widely-used computer OPERATING SYSTEM, developed by Bell Laboratories in the USA in 1969.

unlimited company. A registered company whose shareholders or members are liable to pay any and all debts if the company is wound up.

Unlisted Securities Market (USM). A UK market, created by the London Stock Exchange, upon which shares in new or small limited companies can be sold, without the need for such companies to become fully public. Thus, joining the USM represents a FLOTATION to a limited extent.

unmanned manufacturing. The technology of operating entire manufacturing facilities without the need for human operators (e.g. with the use of robots).

unofficial strike. A work stoppage due to an industrial dispute which has not yet received the formal backing of the trade union(s) concerned.

unproductive time. Time within a certain OPERATING CYCLE during which no productive work is carried out.

unsecured creditor. An individual who is given credit without security.

unsecured loan stock. STOCK issued by a public company which has no guarantee that interest will be paid.

unskilled work. A task for which no special ability or training is required.

unsocial hours. Hours of employment outside the normal SHIFT hours, which are agreed between employer and employee, which disrupt normal social life outside work (e.g. early mornings and late evenings).

unsolicited goods. Items which are received by someone who did not ask for them to be delivered. In the UK, the Unsolicited Goods Act 1971 decreed that the recipient could legally decide to keep such goods without payment, a measure which effectively stopped the practice.

upset price (reserve price). The minimum price at which a client wishes to sell an article at auction, and below which no sale will be agreed to.

urban development corporations (UDCs). In the UK, regional urban bodies set up by central government in 1987 to administer industrial development in specific areas (e.g. existing ENTERPRISE ZONES and REGIONAL DEVELOPMENT areas). Responsible to the Department of the Environment, the UDCs have a broad remit, including the encouragement of industrial investment as well as liaison between other offices (e.g. housing, CHAMBERS OF COMMERCE etc).

Urwick, Lyndall. A writer on SCIENTIFIC MANAGEMENT and dynamic administration. See L. Urwick and E.F.L. Brech, *The Making of Scientific Management,* Vol. I: *Thirteen Pioneers* (London: Pittman), and H.C. Metcalfe and L. Urwick, *Dynamic Administration: The Collected Works of Mary Parker Follett* (New York: Harper & Row, 1941).

usage. The rate at which material is used in a process.

usage classification. An indication of how expensive or important an item is, calculated on the basis of its usage value, usually in terms of Class A, B, or C. *See* PARETO ANALYSIS.

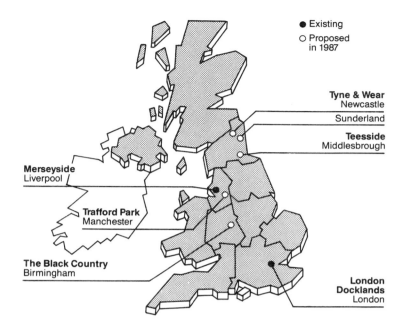

● Existing
○ Proposed
in 1987

Tyne & Wear
Newcastle
Sunderland

Teesside
Middlesbrough

Merseyside
Liverpool

Trafford Park
Manchester

The Black Country
Birmingham

London
Docklands
London

UK urban development corporations

usage value. The value of the amount of an item used during a specific period (e.g. annual usage value). This is used in determining factors relating to that item (e.g. its importance to the firm etc).

usance. The period for which an amount of money is lent.

US Chamber of Commerce. A government organization set up in the USA to monitor factors affecting business performance in the public and private sectors.

user-friendly. A characteristic of a computer (or other system) which makes it easy for a new operator to understand and use.

USM. *See* UNLISTED SECURITIES MARKET.

utility. (1) Usefulness.
(2) A device or office which provides or serves a useful function.

utility function. In OPERATIONAL RESEARCH, a function which relates the value of various quantities of an item to its utility for a company.

utility program. SOFTWARE in the OPERATING SYSTEM of a computer which enables it to carry out its routine functions.

utility theory. A RISK ANALYSIS technique for comparing the monetary and utility values of investments with respect to the risk level involved.

V

value. (1) The amount of money which, it is estimated or known, an item is worth financially (i.e. the price which the consumer is prepared to pay for it).

(2) A personal assessment of the importance or worth of an item – a subjective reasoning.

value added. *See* ADDED VALUE.

value added network (VAN). A computerized communications NETWORK system designed to add value to the information which it is processing by means of a special presentation (e.g. Datastream). *See also* INTEGRATED SERVICES DIGITAL NETWORK.

value added tax (VAT). A tax administered in the UK by HM Customs and Excise, chargeable by most businesses for the provision of goods or services (except those exempted, e.g. food) in respect of the added value in the relevant process. Thus, a business charges VAT to its customers but may claim back VAT charged to it for goods and services received in the process. The result is that it only pays the VAT on the difference (the added value) to the authority, thus acting as a tax collector. Very small businesses are exempt (the 1987 minimum turnover for which VAT registration must be completed was £21,500 per annum).

value analysis. An analysis of the design of a product to determine ways in which cost reductions may be effected without loss of quality or sales, and potential for improving the value of the item to the customer (and hence increase sales revenue) or the company itself (e.g. by improving a profit margin).

value engineering. The process of engineering a product towards maximizing its value while limiting its cost.

value envelope. A project NETWORK ANALYSIS technique designed to compare actual work done with planned activity in terms of its value to the project. The envelope compares the cumulative value of work done if all activities are completed by their earliest date with the same calculation for latest dates. Then, during the project, actual work done may be reguarly compared with this to monitor progress.

VAN. *See* VALUE ADDED NETWORK.

variable cost. A production cost which is proportional in size to the level of production (e.g. material costs).

variable costing. *See* MARGINAL COSTING.

variable expense. A production expense which is proportional to the level of production output.

variable factor programming. A WORK STUDY technique for clerical workers, based upon daily loading, taking into account the variable nature of clerical work (e.g. telephone calls etc).

variable working hours. *See* FLEXIBLE WORKING HOURS.

variance. (1) The degree to which an actual figure differs from a budgeted or forecast figure (e.g. an incurred cost which is greater than a STANDARD COST).

(2) An expression of the dispersion around the mean of a RANDOM VARIABLE PROBABILITY DISTRIBUTION.

(3) The square of a STANDARD DEVIATION.

variance analysis. The use of variances to investigate success in conforming to plans and budgets.

variety. The degree to which a product family contains different designs as a result of PRODUCT DIFFERENTIATION and/or customer specifications being met. For example, a new car is not launched simply as one model, but as a range with different engines, doors, formats etc. Variety is the result of market demand stimulation, but it can produce complexity in manufacture and hence increase costs. It is important to distinguish between real variety — actual differences in product specifications, and apparent variety — apparent differences which are achieved by very minor additions to the specification and thus prove no problems in manufacture. Variety reduction is a major objective in cost-saving exercises.

VAT. *See* VALUE ADDED TAX.

vdu. *See* VISUAL DISPLAY UNIT.

vendor. *See* SUPPLIER.

vendor rating. A customer process of awarding merit points to a vendor for purposes of choosing sources of supply for a new or replaced business. *See also* WEIGHTED POINTS PLAN.

vendor scheduling. A PURCHASING technique of issuing a long-term, BLANKET ORDER to a SUPPLIER, agreeing price, specification and other general supply details, and subsequently requesting delivery quantities and timing by means of a regular schedule.

venture capital. Funds available to a firm, often from another individual or company, for investment, especially in specific projects. In particular, high-risk ventures may require special funding in this way. If an outside party is involved, it is usual for them to share in the profits derived from the project.

vertical integration. A merger or takeover of one company with or by another which is involved in the same business at a previous or subsequent stage in the production/supply process (e.g. a clothing manufacturer taking over a textiles manufacturer, or a chain of high street clothing shops).

very large-scale integration (VLSI). The design and manufacture of microcircuitry involving the fitting of many circuits onto one silicon chip for purposes of space saving, cost reduction and possible quality improvements.

vested interest. A reason, usually connected with potential personal gain, for someone to be other than impartial in a specific decision or choice.

vested rights. Rights which have been put into the ownership of an individual or company by someone else.

vicarious liability. The liability of an employer for the actions of employees while working under instructions.

vice-president. In the USA, the chief of a specific area of a business, usually a board member; roughly the equivalent to a director in the UK.

viewdata. A computerized communications system including the display of transmitted data on a screen. *See also* ELECTRONIC MAIL.

visible exports/imports. The export sale of goods rather than services (imports to the buyer).

Visicalc. A basic, popular on-screen calculating software package for computers, now largely superseded by *Lotus 1 2 3*.

visual display unit (vdu). The part of a computer which provides the visual indication of operation. It consists of a cathode ray tube (colour or monochrome) of high definition, a plasma screen, or a liquid crystal display (on some portable computers).

vital statistics. Facts and figures relating to the essential matters of a company, person or economy.

VLSI. *See* VERY LARGE-SCALE INTEGRATION.

vocational guidance. Advice given to individuals in choosing a new career.

vocational training. Training which is specifically aimed at preparing someone for a particular occupation.

Vogel's Approximation Method. A developed version of the TRANSPORTATION PROBLEM.

voluntary arbitration. An agreement by both sides in an INDUSTRIAL DISPUTE to go to ARBITRATION in an attempt to solve the problem.

voluntary assumption of risk. A legal principle which states that an individual who undertakes something of free will, knowing the risks involved, may not claim recompense for damage or accidents which subsequently occur as a result.

voting rights. The rights of an individual shareholder or member to vote at annual general meetings etc.

voucher. (1) A receipt for payment.
(2) A token which may be exchanged subsequently for goods or services.

Vroom, Victor H. An industrial psychologist, specializing in MOTIVATION and MANAGEMENT STYLE.

W

wage. Money paid for work done by an employee, in respect of a brief period (e.g. a week). A wage is normally used to describe remuneration of non-staff employees.

wage drift. The degree to which the actual amount being paid to operators in a company differs from the rate which is intended, allowing for overtime.

Wages Act 1986. UK legislation which changed the law on the payment of wages, taking away the statutory right of manual workers to be paid in cash (*see* TRUCK ACTS 1831, 1896, 1940). It also meant that at-source deductions from pay were illegal unless covered by statute (e.g. INCOME TAX).

walkthrough. (1) An initial survey of a situation prior to making a prognosis.
(2) An activity carried out by systems analysts and consultants prior to formulating a plan of action for a project.

Wall Street. The New York Stock Exchange (actually a very small street close to it). The term is also used colloquially to refer to the US financial market in general.

WAN. *See* WIDE AREA NETWORK.

wand. A light-emitting, reading device used to read BAR CODES.

want. An item or service which is desired by the consumer to satisfy non-essential requirements (e.g. fashion items of clothing).

warehousing. (1) Holding finished goods in store in order to supply the requirements of customers without delay. Warehousing enables a supplier or distributor to provide a local service to all parts of the country and internationally, even though manufacturing only takes place in one or a few locations.
(2) Storage of materials which are required for a production process.

warrant. (1) A document which instructs and authorizes a specific person to carry out a carefully-defined activity.
(2) On the UK Stock Exchange, a certificate attached to a BOND or SECURITY giving the holder the right to buy shares in the issuer's company at a set price or to subscribe to future bond issues by the same issuer.

warranty. A guarantee that a product will perform in accordance with its specification for at least a certain period after the date of sale, and that corrective action will be taken by or on behalf of the manufacturer should this not be so.

wash sale. A bogus TRANSACTION which is said to have taken place at an artificially high price in a COMMODITY market used by a seller to boost prices.

wastage. The loss of employees due to death, resignation or retirement. *See also* NATURAL WASTAGE.

waybill. A record of contents in a shipment of goods, with special instructions for handling, forwarding etc.

wealth tax. A tax levied (not in the UK) on the personal wealth of an individual after allowed amounts are deducted.

Weber, Max. An important German writer on industrial organizations and the forefather of industrial sociology.

weighted average. A method of reflecting the importance of each of a group of factors in their use within calculations for decision-making by multiplying each by a certain weighting factor. Thus, in calculating the mean, each value of x is multiplied by its weighting factor w before being totalled. This total is then divided by the total sum of all the weighting factors

weighted average
(weighted arithmetic
mean) $= \dfrac{\sum_1^n x_n w_n}{n}$

weighted points plan. A vendor-rating method in which points are awarded to a supplier on the basis of certain factors (e.g. delivery performance, quality problems etc) and then a weighting is applied for the importance of each factor in the context of the overall relationship.

Weights and Measures Act 1963. UK legislation dealing with standard declaration requirements for weights and measures of commerical goods.

wet money. Extra pay awarded for working in wet conditions.

white collar workers. Employees who work in office or staff jobs, as opposed to BLUE COLLAR WORKERS who work in factory environments.

white knight. A friendly company or individual who helps another company to resist an unwelcome TAKEOVER BID by making a better offer for the shares under threat. This may have the effect of frightening off the unwelcome bidder without a change in ownership taking place, However, there is an understanding that should the white knight be forced to make the purchase, no untoward interference in the company would subsequently be made.

white land. Land upon which it is forbidden to erect buildings.

White Paper. A government paper explaining policy of specific subjects. *See also* GREEN PAPER.

Whitley Committee on the Relations of Employers and Employees. A UK government committee which recommended the establishment of councils to act as discussion forums to prevent the rise of conflict in industrial relations at the time of such movements as SYNDICALISM. Whitley Councils were subsequently set up in the civil service, but never became popular in the private sector.

whole-job ranking. A technique in job evaluation which compares one job with another on a total basis (i.e. instead of trying to analyse the function and then award points to elements).

wholesale. (1) Relating to a wholesaler's operation.
(2) Something done on a large scale.

wholesale banking. The provision of banking services to companies on a large scale.

Wholesale Price Index. A monthly published index showing changes in the wholesale price of selected items.

wholesaler. A company or individual who buys goods for resale to someone other than the eventual consumer. A wholesaler may supply to retailers (who will sell the goods to the public), or manufacturing or service operators who use the goods in a process.

wide area network (WAN). A computer NETWORK which has nodes that are geographically widely spread – often internationally. *See also* LOCAL AREA NETWORK; VALUE ADDED NETWORK.

widget. In general discussions on production and selling etc, a standard product, obviating the need to relate the instance to a particular product type.

widows' allowances. In the UK, payments made to a widow for six months after the husband's death, as part of the National Insurance plan. Thereafter, a widow's pension is paid.

wildcat strike. A strike, often unofficial, which occurs without notice, intended to cause the maximum disruption to an operation.

WIMP (Windows, Icons, MOUSE, PULL-DOWN MENUS). USER-FRIENDLY SOFTWARE for computers which communicates by easily understood symbols, rather than the technical wording of an OPERATING SYSTEM.

Winchester. A hard disk data storage device in a computer.

window. An available space in a schedule within which some extra event may be fitted.

wind up. To liquidate a company by arranging for the sale of its assets and the settlement of its accounts. This is usually as the result of a winding-up order by the company itself or its creditors.

wink. In WORK STUDY, a period of .03 seconds.

WIP. *See* WORK IN PROGRESS.

withdrawal. The removal of money from a CIRCULAR FLOW IN INCOME by savings, overseas investment etc.

withholding tax. A tax deducted at source on interest and dividend payments.

with/without profits policy. Life insurance ENDOWMENT policies which do or do not include extra amounts on top of the basic endowment amount in respect of higher premiums (for 'with profits') and the performance of the insurance company over the period of the insurance. A without profits policy starts with a higher guaranteed lump sum endowment, but is overtaken at some point (perhaps half-way through the period) in this respect as the extra amounts added to the with profits policy begin to accumulate.

Woodward, Joan. A writer on manufacturing organizational structure. Her works include *Industrial Organization: Theory and Practice* (Oxford: Oxford University Press, 1965).

woollybacks. Employees who choose not to become involved in INDUSTRIAL DISPUTES. The term, given by more militant employees, denotes acting like a sheep, with the employer as the shepherd or wolf.

word processing. A computerized typing and editing program which enables text to be prepared, corrected, modified and printed in a convenient and time-saving fashion. Introduced in the late 1970s, word processing replaced the use of typewriters in many cases of commercial text preparation.

work. An activity directed towards a useful outcome.

work centre. A physical area arranged for specific work purposes, sometimes treated as one entity for administration purposes.

workers' control. A principle of enabling people employed in a work process to exercise control over its planning and resourcing (i.e. its management). *See* TWO-TIER BOARD.

worker-directors. Members of a company's workforce elected by colleagues to join a board of directors for purposes of industrial democracy. Proposed in the UK in 1976 by the BULLOCK REPORT, the idea did not become popular and was never given the legal requirement status sought for it. However, *see* TWO-TIER BOARD.

work factor system. A WORK STUDY system designed to analyse an operation, similar to a PREDETERMINED MOTION-TIME SYSTEM.

working capital. The difference between a company's CURRENT ASSETS and its CURRENT LIABILITIES (i.e. its net current assets).

working capital cycle. The turnover of working capital − the replenishment of expenditure by income.

working capital ratio. *See* CURRENT RATIO.

work in progress (WIP; goods in process). Items which are currently being worked on. This consists of materials to which some value has been added but which have not been completed. WIP represents a problem for accounting since it is often difficult to tell to what degree value has been added. In general, it is desirable to reduce WIP to the minimum quantity (and thus value) possible.

work measurement. The concept of quantifying effort and time required in specific activities for two purposes: cost accounting and PAY SYSTEMS. Even if remuneration is not linked to work output (which requires quantitative assessment of work done), effective financial control of a physical process still requires some form of work measurement to provide the basis for cost recovery and pricing policy.

workplace bargaining. A bargaining process, usually concerning working conditions, pay etc, which is carried out at the place of work.

work sampling. *See* ACTIVITY SAMPLING.

works councils. Committees of elected members from all areas of a factory which meet to air grievances, discuss ideas of general interest, and make recommendations to management.

work sharing. Two or more people sharing a job. *See* JOB SHARING.

workshop. (1) A place where manual work takes place in a manufacturing sense.

(2) A training group discussion session, concentrating on specific subjects.

works manager. A manager with responsibility for operations within a factory or plant. Specific duties and responsibilities vary widely, from a purely maintenance-based activity to control of all manufacture.

works pension scheme. A PENSION scheme organized by a company for its hourly paid workforce, usually flat-rate and non-contributory.

work station. A physical area designed to provide the best possible environment for a specific set of tasks.

work study (time study). The practice of analysing methods and activities to arrive at data for cost accounting (and possibly payment systems) and to improve methods and efficiency. It consists of WORK MEASURE-MENT and METHOD STUDY. The notion of the 'one best way' of carrying out a task comes directly from SCIENTIFIC MANAGEMENT theories and is intended to provide accurate knowledge of labour costs and capacity. *See* ORGANIZATION AND METHODS; STANDARD HOUR.

work-to-rule. A restrictive practice designed to cause disruption to an operation by withdrawal of co-operation between employees and management above and beyond the basic contractual requirement (the 'rules'). The method may also expose the degree to which the smooth running of the operation relies upon the goodwill of the employees,

since compliance with contractual agreement may not suffice to support the operation.

World Bank (International Bank for Reconstruction and Development). An international organization which began operations in 1946. Its purpose is to provide funds and technical assistance to facilitate economic development in its poorer member countries.

World Confederation of Labour. An international organization, established in 1920, with a membership of over 80 countries, based in Brussels.

World Federation of Trade Unions. An international organization, founded in 1945, with over 50 members, based in Prague.

World Health Organization (WHO). A specialized agency of the United Nations, established in 1948, based in Geneva.

writ. An official Crown instruction document.

write down. To remove an ASSET from a company's BALANCE SHEET by progressively decreasing its value until it is negligible.

write off. To remove an item from a company's BALANCE SHEET for extraordinary reasons (e.g. an ASSET which has been destroyed, or a BAD DEBT which will never be recovered).

written-down value. The value of an asset after DEPRECIATION has been written off to the PROFIT AND LOSS ACCOUNT.

wrongful dismissal. Dismissal which is declared illegal under prevailing employment legislation.

WYSIWYG ('What you see is what you get'). A computer term to describe a system which matches the display on the screen to the printed format subsequently obtained.

X

x-axis. The horizontal axis on a graph – often the timescale.

xerography. The technique upon which photocopiers are based – dry powder deposition and fixing.

Y

Yankee bond. A BOND which is issued in the US market by a non-US company.

y-axis. The vertical axis on a graph.

yearling. A SECURITY, particularly a UK stock issued by municipal authorities, which matures and may be redeemed within one year.

years' purchase. The cost of an investment in terms of the number of years' income which will be obtained from it.

yellow dog contract. A written agreement by an employee not to join a trade union.

yield. A RATE OF RETURN. The yield produced by SHARES is equal to the DIVIDEND divided by the price paid for the shares, expressed as a percentage.

yield variance. The degree to which a yield departs from a forecast yield.

YOP. *See* YOUTH OPPORTUNITIES PROGRAMME.

Young Workers Scheme. In the UK, a government subsidy paid to employers who take on school-leavers. Set up in 1982, by 1985 the level had increased to £15 per week for those paid less than £50 per week total.

Youth Opportunities Programme (YOP). A UK government scheme for work experience and training for unemployed school-leavers. Administered by the MANPOWER SERVICES COMMISSION, and paid for by the EEC Social Fund, the YOP scheme was successful in that two-thirds of its trainees stayed on to work with the companies which had trained them. It was replaced in 1982 by the YOUTH TRAINING SCHEME.

Youth Training Scheme (YTS). A UK government programme, funded partly by the EEC Social Fund, to encourage employers to find work for unemployed school-leavers. A small weekly wage is paid by the government to the trainee. Most trainees go into fully-paid employment after the one-year training period. Set up in 1982–3, YTS has been claimed as a success by the government which installed it (the period of training was extended to two years in 1986), but discounted by its critics as a political expedient to hide the true levels of youth unemployment.

YTS. *See* YOUTH TRAINING SCHEME.

yuppies (young, upwardly-mobile professionals). A mildly derogatory reference to successful but status-conscious business (or other professional) people.

Z

zaibatsu (grupu). A group of companies in Japan which co-ordinates their activities to mutual advantage. The companies are usually linked by ownership of equity, but this is limited to each company owning only a small stake (e.g. five per cent) in every other company. One company may be the dominant partner in the group, sometimes epynonymous. Each group usually includes a trading company, a bank, and other service companies to support the main activities of manufacture.

Z-chart. A graphical method employed in time series analysis to compare observed periodic (monthly) values of a variable, their cumulative total, and the moving annual total.

zero-based budgeting. Budgeting which classifies all future expenditure as new items, rather than simply more easily approvable increments on existing budgets.

zero-based review. A zero-based budgeting technique, developed into a formal management planning process.

zero coupon bond. A BOND which is issued without the normal interest coupon, but at a reduced price which will result in an attractive interest total by the time it is due for redemption.

zero defects policy. A quality policy which is aimed at removing all defective items from production and to delivering 100 per cent correct items. This is in contrast to the tradition of making allowances for poor quality and working with an 'acceptable quality level' of less than 100 per cent.

zero sum. In GAME THEORY, a situation in which the size of a resource is fixed. Thus, one player can win only if another loses.

zero time activity. A dummy activity in a critical path network.

zone circles. A version of the problem-solving technique, QUALITY CIRCLES in which employees are grouped into self-regulatory teams in order to improve motivation and benefit from a joint approach to operating difficulties.

zone curve chart. A graphical chart which has, for each point, two values, one vertically above the other (e.g. maximum and minimum). When the lower and upper lines are drawn, a zone of varying size is shown between them. It is the nature of this difference, rather than the absolute value of either line, which is of interest.